LEARNING TO COLLABORATE, COLLABORATING TO LEARN

LEARNING TO COLLABORATE, COLLABORATING TO LEARN

KAREN LITTLETON, DOROTHY MIELL
AND DOROTHY FAULKNER
EDITORS

Nova Science Publishers, Inc.
New York

Senior Editors: Susan Boriotti and Donna Dennis
Coordinating Editor: Tatiana Shohov
Office Manager: Annette Hellinger
Graphics: Magdalena Nuñez
Editorial Production: Marius Andronie, Robert Brower, Maya Columbus,
           Vladimir Klestov, Matthew Kozlowski and Lorna Loperfido
Circulation: Luis Aviles, Raymond Davis, Melissa Diaz, Ave Maria Gonzalez,
           Marlene Nuñez, Jeannie Pappas, Vera Popovic and Frankie Punger
Communications and Acquisitions: Serge P. Shohov
Marketing: Cathy DeGregory

Library of Congress Cataloging-in-Publication Data
Learning to collaborate, collaborating to learn / Karen Littleton, Dorothy Miell and Dorothy
    Faulkner (editors)
      p. cm.
  Includes bibliographical references and index.
  ISBN: 1-59033-952-5 (hardcover)
  1. Group work education. 2. Learning. I. Littleton, Karen. II. Miell, Dorothy. III. Faulkner,
Dorothy.

LB1032.L364 2004
371.36—dc22
                                             2004003041

The publisher has taken reasonable care in the preparation of this book, but makes no expressed or implied warranty of any kind and assumes no responsibility for any errors or omissions. No liability is assumed for incidental or consequential damages in connection with or arising out of information contained in this book.

This publication is designed to provide accurate and authoritative information with regard to the subject matter covered herein. It is sold with the clear understanding that the publisher is not engaged in rendering legal or any other professional services. If legal or any other expert assistance is required, the services of a competent person should be sought. FROM A DECLARATION OF PARTICIPANTS JOINTLY ADOPTED BY A COMMITTEE OF THE AMERICAN BAR ASSOCIATION AND A COMMITTEE OF PUBLISHERS.

Printed in the United States of America

ACKNOWLEDGMENTS

The editors would like to thank Elaine Richardson for her careful preparation of the final manuscript and the staff at NOVA for their encouragement and support through the production process. We would especially like to thank Frank Columbus for approaching us to produce a book on this theme.

CONTENTS

CONTRIBUTORS

Maarit Arvaja is a doctoral student in the Institute for Educational Research at the University of Jyväskylä, Finland. She works within the research group addressing the role of 'ICT in Learning and Working Environments'. Her doctoral thesis deals with collaborative learning in secondary school settings. She is especially interested in social and contextual aspects of collaboration.

Karin Bachmann is a research assistant in the Department of Psychology at the University of Lausanne, Switzerland. Her doctoral dissertation (in progress) concerns an extensive psychosocial and interactional analysis of an educational project on peer-tutoring. She is also a teacher and researcher in psychology in a nursery school.

Curtis J. Bonk (*http://php.indiana.edu/~cjbonk/*) is Professor of Educational Psychology as well as Instructional Systems Technology at Indiana University (IU), USA. He is a core member of the Center for Research on Learning and Technology at IU and a Senior Research Fellow with the Army Research Institute. Curtis received the Burton Gorman Teaching Award in 1999, the Wilbert Hites Mentoring Award in 2000, the CyberStar Award from the Indiana Information Technology Association in 2002, and the Most Outstanding Achievement by an Individual in Higher Education award from the U.S. Distance Learning Association in 2003. He also received a State of Indiana award for Innovative Teaching in a Distance Education Program in 2003. Curtis has published widely on e-learning and is in demand as a conference keynote speaker. He is President and Founder of CourseShare and SurveyShare and can be contacted at *cjbonk@indiana.edu*.

Sarah Brown is a Senior Lecturer in Psychology in the School of Health and Social Sciences at Coventry University, UK and the course director of the MSc in Forensic Psychology. As a Chartered Forensic Psychologist, Sarah's main area of expertise is Forensic Psychology; however she has used WebCT (the on-line learning facility available at Coventry University) extensively since she joined the University in November 1999. Sarah produced a Learning Environments and Pedagogy (LEAP) case study of her use of WebCT in the delivery of an undergraduate Psychology and Crime module for the UK Psychology Learning and Teaching Support Network (LTSN), which is available on the LTSN website, and presented the case study at the associated conference in February 2003.

Pav Chera is a Senior Lecturer and Post Graduate Curriculum Leader for the Business Information Systems group in the School of Computing Science at Middlesex University UK. She has been teaching a range of IT, business and educational subjects for a number of years at undergraduate, professional and post graduate levels. Currently, her teaching involves MSc students in London but also, as a member of the Global Campus Team, she is involved in the delivery and (evaluation) of distance learning programmes, specifically, MSc BIT and MSc ECommerce to students in Cairo, Hong Kong, Shenzhen, Shanghai, and Singapore. This has provided an area of active research into the use of Virtual Learning Environments (VLEs), distance learning and CAL in higher education. Other research interests centre around designing and developing multimedia educational CAL software for young children, which involved extensive research, evaluation and liaison with schools and practitioners during her inter-disciplinary doctoral studies. This research and interactive 'Talking Books' software has been extended since, via an active collaborative project with colleagues at The Open University. She is also the convenor of the Adaptive Learning Environment Research Team (ALERT) research group within the School which conducts theoretical and applied research into the use and development of learning environments to enhance and transform learning.

Gillian Cross obtained a BA in Psychology at Strathclyde University in 2000. She went on to research children's collaborative learning with Professor Christine Howe and Dr. Donna McWilliam. From 2002–2003 she was employed as a researcher and speech and language therapy assistant on a project which aimed to explore different modes of speech and language therapy for children with primary language impairment. She is currently studying to gain an MSc in Educational Psychology at Strathclyde University, UK.

Lyn Dawes began work as a secondary science teacher 1972, subsequently re-training to teach primary science and ICT. From 1997 – 2000 Lyn undertook research investigating the integration of computers into classrooms, gaining a doctorate before taking a post with The British Educational Communications and Technology Agency (Becta) as Education Officer for Software. In 2001 Lyn joined De Montfort University, UK as a Senior Lecturer in the School of Education where she is currently working with PGCE and BEd students on the Science and language programmes. Lyn has been involved since 1990 with the Open University's 'Thinking Together' action research program, as teacher-researcher, author and consultant. She contributes regularly to *Junior Education*.

Anneli Eteläpelto is Professor of Education in the Department of Education at the University of Jyväskylä, Finland. She has researched professional learning and developing professional expertise in schooling and working life environments, and has published extensively in these areas. She has conducted research on learning professional competencies in design, programming, and teaching. Recently she has researched project-based learning and teachers' role in promoting collaborative learning. Anneli has co-edited several books in Finnish and has also edited *Learning and Collaboration in Virtual Environments* (2002) with Jeanette Bopry. She has taken responsibility for organizing several scientific meetings and is a founding member of EARLI-SIG Learning and Professional Development. From 1994-99 she was a member in the European Science Foundation's 'Learning in Humans and Machines' programme.

Dorothy Faulkner is a Senior Lecturer in the Centre for Childhood, Development and Learning, Faculty of Education and Language Studies, at The Open University, UK. She has carried out a number of studies that have investigated the impact of friendship and peer relationships on classroom-based, collaborative activity in young children. Focusing particularly on young children's cognition, Dorothy's research focuses on the relationship between socially constructed knowledge and individual learning, memory and problem-solving. Most recently she has been developing a research programme to investigate whether collaborative activity is influenced by the established social roles children adopt in relation to their peers. She is a member of the editorial board of the *International Journal of Early Years Education* and, was a co-editor of the Special Issue *'Learning to Collaborate and Collaborating to Learn'* for the *European Journal of the Psychology of Education, 2000, XV* (4). Together with Karen Littleton and other colleagues at The Open University she co-edited, *'Learning Relationships in the Classroom'* (Routledge, 1998) and *'Rethinking Collaborative Learning'* (Free Association Press, 2000).

Michèle Grossen is Professor of Psychology in the Department of Psychology at the University of Lausanne, Switzerland. Her research began with a concern with the role of peer interaction in development and learning and more generally teaching and learning from a sociocultural perspective. For some years, she has also been working on therapist-patient verbal interactions in clinical interviews and developing a dialogical approach to therapeutic situations. She is currently involved in three main research projects concerning the use of new technologies in schools, test situations considered from a sociocultural perspective and, more recently, the issue of language in social representations.

Päivi Häkkinen is a professor at the Institute for Educational Research, University of Jyväskylä, Finland. She is currently leading the research group on ICT in Learning and Working Environments. Her main research areas are collaborative learning, computer-supported collaborative learning, design and evaluation of computer-based learning environments, as well as methodological innovations in research on learning environments. Päivi has actively published in national and international journals, and she has also been involved in many national and international scientific tasks (e.g. member of international programme committees of conferences, referee for journals). From 1996–99 she participated the European Science Foundation's 'Learning in Humans and Machines' programme, and from 1998–99 she worked as a visiting Research Fellow at the Institute of Educational Technology in the Open University (UK).

Christine Howe is Professor of Psychology and Vice-Dean (Research) at Strathclyde University, UK. In addition to children's collaborative learning, her current research interests include conceptual mastery in mathematics and physics, first language acquisition, communication and social relations in children, gender and dialogue, computer-supported collaborative learning, and young people's experience of racism. She has published extensively, with over one hundred journal articles and book chapters. Her books include *Acquiring Language in a Conversational Context* (1993), *Language Learning: A Special Case for Developmental Psychology?* (1993), *Group and Collaborative Learning* (1994), *Gender and Classroom Interaction: A Research Review* (1997), and *Conceptual Structure in Childhood and Adolescence* (1998). Christine is Associate Editor of the journal *Social Development*.

Sinikka Kaartinen is a Senior Lecturer in Mathematics Teacher Education at the University of Jyväskylä, Finland. She has researched collaborative learning in science and mathematics across age levels. She has co-authored (with Kristiina Kumpulainen): *Negotiating meaning in science classroom communities: Cases across age levels* (2001), *Collaborative inquiry and the construction of explanations in the learning of science* (2002), *Situational mechanisms of peer group interaction in collaborative meaning making: Processes and conditions for learning* (2000), and *The interpersonal dynamics of collaborative reasoning in peer interactive dyads* (2003). Her doctoral thesis was entitled 'Learning to participate-Participating to learn in science and mathematics classrooms' (2003).

Kristiina Kumpulainen is an Academy Research Fellow of the Academy of Finland. She is also a Senior Lecturer at the University of Oulu, Department of Educational Sciences and Teacher Education, and a Docent at the University of Turku. The core themes of her scientific research work deal with collaborative learning, conceptual learning, multimedia-based learning, sociocultural learning theories, and qualitative research methods with a specific interest in the analysis of social interaction and discourse. Her recent publications include *Classroom interaction and social learning* (2002) co-edited by David Wray, *Negotiating meaning in a community of learners* (2001) co-edited by Geerdina van der Aalsvoort, *Collaborative inquiry and the construction of explanations in the learning of science* (2002), co-authored with Sinikka Kaartinen, and *The dynamics of children's science learning and thinking in a social context of a multimedia environment* (2003) co-authored with Marjatta Kangassalo. She has directed several research projects funded by the Academy of Finland and EU. Her recent research project is part of the Finnish 'Life as learning' national research programme. She is currently a board member of the European Educational Teacher Education Network (ETEN) and a co-ordinator of the European Association for Research on Learning and Instruction (EARLI) Special Interest Group focusing on social interaction in learning and instruction.

Jaana Lahti is a researcher at the Virtual University and is a PhD student in the Unit of Educational Psychology at the University of Helsinki, Finland. She worked for ten years as a teacher of philosophy, psychology and theology at senior high school level and has also tutored at the Teacher Training School. She innovates, implements and evaluates ICT and researches processes of teaching/learning in various learning environments. Her current research is an evaluation of a learning community-based teacher education program (in collaboration with Professor Anneli Eteläpelto and Lic. Ed. Sanni Siitari). These studies are funded by the Academy of Finland and the Ministry of Education.

Karen Littleton is a Senior Lecturer in Developmental Psychology in the Centre for Childhood, Development and Learning at The Open University, UK, and Visiting Professor at the University of Helsinki. She has researched children's collaborative learning, often with reference to new technologies and gender, and has published extensively in this area. Karen co-edited *Learning with computers* (1999), with Paul Light, and *Rethinking collaborative learning* (2000) with Richard Joiner, Dorothy Faulkner and Dorothy Miell. She is the co-author, with Paul Light, of *Social processes in children's learning* (1999). From 1994–99 she was senior scientist in the European Science Foundation's 'Learning in Humans and Machines' programme. She is currently the lead editor for the book series *Advances in Learning and Instruction*.

Raymond MacDonald is Lecturer in Psychology at Glasgow Caledonian University, UK. He researches a number of areas within the general field of the psychology of music and has published and presented his research widely. He has also been Artistic Director for a music production company, Sounds of Progress, working with individuals who have special needs. He is an experienced jazz saxophonist and was awarded Scottish jazz musician of the year in 2002 by The Sunday Herald.

Kati Mäkitalo is a doctoral student of education in the Institute for Educational Research at the University of Jyväskylä, Finland. She works with the research group, ICT in Learning and Working Environments. Her research area examines the grounding process, with reference to virtual interaction and collaborative activity, in the context of higher education.

Donna McWilliam is a Lecturer in Psychology at the University of Strathclyde, UK, teaching cognitive development and dialogue analysis. Previously she was employed as an associate lecturer and tutor in the Open University's Faculties of Social Science and of Education and Language Studies. Her doctorate, supervised by Professor Christine Howe, was completed in 1999 and focused on the discussion skills of pre-school children in conflictual, co-operative and intervention contexts. Results of the first PhD study (conflictual context) were published in a special edition of the *Journal of Language and Social Psychology* (2001). Since the completion of her PhD, Donna has been involved in research projects concerned with children' s collaborative learning, the discussion skills of school-aged children, and body image in women.

Dorothy Miell is a Senior Lecturer in Psychology in the Faculty of Social Science, The Open University, UK. Her research interests lie in studying close relationships, particularly the effects of such relationships on identity development and on the nature of collaborative working in creative tasks such as music making. She has recently edited *Musical Identities* (2000) with Raymond MacDonald and David Hargreaves and is now working on *Collaborative Creativity* (with Karen Littleton, Free Association books) and *Musical Communication* (with Raymond MacDonald and David Hargreaves, Oxford University Press).

Maria Luisa Nigrelli is a consultant for Telecom Italia Learning Services, Italy, which specializes in Enterprise e-learning and knowledge management process solutions. She was a consultant for KPMG Italy in 2002 where she carried out a study for Enterprise Application Integration within a portal framework for information management and application sharing. She graduated from the University of Palermo in 2001 and received a master' s degree in Science and New Media Technologies at the University of Pavia in 2003. During 2002, she was a visiting scholar at Indiana University Bloomington. Presently, her research interests are in instructional systems design, communities of practice, and knowledge management.

Claire Sams began work as a primary school class teacher in 1986, later specializing in teaching children with moderate learning difficulties in mainstream settings. In 2000 Claire joined the 'Thinking Together' research team at the Open University, UK, and managed a Key Stage 2 project in Milton Keynes schools on ICT and Talk in the Primary Curriculum, which focussed on Science and Maths. Claire is currently working on the latest 'Thinking Together' project in conjunction with 'SMILE' mathematics software developers. She is a co-author of teachers' materials and articles relating to these projects. Claire is also an Associate Lecturer for the Open University working with teacher assistants and trainee teachers.

Sanni Siitari is a lecturer in Educational Psychology at the Research Centre for Educational Psychology, Department of Teacher Education at the University of Helsinki. Sanni previously worked as a primary school teacher. She obtained her Licenciate in Education degree (educational psychology as her main subject) in 2001, having researched teachers' and parents' common process of creating a curriculum for their school. Recently her research work has focused on pedagogical leadership and organisational development. She is currently studying for a doctorate in educational psychology at Helsinki University.

Nigel Wilson is a Senior Lecturer in Psychology at Coventry University UK and has been teaching in higher education for over 10 years. At Coventry, he is Course Leader for Joint Degrees involving Psychology and Module Leader for modules in Physiological Psychology and Psychopharmacology. Nigel also contributes to modules in Research Methods in Psychology. He has research interests in the behavioural effects of drugs and also in teaching and learning in higher education, particularly the use of on-line learning facilities. He has published articles on the role of neurotransmitters in anxiety and is currently researching aspects of nicotine addiction. He is a Chartered Psychologist and Associate Fellow of the British Psychological Society.

Robert Wisher is the Director of the Advanced Distributed Learning Initiative within the U.S. Department of Defense. Bob has more than twenty years of experience as a research psychologist, examining the training effectiveness of emerging distributed learning technologies. Bob received a B.S. degree in mathematics from Purdue University and a Ph.D. in cognitive psychology from the University of California, San Diego. He has published more than 90 technical reports, book chapters, and journal articles related to training technologies and the learning sciences. In 1999, he received the Most Outstanding Achievement Award by an Individual from the U.S. Distance Learning Association.

Clare Wood is Lecturer in Developmental Psychology in the Centre for Childhood, Development and Learning at the Open University, UK. Her main research interests are concerned with the development of reading ability and reading difficulties, including children's ability to benefit from contact with educational technology. In May 2000 she was awarded the International Reading Association' s Literacy / Reading Fellowship, and she is currently a co-editor of the *Journal of Research in Reading*. She has been teaching psychology full time to students in Higher Education since 1996, and as a member of the Institute of Learning and Teaching continues to develop her interests in improving the quality of teaching and learning to these students.

Chapter 1

'LEARNING TO COLLABORATE, COLLABORATING TO LEARN': EDITORIAL INTRODUCTION

Karen Littleton and Dorothy Miell

INTRODUCTION

The study of collaborative learning has a relatively brief history, yet there have been notable changes in the nature of the research being undertaken in this field. Initially, the primary aim was to determine whether and when collaborative learning was more effective than learning alone (Dillenbourg, Baker, Blaye & O'Malley, 1995) and there is a substantial body of empirical evidence demonstrating that, whilst not an educational panacea, there can be positive effects of social interaction for learning (see Light, Littleton, Messer, & Joiner, 1994; Littleton & Light, 1999; Joiner, Littleton, Faulkner & Miell, 2000). More recently, however, interest has shifted away from considering just the outcomes and products of collaborative work, towards analysing the interactions themselves. This shift to a more process-oriented account of productive group-work has brought with it an interest in understanding the nature of productive talk and joint activity and researchers have attempted to identify interactional features which are important for learning and cognitive change. Researchers with different theoretical backgrounds and different methodological approaches have emphasized different facets of interaction with some highlighting the important role of conflict, others planning, negotiation, exploratory talk, transactive dialogue and so on (see Joiner, Littleton, Faulkner & Miell, 2000; Littleton & Light, 1999, for details of relevant work).

Underpinning many researchers' interest in exploring and conceptualizing the nature of productive interaction is the notion that we need to understand how better to support learners' joint endeavours, such that we can promote effective opportunities for collaborative learning and design strategies for optimizing collaboration. This desire to create effective opportunities for collaborative learning has brought about a further shift in research. Increasingly, in addition to studying how certain modes of peer collaboration may promote learning ('collaborating to learn'), researchers are also asking how collaboration is and can be learned in order to make peer interaction an opportunity for learning ('learning to collaborate') (see Grossen & Bachmann, 2000). This interest in 'learning to collaborate' recognizes that learners not only have to acquire knowledge, they also have to regulate the processes of acquiring knowledge (Elbers & Streefland, 2000). It is this need to understand both how learners 'learn to collaborate' and 'collaborate to learn' which sits at the heart of this book.

The book brings together contributions from researchers, working across Europe and North America, who have interests in collaborative learning. The work presented here is united through the contributors' shared desire to understand and promote educationally productive collaborative work, whilst investigating this in diverse ways, for example with respect to the particular contexts, learning communities and the age of the learners being studied.

The book opens with two chapters that examine young children's collaborations. The first of these examines the context and interactional dynamics of joint story creation (Chapter 2: Dorothy Faulkner & Dorothy Miell) whilst the second (Chapter 3: Karen Littleton, Clare Wood & Pav Chera) looks at the modes of interaction observed during the paired reading of a talking book. Taken together, these two chapters highlight that effective collaboration is a highly situated achievement. The efficacy of collaborative work is resourced or constrained by factors such as individual differences, the nature of young learners' relationships with each other and the task and the processes involved in the ongoing negotiation of a shared, educationally appropriate, understanding of both the task and co-workers' expectations and needs. Whilst researchers often assume that educational tasks are 'givens', Chapter 2 highlights that task meaning is negotiated and contested in interaction and we cannot assume that a particular task has the same salience for different partners, for example, boys and girls, friends and acquaintances. Through the analyses presented in Chapter 3 we see that whilst collaborative interactions are framed by the institutional, cultural and historical contexts within which they are located and positioned, contexts for collaboration are also partly constituted within interactions and through the effects of participants' interactional work (Grossen & Bachmann, 2000, p.492).

Chapter 4 (Christine Howe, Donna McWilliam & Gillian Cross) makes it clear that researchers need to understand a multiplicity of 'relationships' if they are to make further progress as regards the issue of 'collaborating to learn'. Starting from the premise that there is now a substantial body of evidence that peer collaboration can have positive consequences for individual learning, these authors note that far less is known about the processes by which such positive consequences occur. It is argued that in some circumstances they almost certainly involve the creation, during collaboration, of superior insights that are then individually internalized. However, the authors assert that internalisation cannot be the only mechanism, as individual learning can take place even when collaborative 'products' are inferior to the ideas that the individuals began with. When learning takes place in these circumstances, it tends not to be apparent until some weeks after the collaborative experience, i.e. it requires 'incubation'. The work reported here relating to conceptual growth in science in 9-12 year-old children, suggests that incubation occurs because peer collaboration primes individuals to look differently at relevant events in their everyday lives. Crucially, it is suggested that greater attention needs to be paid to the relationships between the claims that are made during interaction and those between the beliefs of the participating individuals. It is suggested that one of the reasons why the centrality of these relationships is seldom recognized may be the over-emphasis placed on collective insights as an explanation for productive interaction.

The detailed analyses of contrasting case dyads engaged in mathematical problem-solving activities presented in Chapter 5 (Kumpulainen & Kaartinen) demonstrate the sheer complexity of interactional dynamics and illustrate that the social and cognitive processes inherent in peer problem solving and shared meaning making are; 'highly dynamic in nature, shaping collaborative activity on a moment-by-moment basis' (p.88). Through the micro-analyses presented, we see very clearly the 'myriad of interactional spaces' (p.89) the twelve-year-old partners have to negotiate as they 'adjust to each other's topics, emotions and tempos in order to establish shared meaning' (p.89). The interaction processes and factors supporting and challenging shared meaning making also become apparent and we begin to see how the practice of collaborating to learn is tightly interwoven with the practice of learning to collaborate. The work reported here suggests that if students are to learn how to collaborate and collaborate to learn they need to be helped to engage in meta-reflection during collaborative problem-solving so that they become aware of the attentional engagement of themselves and their interacting partners whilst solving problems together. It is also noted that there is a 'need to help students develop strategies for establishing a shared understanding during joint problem solving particularly during moments of confusion, domination and/or conflict' (p.88).

In Chapter 6 (Dawes & Sams) we see how the shift towards a research interest in 'learning to collaborate' has led some scholars to reverse the original empirical research paradigm by 'teaching students the modes of collaboration and the types of discourse [earlier research] had showed to be efficient in promoting learning' (Grossen & Bachmann, 2000 p.492). Dawes and Sams discuss the nature and impact of the 'Thinking Together' approach, designed to teach primary school children a kind of educationally productive talk described as 'exploratory talk'. Clearly, teaching a particular kind of talk cannot be fully equated with the appropriation of a given body of knowledge and making sense of it (Grossen & Bachmann, 2000, p.503). Recognizing this, however, Dawes & Sams argue that direct teaching of exploratory talk can provide children with the essential language tools for raising individual achievement. Their account stresses the ways in which teachers can create 'a talk-focused classroom community where discussion supports all the learning that takes place' (p.108).

The notion of the complexity of collaborative interactions raised in Chapter 5 is returned to in Chapter 7 (Bachmann & Grossen). Here the analyses of secondary school pupils' peer tutoring episodes, and the associated consideration of explanations as a situated activity, show that explanation is 'a discursive device used to transform the tutees' problematic state of knowledge into an unproblematic state' (p.129). It is argued, however, that explanation is also an 'interactional resource through which the asymmetry and complementarity of the tutor-tutee relationship is accomplished and through which the tutors construct their legitimacy. Explanation is also a semiotic tool that tutors use to self-regulate their cognitive activity and thus has a meta-cognitive function' (p.129).

Grossen and Bachmann's chapter clearly highlights the multi-functionality of discursive episodes and this theme is echoed in MacDonald and Miell's contribution (Chapter 8). Drawing on data relating to collaborative music-making and music listening in diverse contexts we see how participants situate themselves in relational activities with others and 'that much of discourse and thus [much] of cognition serves to situate an individual with respect to others, to establish a social role or identity' (Resnick, Pontecorvo & Säljö, 1997, p.9). This suggests that a consideration of identity work should be integral to our analyses of collaborative activity – episodes of collaboration are not just about the construction and negotiation of understanding, they are fundamentally about the subtle processes involved in the moment-to-moment negotiation of identity.

The inextricable interrelationship between the construction of knowledge and the construction of self is discussed further in Chapter 9 (Lahti, Eteläpelto & Sittari), where a study of intensive, group-based learning amongst student teachers is reported. Taking the theme of 'conflict as a challenge to productive learning', these authors consider the significance of conflict for collaboration. They argue that 'by becoming attuned towards the viewpoints of others in the group, group members can give support to each individual's process of becoming a subject of his or her own learning and taking on the professional identity of teacher' (p.160).

At this point in the book there is a shift away from considering face-to-face collaborative activity, and Chapters 10 (Häkkinen, Arvaja & Mäkitalo), 11 (Brown, Wilson & Wood) and 12 (Bonk, Wisher & Nigrelli) discuss collaborations mediated *through* computer-technology. In considering the recent research on collaborative learning and Computer Supported Collaborative Learning (CSCL) Häkkinen, Arvaja and Mäkitalo point out that the use of computer technology can transform the cognitive and communicative requirements of learners' actions and interactions. They argue that the use of computers can re-structure social interaction and joint knowledge building, and can give rise to new kinds of learning culture. However, they also point to the gap between the potential afforded by CSCL and the difficulty of moving from research-led initiatives to implementation with teachers and practitioners. The associated problems of 'scaling up' from intensive pilot experiments are also highlighted.

The issue of institutional support of and commitment to the use of new technologies to support collaborative learning is raised by Brown, Wilson and Wood (Chapter 11). These authors present a case study of how university undergraduate psychology students use web-based module-specific conference areas to support their learning in the context of an institutional setting that encourages the use of such resources. Presenting comparative data derived from an analysis of two Web-based module related conference areas on WebCT, it is suggested that for collaboration to be effective in this context, amongst other things, the way that the tutor casts themselves and the function of the environment is critical, as is the clarity of the induction regarding the nature and purpose of the WebCT conferencing environment. The issue of the inter-relationship between on-line activities and individualized off-line activities such as essay writing and examination preparation is also explored.

Finally, the chapter by Bonk, Wisher and Nigrelli (Chapter 12) draws on data derived from a number of research projects, conducted with adult learners, to detail the emerging principles of on-line collaborative learning communities as well as the methods for researching them. The authors end their contribution by speculating 'what is next' in terms of work in this field.

REFERENCES

Dillenbourg, P., Baker, M., Blaye, A., & O'Malley, C. (1995). The evolution of research on collaborative learning. In H. Spada & P. Reimann (Eds.), *Learning in humans and machines* (pp.189–211). Oxford: Elsevier.

Elbers, E., & Streefland, L. (2000). Collaborative learning and the construction of common knowledge. *European Journal of Psychology of Education, XV*(4), 479–490.

Grossen, M., & Bachmann, K. (2000). Learning to collaborate in a peer-tutoring situation: Who learns? What is learned? *European Journal of Psychology of Education, XV*(4), 491–508.

Joiner, R., Littleton, K., Faulkner, D., & Miell, D. (2000). *Rethinking collaborative learning.* London: Free Association Books.

Littleton, K., & Light, P. (1999*). Learning with computers: Analysing productive interaction.* London: Routledge.

Light, P., Littleton, K., Messer, D., & Joiner, R. (1994). Social and communicative processes in computer based learning. *European Journal of Psychology of Education,* 9, pp.93–109.

Resnick, L., Pontecorvo, C., & Säljö, R. (1997). Discourse, tools and reasoning. In L. Resnick, R. Säljö, C. Pontecorvo, & B. Burge (Eds.), *Discourse, tools and reasoning: Essays on situated cognition.* Berlin and New York: Springer-Verlag.

Chapter 2

COLLABORATIVE STORY TELLING IN FRIENDSHIP AND ACQUAINTANCESHIP DYADS

Dorothy Faulkner and Dorothy Miell

INTRODUCTION

It is generally accepted that, under favourable circumstances, when children work collaboratively their cognitive understanding of the task or problem they have been working on is enhanced (see Howe this volume). It has also been established that a key feature of successful peer collaboration is the degree of mutual engagement with each other's ideas and perspectives that children are able to establish and maintain through transactive dialogue, (e.g. Kruger, 1993; Miell & MacDonald, 2000). Miell and MacDonald (2000) have pointed out, however, that we still do not completely understand how children's pre-existing relationships within their peer group influence the nature and quality of their interaction in collaborative contexts. Furthermore, as Kutnick and Manson (1998) argue, "the nature of children's social pairings (used to promote cognition) will be affected by the pupil's emotional and social responses to the 'working conditions' in which they undertake the assigned cognitive tasks" (p.166). This suggests that consideration of the nature of the learning context is also important for understanding children's willingness to participate in collaborative learning contexts. For example a number of studies have demonstrated the positive effects of friendship on joint problem solving, collaborative story writing and musical composition (e.g. Azmitia & Montgomery, 1993; Hartup, 1998; Miell & MacDonald, 2000). These studies have demonstrated that tasks need to be challenging, (but not too challenging), and that they need to engage children's creativity and imagination. Where this is the case friendship pairs are more likely than other children to engage in transactive dialogue, pose alternatives to and/or provide elaborations of their own and each other's ideas, agree with each other and resolve conflicts and disagreements to reach a mutually acceptable solution. Reviewing the existing evidence, Hartup (1998, p. 148) suggests that four cognitive and motivational conditions can account for the distinctive interactions of friends:

1. 1 Friends know one another better than non-friends and are thus able to communicate with one another more efficiently and effectively;
2. 2 Friends and nonfriends have different expectations of one another, especially concerning assistance and support;
3. 3 An affective climate more favourable to exploration and problem solving exists between friends and than between nonfriends – namely a "climate of agreement";
4. 4 Friends more readily than nonfriends seek ways of resolving disagreements that support continued interaction between them.

This suggests that children with established friendships will have a head start when it comes to learning how to collaborate compared to children without such friendships. Firstly they will be more used to offering each other assistance within a supportive affective climate. Secondly, as existing research shows, within a friendship dyad, children display the kind of sophisticated language and communication skills that are the hallmark of successful collaboration. Finally, by virtue of having developed a history of shared experiences, children within friendship dyads should find it easier to operate on each other's ideas and establish a degree of intersubjectivity. Existing research on the influence of friendship on collaborative learning, however, has not investigated whether the children from friendship dyads are able to communicate effectively and establish productive working partnerships with nonfriend peers. Nor have there been many attempts to establish whether interaction with a child who is socially able (within the context of a friendship dyad) is one way that less able children might acquire the 'rules' of successful collaboration. This is surprising given Vygotsky's (1978) claim that when children engage in collective activity they can imitate a variety of actions and behaviours that go well beyond the limits of their own capabilities. It is also surprising in the light of the large body of research that shows that other kinds of intimate, supportive relationships such as those between siblings can lead to both cognitive and social growth, (Azmitia and Hesser, 1993; Hartup, 1989). Evidence that children can acquire positive social behaviours through interaction with other, more socially skilled children comes from a recent study by Gumpel and Frank (1999). This study demonstrated that socially isolated, five year-old boys can benefit from participating in social skills training sessions delivered by older boys and that there are long-term benefits to both tutees and tutors in terms of an increase in prosocial behaviour. Our own previous research also indicates that isolated and rejected children work better with popular children and children from friendship pairs in the context of collaborative tasks, (Faulkner & Miell, 1994; Murphy & Faulkner, 2000).

AIMS AND DESIGN OF THE CURRENT STUDY

This chapter reports an exploratory study of five year-old children's creative collaboration in the context of a joint story creation task that was designed to investigate whether working with different partners would affect the nature of children's collaborative activity. As the main focus was on processes of creative collaboration and shared meaning making through dialogue and conversation, asking children to make up a story together seemed to be an appropriate task for several reasons. Firstly, in their study of the influence of friendship on 11-12 year olds creative collaboration in the domain of musical composition, Miell and MacDonald (2000) point out that few studies have examined children's styles of interaction on open-ended creative tasks although this style of working is common in English primary schools. Group storytelling is also a common phenomenon in early childhood education in the US (Hayes & Casey, 2002). Secondly, during early childhood, children are actively encouraged to tell their own stories and to contribute to shared narratives created during family conversations, pretend play with peers and school-based literacy activities, (e.g. Engel, 1999; Hayes & Casey, 2002; Middleton & Edwards, 1990; Vass, 2002). As Engel, (1999) remarks, "Listening to and telling stories are cultural activities. As children learn the story form, they also learn about their culture. In turn, through stories, aspects of their culture shape the way they think about and remember experiences" (p.10). Inventing stories therefore is a familiar and natural activity for young children . Also they structure their play through narratives that reveal the influence of culture on their thinking and imagination, (Wells, 1986). In this chapter, however, the nature and content of the stories children make up will not be of central concern. The main focus will be on the nature of the children's collaborative activity.

As mentioned above, the main aim of the study was to investigate how different kinds of relational pairing might affect the quality of social interaction observed between children. To this end we designed a study that would allow us to compare individual children's collaborative activity and talk both with a mutual best friend and with nonfriend classmates. A secondary aim was to investigate whether socially isolated children's ability to engage successfully in collaborative activity would be influenced by the friendship status of their partner. It was predicted that these children would benefit from being paired with a child from a friendship dyad if friends are able to create positive cognitive and motivational climate with nonfriend partners as well as with their friends.

Five year-old children from two British primary schools participated in the study. The schools were located in Milton Keynes, a new city approximately 90 miles north of London. A sociometric, peer rating procedure (Asher & Hymel, 1981) and a peer nomination friendship interview was used to select eight pairs of children who nominated each other as best friends (four girl/girl dyads and four boy/boy dyads). The views of the children's class teachers were solicited to confirm that children in these Friendship dyads had been best friends since they started attending school. Eight of the 16 children from the Friendship Dyads, one per dyad, were also allocated to a Friend/Acquaintance Dyad by matching them with eight, same-gender peers on the basis of sociometric friendship ratings and verbal age[1]. No child in a Friend/Acquaintance dyad nominated his/her partner as being a mutual friend or a best friend. Also, the children identified as acquaintances did not themselves belong to a mutually reciprocated friendship pair although they all received positive friendship ratings from at the majority of their peers. The other eight children from the Friendship dyads were each paired with a same-gender, 'socially isolated' child who received few positive friendship ratings from his/her peers (Friend/Isolate Dyad). Finally, pairing the eight socially isolated children with the eight children selected as acquaintances resulted in a fourth set of Acquaintance/Isolate Dyads[2].

This design meant that 32 children were initially involved in the study, 16 children from friendship dyads, eight nonfriend acquaintances, and eight socially isolated children.

---

[1] Verbal age was measured using the British Picture Vocabulary Scale, (Dunn & Dunn, 1982).

[2] It was not possible create exact verbal age matches for the socially isolated children as only ten of these children were identified in total across four classes in two schools. Mean verbal age for the 'friends', 'acquaintances' and 'socially isolated' children was 63.3, 62.2 and 50.7 months respectively.

Originally it was planned that each child would participate in two story creation sessions with a different partner on each occasion. Due to absenteeism, however, not all children were able to participate in two sessions and the final design of the study included eight Friendship Dyads, eight Friend/Acquaintanceship Dyads, six Friend/Isolate Dyads and six Acquaintance/ Isolate Dyads. The order in which dyads were allocated to the two story creation sessions was randomized to control for possible practice effects.

The story creation sessions took place in a small, quiet room adjacent to the children's normal classrooms and began with the researcher introducing (or reintroducing) two finger puppets, Mo Monkey and Ollie Owl. Children were told that Mo and Ollie were good friends and that they liked going on adventures together. Children were invited to choose which character they wanted to be and were asked to make up an adventure story about Mo and Ollie. To help them several toy 'props' similar in scale to the puppets (e.g. small vehicles, farm animals, wooden buildings and trees, miniature utensils) were also available. These were provided as previous research has shown that 3-5 year old children produce more coherent and cohesive stories when provided with pictures or other kinds of prop that provide structural cues, (e.g. Shapiro & Hudson, 1993). Children were given a couple of minutes to familiarize themselves with the puppets and toy props and to 'plan' their story. The researcher emphasized that they should 'make up the story together'. The sessions, (lasting approximately 10 – 15 minutes) were tape-recorded[3] and the children's conversations were transcribed for subsequent analysis.

ANALYSIS AND FINDINGS

The transcripts of the children's conversations yielded a substantial quantity of data that could be explored in a number of different ways and at a number of levels. The first set of quantitative analyses offers a descriptive account of features of children's interaction at the level of the dyad. It allowed us to examine group differences in the nature of the conversations taking place in the four different types of dyad: Friendship Dyads (FR+FR); Friend/Acquaintance Dyads (FR+AQ); Friend/Isolate Dyads (FR+IS) and Acquaintance/Isolate Dyads (AQ+IS). It should be noted, however, that a statistical treatment of the data was precluded due to the loss of 8 participants as this reduced the number of boy AQ+IS dyads from 4 to 2. Also, initial inspection of the data revealed large differences in variability between the four Dyad Types and between boy and girl dyads within these Dyad Types.

The second set of analyses offers a qualitative account of some of the conversations that took place within dyads in order to illustrate how a change of partner influenced the nature and style of individual children's talk in the two sessions. These analyses will also build on key differences between girl and boy dyads identified from the quantitative analyses.

---

[3] Pilot work had established that video recording was not feasible in the rather confined space where the sessions took place in one school.

Conversational Turn Analysis

Our first analysis compared the mean number of conversational turns in each dyad. A *Conversational Turn* was defined as a complete utterance, or set of utterances by one child or the researcher followed by a change of speaker, or followed by a pause of at least 15 seconds where there was no change of speaker. Two features of the conversations immediately became apparent. Firstly, as mentioned above, there was substantial variability with the number of conversational turns per dyad ranging from 20 to 139, (mean = 59). Secondly, although the researcher had been instructed to intervene as little as possible, there was considerable variation in the amount of adult involvement in the story telling sessions, so much so that for the majority of dyads the conversation was essentially triadic rather than dyadic (see Table 1).

Table 1: Mean number of conversational turns attributed to
child partners and adult experimenter as a function of Dyad Type and Gender

Dyad	n	Conversational Turns	
		Children	**Adult**
FR+FR			
Girls	4	53	6
Boys	4	42	27
FR+AQ			
Girls	4	35	20
Boys	4	35	9
FR+IS			
Girls	3	52	23
Boys	3	35	33
AQ+IS			
Girls	4	41	22
Boys	2	23	19

Note: Values have been rounded up or down to the nearest whole number for ease of comparison.

Table 1 shows that children in girl dyads generated more turns than those in boy dyads except when a girl from a friendship dyad was paired with a non-friend acquaintance (FR+AQ). The table also shows much greater adult involvement with boy FR+FR dyads than with girl FR+FR dyads. This finding was reversed in the FR+AQ dyads where girls appeared to require more adult support than boys suggesting that, for these 5 year-old children, there is only an advantage in working with one's best friend if one is a girl. All dyads containing a socially isolated child also showed a lot of adult involvement. In the case of boy FR+IS and AQ+IS dyads, the adult contributed almost as many turns as both children together.

Although children were instructed to take turns we also considered the possibility that the children predicted to be more socially competent (i.e. the children from best friend dyads) might dominate the interaction when paired with an acquaintance or isolated child. When we compared the mean number of conversational turns contributed by each child, however, there was no evidence to suggest that one or other partner was dominating the interaction in any Dyad Type. Boys and girls contributed equally to the interaction regardless of whether their partner was their best friend, an acquaintance or a socially isolated peer. This may be due to the task instructions and adult involvement, however, both of which emphasized that children should take turns in contributing to the story.

Table 2: Coding scheme used to categorise adult's utterances

Utterance Codes	Definition	Examples
Adult Questions Information Questions	Questions that ask child or pair to clarify or elaborate aspect of the story or actions performed with the finger puppets Mo and Ollie.	What are you going to say to Mo? What are you going to do about that Ollie? Are you a woodchopper? Are you going on a boat or a plane to do that?
Maintenance Questions	General questions that encourage children to maintain the flow of their story.	What happens next? What does Ollie do now? What are Mo and Ollie going to do now they've fed the animals?
Specific Suggestions	Adult makes a specific suggestion to the child/pair regarding a possible story action or event.	What about you are you having a big bag of chips too? Are you going to help make the garden? What about these [animals]? Can you do anything with these?
Opening and Closing Questions	Question to pair or child that encourages them to begin or end their story.	What can Mo and Ollie do together? Now, what do you think you could start the story with? Is that the end of the story now? Is it time for them to go home now?
Rhetorical Questions	Question that does not require an answer or that describes a child's immediately previous actions or utterance.	That's a big adventure isn't it? She makes him a drink does she? Yes, monkeys like bananas, don't they?
Opinion Questions	Question that asks child for her/his views on something.	Is that a good idea do you *think*? What do you *think* they'd say to each other if they were lost? What would *you* like to do Mo?
Smoothers	Confirmatory utterances, confirmatory repetitions, reformulations or utterances that smooth over a potential problem.	How lovely. He's eating peas and chips, lovely. Flies to New York, Wow that'll be good. Perhaps Mo can go in the lorry and Ollie can go by boat.
Prompts	Utterances that prompted the next action or part of the story or reminded children to take turns.	You suggest something for the Owl. See what he wants to do. You tell me what he's doing. Now it's Mo Monkey's turn.

Analysis of Adult Utterances

Given that the researcher made a substantial contribution to the conversation for all Dyad Types with the exception of girl friendship and boy friend/acquaintance dyads, we next carried out an analysis of Adult utterances according to Dyad Type and Gender. Adult utterances could be broadly categorized as *Adult Questions to Child* (AQC), *Prompts* (P) *or Smoothers* (S). Table 2 shows the detailed coding scheme used to categorize the adult's utterances. This scheme accounted for 85% of all adult utterances. The remaining 15% related to managerial aspects of the task situation such as reminding children to speak clearly for the tape recorder.

While six different categories were identified that could exhaustively account for all adult questions, *Information Questions* and *Maintenance Questions* accounted for 90% of all adult questions. Maintenance questions served as general reminders to the children to maintain the flow of the story. Information questions asked children for verbal clarification of actions that the puppets were miming or asked for specific information about what was happening in the story. Table 3 gives the mean number of adult questions, prompts and smoothers, (the latter categories have been combined), by Dyad Type and Gender.

Table 3: Mean number of adult utterances categorised as Questions (AQC), Prompts and Smoothers (P&S) as a function of Dyad type and gender

Dyad	n	Adult Utterances	
		AQC	P&S
FR+FR			
Girls	4	4	7
Boys	4	23	34
FR+AQ			
Girls	4	14	24
Boys	4	7	10
FR+IS			
Girls	3	13	22
Boys	3	20	27
AQ+IS			
Girls	4	15	25
Boys	2	16	14

Note: Values have been rounded up or down to the nearest whole number for ease of comparison.

As with the Conversational Turn analysis, the data presented in Table 3 indicates that girls from best friend dyads (FR+FR) and boys from FR+AQ dyads did not receive as much adult support as other Dyad Types. Most of the time the conversation between these children was genuinely dyadic. They took turns, built on each other's suggestions and tried to create more or less coherent 'adventures' for the two story characters. For other Dyad Types, however, both children needed considerable assistance from the adult to generate and maintain the flow of their 'stories'.

Analysis of the Children's Utterances

Kruger's (1992) coding scheme has been successfully adapted by Miell and MacDonald (2000) to analyze the transactive communications that take place when friendship dyads are engaged in creative collaborations concerning musical composition. Due to the extent of adult involvement and the triadic nature of so many of the interactions this scheme did not lend itself easily to our data as it requires the identification of 'self' and 'other' transactive statements, questions, and responses within the context of two-way interactions. Instead, a coding scheme was developed that identified child utterances as falling into three broad categories: *Productive, Non-productive* or *Adult Directed*. Productive utterances were those that made a positive contribution to the joint interaction between children and included Child Initiated Sequences, Child Contingent Utterances, Child Agreements and Child Questions. Non-productive utterances were those that contributed little to the stories children were developing, such as Child Repetition, those that signaled Child Disagreement and/or non-negotiated changes of topic, and Child Non-contingent Utterances. Adult Directed utterances were those made in response to adult questions and suggestions and could be categorized as 'Adult Contingent' or Adult Non-contingent. Definition of these categories and their sub-categories are given in Table 4. This coding scheme was able to account for over 90 % of children's utterances. As with the scheme derived for adult utterances, however, the frequency of utterances in some sub-categories was substantially greater than in other sub-categories.

Child Contingent, and Adult Contingent were the most frequent types of Productive Utterance observed. Child Contingent utterances are arguably the most important category as the definition of 'contingent' adopted here applied to utterances where the "Child offers a contribution that builds on or elaborates own or partner's (or adult's) immediately preceding utterance or suggestion". This is similar to Miell and MacDonald's (2000) definition of transactive communication: "Transactive communication is where the child extends, elaborates or otherwise works on ideas that have already been raised in the interaction – either by themselves or by their partner" (p. 353). We would argue that, in the context of our story creation task, the definition of 'Contingent' is equivalent to the notion of transactive communication. We were interested in comparing the frequency of Child Contingent utterances across Dyad Types as this type of communication is more often found in interactions between friends than between acquaintances. It is also one of the features of successful collaboration. We predicted, therefore, that this type of utterance would be observed more frequently for FR+FR dyads than other Dyad Types if, as Hartup (1992) suggests, "Friends engage in more frequent positive exchanges […] than unselected partners or children who don't like each other" (p.185). We also predicted that contingent interactions would be more frequent in FR+AQ and FR+IS dyads compared with AQ+IS dyads. This prediction was based on our previous research that demonstrated that popular, socially competent children can extend their highly successful communication strategies to working with other, less socially skilled children, (Murphy & Faulkner, 2000).

Table 4: Coding scheme used to categorise children's utterances

Utterance Codes	Definition	Examples
Productive		
Child Initiates Sequence	Child suggests how the story or a new event sequence could start.	C: Hello, let's go and play with the horses. C: Let's go to the seaside and the park.
Child Contingent	Child offers a contribution that builds on or elaborates own or partner's immediately preceding utterance or suggestion.	C1: Oh no, the play park's on fire. C2: That was where the aeroplane was. Look the aeroplane is on fire too.
Child Question	Child asks partner for information or clarification.	C: What shall we do now? C: Will you go up to the zoo?
Child Agreement	Child agrees with partner's suggestion	C1: Let's climb up the trees. C2: Good idea. C1: We're gonna have some breakfast aren't we? C2: Yeah lets have some breakfast.
Non-productive		
Child Non-contingent	Novel or irrelevant contribution that does not build on partner's immediately preceding utterance.	C1: I'm going to have a drink first before I go. C2: Look a chicken. C1: I'm going to the mountains. C2: Where's my garage.
Child Repetition	Contribution that is a simple repetition of own or partner's immediately preceding utterance.	C: I ate them all. I ate all of them C1: Aliens invading. C2: Aliens invading.
Child Disagreement	Child disagrees with partner.	C1: Hey – wait for me. C2: No, I'm going to the shops. C1: Do you want to come on my aeroplane? C2: No, I want to stay here.
Adult Directed		
Adult Contingent	Child offers a contribution that builds on or elaborates adult's immediately preceding utterance or provides a relevant answer or adult's question.	A: Are you going to tell that owl to go away? C: Owl, go away. You're supposed to be a night animal. A: What would you like to do, Monkey? C: I would like to go to the woods.
Adult Non-contingent	Novel or irrelevant contribution that does not build on adult's immediately preceding utterance or is an irrelevant answer to adult's question.	A: How's this story going to end? C: Tonight, tomorrow. A: Is Ollie Owl sitting beside his pal? C: I'm starting to put things back.

Table 5 gives the percentages of all child utterances categorized as Child Contingent or Child Non-contingent for the various Dyad Types. It can be seen that the data only partially supports these predictions. Collapsing across gender, the percentage of Child Contingent interactions in FR+FR, FR+AQ and FR+IS dyads is greater than that for AQ+IS dyads (34.5%; 28.5%, 26.5% and 20% respectively) thus confirming one of our predictions. It is apparent, however, that contrary to the prediction that FR+FR dyads would show the greatest amount of contingent interaction, boy FR+FR dyads generated fewer contingent utterances than boy FR+AQ and FR+I Dyads. Contrary to expectations, boys in best friend dyads solicited the highest number of Adult Questions, Prompts and Smoothers of all dyads, (see Table 4) suggesting that, for these children, working with a best friend is not an optimal working context. The boys from FR+FR dyads appeared to find working with a nonfriend acquaintance easier even where the acquaintance was a child regarded as socially isolated by his peers. By contrast girls in FR+FR dyads showed the greatest percentage of contingent utterances and lowest amount of adult involvement over all Dyad Types suggesting that for girls, as predicted, engaging in creative activity with a best friend is an optimal working context. These gender differences were unanticipated and will be discussed in more detail later in the chapter.

Table 5: Mean percentages of children's utterances that were contingent or non-contingent as a function of Dyad type and gender

Dyad	n	Utterance	
		Child Contingent	Child Non-Contingent
FR+FR			
Girls	4	47	13
Boys	4	22	8
FR+AQ			
Girls	4	24	9
Boys	4	33	15
FR+IS			
Girls	3	23	20
Boys	3	30	7
AQ+IS			
Girls	4	17	9
Boys	2	23	2

Note: Values have been rounded up or down to the nearest whole number for ease of comparison.

Child Non-contingent utterances were much less frequent than Child Contingent utterances. The largest percentage of non-contingent interactions was observed for girl FR+IS dyads. This, together with the observation that girls in this type of dyad solicited a high proportion of Prompts and Smoothers from the researcher, suggests that this working relationship was particularly problematic for them.

Findings for children working in AQ+IS dyads are somewhat mixed. As with other girl/girl pairs, girl AQ+IS dyads had a higher number of conversational turns than boys, (see Table 1), but they also solicited a fairly high degree of adult involvement and showed the smallest percentage of contingent utterances. Transcripts for boys in AQ+IS dyads were only available for two pairs. This meant that differences between these two pairs, girl AQ+IS dyads and other types of dyad could be to attributable to individual variation and should be treated with caution.

The Effect of Different Partners on Children's Collaboration

The preceding analyses only indicate between dyad differences. They do not reveal whether a change of partner affected children's ability to collaborate successfully. This was explored by comparing the percentage of Productive and Non-productive utterances generated by individual children across the two story telling sessions that they took part in. Thus for any one child it was possible to compare whether the nature of his/her contribution changed as a result of a change of partner. In this section, this analysis, together with extracts from the children's conversations and stories will be presented. The conversational extracts illustrate how the nature of individual children's collaboration attempts was affected by changes of partner.

Girls with their Partners
Figure 1 shows how the relational status of their partner affected the percentage of Productive and Non-productive interactions generated by best friends. It confirms the finding that those girls from best friend dyads generated a higher percentage of productive utterances with their friend than with either an acquaintance or a socially isolated child. Conversely, for the boys in FR+FR dyads, a partnership with either an acquaintance or a socially isolated child yielded a greater percentage of productive contributions than the partnership with their best friend.

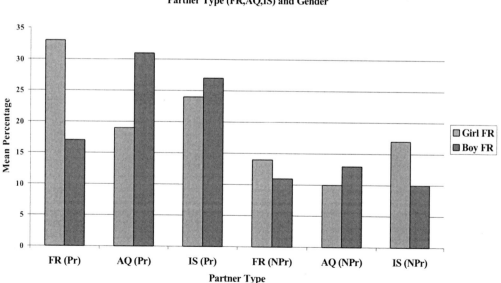

Best Friends - Productive (Pr) and Non-Productive Utterances According to
Partner Type (FR,AQ,IS) and Gender

Figure 1

Figure 1 also shows that Non-productive interactions were greatest for girls from friendship dyads when they partnered a socially isolated girl although they were also relatively frequent between best friends. This latter observation is not too surprising given that other studies have reported that disagreements occur more frequently between friends than nonfriends, (see Schneider, 2000 for a review). Also it has been found that friends repeat their own and the other's contributions more often than nonfriends, when generating stories, (Hartup, Daiute, Zajac & Sholl, 1995, cited in Hartup, 1998). In the present study, however, For both FR+FR and FR+IS dyads, disagreements accounted for less than 5 % of individual children's utterances in the majority of cases. Repetition of a partner's utterances and ideas was much more frequent. This suggests that although we categorized repetitions as Non-productive children might, as Hartup et al. (1995) suggest, use repetition to signal positive engagement with the task and with their partner.

Extract 1 is an example of a highly productive interaction between two best friends Helen and Laura. It comes at the end of a long sequence where Monkey has been persistently annoying Owl who has been trying to sleep. Sixty-eight % of Helen and Laura's utterances were contingent and there was minimal adult involvement in their story telling session.

Extract 1: Laura and Helen (FR+FR) – Monkey gets arrested

Laura (Mo):	Knock knock. Knock knock.
Helen (Ollie):	[Shouting] "Who's there"?
Laura:	"Your friend".
Helen:	[Mock annoyance] "Just get out of my house. I'm not interested"!
Laura:	"I'll break the door down in a minute".
Helen:	"No you will not. I'm going ups… I'm going into my bedroom".
Laura:	[Laughing] "I'm here now". [Inaudible] "Watch out, before I get my carving knife and stab you".
Helen:	"I'll phone the police then" [Telephone noise?]
Laura:	"Go on then, I don't care".
Helen:	"481243, hello Police. Can you come to Monkey's house? She's going to kill me". [They're] coming. [inaudible] I've got the police. There you are, saw you. Whaaw, you're under arrest. Clip clop. You're in jail now. *End of story*

What is notable about this extract is that the story action is created through dialogue rather than through a descriptive account of a series of loosely connected events. This is highly sophisticated and signals that a considerable rapport exists between these two children within the context of their friendship.

The next extract shows what took place when Helen was paired with Charlotte, a socially isolated child. Charlotte began this dyad's session by making Ollie Owl crash the aeroplane into all the toys. Mo (Helen) escaped this mayhem by going to the mountain where he enjoys some refreshment before returning. Extract 2 shows what happened next.

Extract 2: Helen and Charlotte (FR+IS) – Going to the mountain

| Helen (Mo): | Sit on the chair and have lemonade. Then he stood up. Then he comes back to see the farm and ride on horsey. Clip clop. |
| Charlotte (Ollie): | I go to the mountain. |

Helen:	I think you're copying me.
Charlotte:	Go back to the farm and get on the horse. Clip clop.
Charlotte:	I'm going to fly.
Adult:	Owl's can fly can't they? So that's OK.
Helen:	Then I jump on the lamb, stick it in the boat.
Helen:	Put it in the boat and go home. Put it on the chair and let it have some lemonade, then take it back there. Then fell down!
Charlotte:	Fly, pick that up [inaudible] What?
Helen:	What?
Charlotte:	Do you think I'm copying you?
Helen:	Yeah.
Charlotte:	Go back home. Oh, forgot the lamb and go back home. [Flying noises] Get that back. Mr Puppet knocks all that down.
Helen:	[Laughs].

The sustained 'pretend' dialogue observed between Helen and her best friend Laura in Extract 1 was completely absent from her interaction with Charlotte. While Helen was clearly trying hard to develop a story the only way that Charlotte appeared to be able to contribute was by repeating Helen's story. Thirty-two per cent of Charlotte's utterances were either non-contingent utterances or straightforward repetitions of Helen's contributions. Fortunately, as Extract 2 shows, Helen appeared to accept this with good-humor and, as with her session with Laura, adult involvement was minimal. This suggests that although this pair did not manage to produce a jointly created story, they did manage to establish a positive emotional climate. Unfortunately, as Extract 3 shows, the same can not be said of the interaction that took place between Laura and Fiona who were the FR+AQ pair for this particular set of children. The story session starts with Mo in the aeroplane knocking down trees and animals.

Extract 3: Laura and Fiona (FR+AQ)

Adult:	Monkey is feeling very angry today is he? So what does Ollie Owl do?
Fiona (Ollie):	Goes on the bus.
Adult:	Goes on the bus?
Fiona:	[Inaudible]
Adult:	Pardon, I can't hear you?
Fiona:	[Inaudible] and climbs up onto the mountain.
Adult:	Oh, he's climbing the mountains. Yes that's good isn't it? So, what does the Monkey do now? Gets on the van? What does he do? You tell me what he's doing.
Laura (Mo):	[Whispering] He's trying to driving. [Clattering as houses are knocked over].
Adult:	Oh my goodness – drives and knocks all the houses down.
Laura:	[Giggles]
Adult:	I think Monkey is a bit vicious. Right, now. What happens now Ollie? Sitting on your chair.
Fiona:	That's right. Drinking a cup of tea.
Adult:	Drinking a cup of tea. Lovely cup of tea – mmmm.
Fiona:	He eats his dinner.

Adult:	Eats his dinner, yes.
Fiona:	Then he goes out for a walk on the horsey.
Adult:	Oh, he's going for a ride on the horse – that's a very clever Owl, isn't it? Very good.
Fiona:	And then he sees the goat and gives him a ride.
Adult:	How lovely. Come on then Monkey. What do you want to do?
Laura:	Nothing.

During the session involving Laura and Fiona, 56 % of all of their utterances were Adult Directed. None of Laura's (FR) utterances were directed to Fiona (AG). As Extract 3 shows, there was an extremely high level of adult involvement in this session although even the researcher failed to draw Laura into the interaction. The 'story' here is essentially created between Fiona, and the researcher. Of course while we have no way of knowing why Laura chose not to participate in this session, she may simply have been tired or bored, the tone of her interaction with Fiona stands in marked contrast with that of the lively creative session with her friend Helen. It also contrasts with the session reproduced in the next extract where Fiona partners Charlotte. Extract 4 shows, that although this dyad needed as much adult support as Laura and Fiona, the tone of their interaction was more positive with much laughter and clownish behaviour.

Extract 4: Fiona and Charlotte (AQ + IS) – Knocking the woods down

Adult:	Now what are you going to do? I mean [...] Ollie Owl, it's your turn. What's going to happen in their adventure?
Fiona (Ollie):	He's going for a flight.
Adult:	He's going for a flight. OK. Get on the aeroplane. Are you on the aeroplane?
	[Aeroplane noises]
Adult:	And where have you landed?
Fiona:	Near the woods.
Adult:	The woods. What happens in the woods?
	[Pause and clattering]
Adult:	Ooh – knock all the woods over. Are you a wood chopper? Ollie Owl the wood chopper. [Laughs]
Adult:	Now, Mo Monkey. What happens next?
Charlotte (Mo):	I'm going on a flight.
Adult:	You're going on a flight are you?
Charlotte:	Hmm. Near the woods. [Giggles]
Adult:	Oh, you've knocked down the woods as well.
Charlotte:	Yeah, I've knocked two over.

Note how in this extract, Charlotte again adopted the strategy of copying her partner just as she did when interacting with Helen. Twenty per cent of her utterances were repetitions. It would be tempting to suggest that imitation and repetition might be a coping strategy that socially isolated children adopt when they are required to cooperate with other children. Of the seven socially isolated children participating in this study, however, Charlotte was the only child who adopted this strategy almost exclusively although children in other dyads also imitated their partners' utterances and activities.

Boys with their Partners

As Figure 2 shows, when a boy acquaintance worked with a child from a friendship pair, the interaction was characterized by a higher percentage of productive interactions than when they worked with a socially isolated child. This was the case for both girl and boy acquaintances. Extract 5 is taken from a very long session with Ben (AQ) and Daniel (FR). This extract occurs at the end of the session. Daniel's puppet Mo has just built a tower and Ben's puppet Ollie has flown off with its roof.

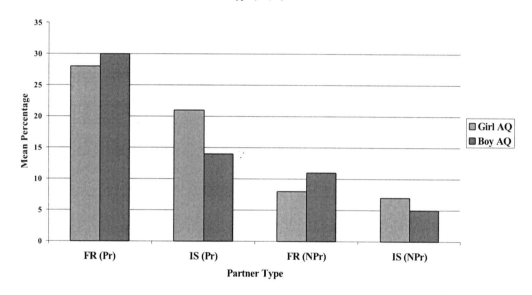

Acquaintances - Productive (Pr) and Non-productive (NPr) Utterances According to Partner Type (FR,IS) and Gender

Figure 2

Extract 5: Daniel and Ben (FR+AQ) – Stealing from Monkey

Adult:	So what are you going to do?
Daniel (Mo):	Hmm. [Pause] If he doesn't give me that button I'll shoot him.
Adult:	My goodness. Right Ollie what are you going to do about that?
Ben (Ollie):	I'll take that back and take his chicken in.
Adult:	Now what are you going to do?
Ben:	Now I'm going to stay and eat all the toys.
Adult:	Ah, so he can't come and pinch anything now can he?
Ben:	[Growling] "Don't let me see you again".
Adult:	Tell me what's happening, Monkey?
Daniel:	I'm going to get a knife and cut his head off.
Adult:	If he doesn't stop stealing your things you're going to get a knife and cut his head off?
Daniel:	Yeah.

Adult:	Well Ben, what are you going to do about that?
Ben:	Take his chair.
Adult:	You just keep stealing his things! Hello, he's coming, attacking you.
	[Pause and clattering]
Adult:	So Ben, how does the adventure end?
Ben:	Bring his chair back. The end.
Adult:	He just brings the chair back at the end. What does he say to Monkey?
Ben:	"Sorry".
Daniel:	[Growling] "No you're not".
	End of story

While Ben and Daniel's attempts to act out a story about Mo and Ollie are somewhat repetitive, 48 % of their utterances were productive although Ben (AQ), in particular needed quite a lot of support from the researcher to sustain his contribution to the interaction. Thirty-five percent of this dyad's utterances were Adult Directed and of these Ben contributed 26 %. As the extract shows, the researcher mediated the interaction by locating the boys' role-play within a scenario where Ollie steals things from Mo. Daniel enters into this scenario by threatening to chop Ollie's head off although Ben, in his role as Ollie is a rather timid burglar. He returns what he has stolen only to fly off with something else. Like Laura and Helen the best friends in Extract 1, Ben (AQ) and Daniel (FR) also invent dialogue for their characters although they do not sustain it as effectively as the girls.

Building a tower also featured in the interaction between Daniel and his best friend Matthew. Unlike Daniel and Ben, however, only 27 % of this dyad's interaction could be classed as Productive and 58 % of their utterances were Adult Directed.

Extract 6: Matthew and Daniel (FR+FR)

Adult:	[...] what happened next Mo Monkey?
Matthew (Mo):	And I went back home.
Adult:	You went back home. Yes, what did you do when you got home? Do you know what happened next? Well, look at all the things you could have. What do you think you could do next?
Matthew:	Um, play on the aeroplane.
Adult:	Right, you've found and aeroplane to play on. So what happened then Ollie Owl?
	[Long pause]
Adult:	What's happening?
Daniel (Ollie):	He's in the lorry, playing.
Adult:	He gets in the lorry and plays. Yes, where does he go in the lorry?
Daniel:	Sit in the lorry and drive.
Adult:	Err, right. So what does Mo Monkey say when he sees that?
Matthew:	He gets in it and he goes.
Daniel:	He's copying me!
Adult:	Remember these animals are best friends. Are they going to do anything together? So what does Ollie Owl [...]
M & D Together:	[Interrupting] He shouts.
Daniel:	He shakes.

Adult:	He's shaking his head. What does Ollie Owl do now? They've both had a ride in the lorry?
Daniel:	Guess what I got for my birthday yesterday. I got [inaudible] and I got two water pistols and I got a ice cream.

In common with other boy FR+FR pairs Matthew and Daniel's 'story' consisted of one, barely connected sequence of events in which Mo and Ollie almost appeared to act as independent agents. Only 19 % of their utterances could be classed as Child Contingent and the transcript did not convey a sense that the boys were sharing and extending each other's ideas. Note Daniel's "He's copying me". As the Extract shows, the researcher frequently had to remind them of what they were supposed to be doing. In common with other boy FR+FR pairs, Matthew and Daniel required substantially more adult input in terms of Adult Questions, Prompts and Smoothers than any other Dyad Type, (see also Table 3). Neither boy could be said to be fully engaged with the task and the session ended shortly after Daniel introduced the topic of his recent birthday, signaling that he no longer wanted to participate.

A comparison of Extracts 5 with Extract 6 offers confirmation of the finding that collaboration between boys is more successful when their partner is a nonfriend acquaintance rather than a best friend. And a comparison of Extract 6 with Extract 1 highlights the differences in the quality of the interactions that took place between girl and boy friendship pairs.

Earlier in this chapter we predicted that if friends are able to extend their highly successful communication strategies to working with other children then socially isolated children should benefit more from being partnered by a child from a friendship dyad than with a nonfriend acquaintance. The data in Figure 3, however, does not offer unequivocal support for this prediction. Once again substantial gender differences appear to be operating. Socially isolated girls generate slightly more Productive utterances when partnered with a child from a friendship dyad than when partnered with an acquaintance but they also generate more Non-productive utterances with a friend. As the discussion of Helen and Charlotte's interaction presented earlier, (Extract 2) showed, Charlotte openly acknowledged using non-productive repetition as her preferred strategy. For all girl FR+IS dyads, Non-productive Child Non-contingent utterances were more frequent than Productive Child Contingent Utterances and repetition was used between 10 and 15% of the time by the partners of the socially isolated girls.

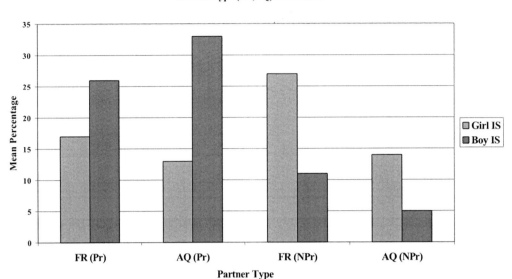

Figure 3

By contrast, socially isolated boys appear to engage in more productive collaboration with an acquaintance than with a child from a friendship pair as a comparison between Extracts 7 and 8 show.

Extract 7: Ben and George (AQ+IS) – Taking the animals on a picnic

Adult:	Ok Ben. What happens next?
Ben (Ollie):	Oh, there's this one left [goat], I think I'll take him to the picnic.
Adult:	Take the goat to join the picnic. Then what happens Monkey?
Ben:	"I brought the other one back".
George (Mo):	"Oh, thank you". Shall I bring the picnic things?
Ben:	Yes, come on, I'll go. Ok, nearly done. Brmm brmm, brmm brmm. Got them.
Adult:	Right Monkey, what happens next?
Ben:	Let's eat the picnic.
George:	Ok. Would the Owl like to get out to eat the picnic? Don't worry. Let's have a bit. Let me have a bit.
	[Pause while George tries to get an animal to stand up]
George:	Ok. "Have you finished"? "Have you"? "Good, bye-bye".

The transcript for this AQ+IS dyad showed that while 35 % of their utterances were contingent, George contributed approximately two thirds of these. Extract 7 shows, however, that although Ben's contributions were fairly brief, his utterances elicited fairly detailed contingent responses from George that allowed him to build on Ben's picnic theme. The next interaction between Matthew (FR) and George (IS) was much less coherent and showed little attempt by Matthew to collaborate. Extract 8 shows how George tried valiantly to engage Matthew's participation in the business of taking the hen for a ride.

Extract 8: Matthew and George (FR+IS) –
Mo takes hen for a ride and Ollie builds a tower

Adult:	Right Matthew you can start the adventure off. What's going to happen?
Matthew (Ollie):	He's sitting on the hen.
Adult:	What? Ollie owl is sitting on the hen? What's he doing sitting on the hen?
George (Mo):	He's warming the hen up.
Adult:	He's warming the hen up, oh. Well come on then Monkey. What's going to happen next?
George:	"Hello friend, want to come with me for a ride"?
Adult:	So what happened? The hen gets in the lorry.
George:	[Driving lorry] Brmm, brmm. Brmm, brmm. I'll go and get the plane.
Adult:	So then what happens Ollie Owl? Your turn.
George:	"Come on Owl, let's have a drink".
Matthew:	He's drinking his drink.
Adult:	Oh, he's drinking his drink at the picnic. And then what happens? Then what happens?
Matthew:	He's building a tower.

As when Ben (AQ) was his partner, George contributed two thirds of all Child Contingent interactions when he partnered Mathew (FR). Unlike Ben, however, Matthew's contributions did not give George anything that he could build on although his suggestion that Ollie Owl (Matthew) was sitting on the hen to warm it up was an ingenious attempt. Matthew clearly wanted to build a tower and the interaction that followed on from this extract mainly involved interaction between Matthew and the researcher. Like Daniel in Extract 6 and Laura in Extract 3, Matthew effectively refused to co-operate with either George or the researcher and this session was very brief.

SUMMARY AND CONCLUSIONS

The main aim of the study presented in this chapter was to examine the effects of different types of interpersonal relationships on the collaboration of five year-old children. We also wanted to investigate whether less socially skilled children's ability to engage in collaborative activity would benefit from being paired with a socially competent peer. The evidence that we have presented suggests that children's ability to participate in collaborative activity is profoundly influenced by the nature if the social relationship that exists between themselves and their partner. We have also shown that for young children, dyadic interaction between friends does not inevitably foster a positive emotional climate that allows rich and meaningful transactive dialogue to occur. Our study revealed substantial differences in the nature of the collaboration between girl and boy best friend dyads. For girls, effective participation in collaborative activity was facilitated when they worked with a best friend. For boys, however, being paired with a best friend was positively detrimental. Girls in Friendship dyads created sophisticated stories through joint interactions that appeared to draw on a shared understanding of both story form and content. They realized characters for their puppets through invented dialogue and developed meaningful and coherent event sequences that had well-developed beginning and end points. What is more, they did this with minimal adult assistance. The interaction that took place between boys and their best friends was of a completely different nature. They appeared to be much more interested in exploring the properties of the toy props provided than in working collaboratively. They built towers and knocked them down, they made their puppets crash into things and conducted their activity through action and mime rather than pretend dialogue. They made their puppet characters operate individually rather than together and even substantial adult input providing specific suggestions did not facilitate their effective participation in this kind of joint activity.

One explanation as to why this was the case might be that perhaps the task itself was not gender-neutral. Story creation was chosen as the task for this study as it seemed to be a culturally meaningful activity for children of this age. It did, however, require children to develop a pretend play story scenario with small-scale toys and puppets, an activity that is arguably more attractive to girls than it is to boys. However, this does not seem the most likely explanation for the differences observed between boy and girl best friend dyads for two reasons. Firstly, the boys from best friend pairs were able to develop meaningful stories when their partner was a non-friend acquaintance suggesting that the task was not particularly gender specific. Secondly, when girls from best friend pairs were partnered with an acquaintance they were not able to display the same level of sophisticated story telling without substantial adult input, suggesting that even if the task could be seen as being 'gendered', it did not necessarily promote successful collaboration between girls.

A recent study by Kutnick and Kington (2003) suggest an alternative interpretation. Their study was designed to investigate friendship effects in primary school classrooms through the naturalistic observation pairs of friends and non-friends working on scientific reasoning tasks. They observed children aged 5 to 11 years and report similar findings to the ones presented here, and state that at all ages, " Girls partnered with (female) friends provided the highest level of performance, followed by boys in non-friendship pairings, then girls in non-friendship pairs. *The poorest paired performance was boys working with (male) friends*". Kutnick and Kington also interviewed the children in their study about the qualities and activities that characterized their friendships. These interviews revealed that boys' and girls' friendships are located in different cultural contexts. Boys' friendships were action oriented and based on activities with others outside the school classroom. They excluded school collaboration from their interview accounts and did not consider it as a legitimate activity within the context of their friendships. Girls, on the other hand, located their friendships within a relational context based on loyalty, trust and joint problem solving and they frequently mentioned school based collaboration as a legitimate friendship activity.

We would suggest, therefore, that when they were working with their best friend, the boys in our study did not perceive joint story creation as a legitimate activity within the context of their friendship. Kutnick and Kington's findings also suggest that whereas boys perceive school-based collaborative activity with an acquaintance as being an appropriate activity, girls do not. For girls, friendships are located in an positive climate of mutual trust where there is the expectation that friends will help each other share information. In our study, girls only seemed to be able to create this type of climate when paired with their best friend. When their partner was an acquaintance or a socially isolated girl, the girls from best friend pairs could only collaborate effectively through an adult third party.

Our findings only partially supported the prediction that socially isolated children would benefit from working with a partner from a friendship dyad. Again there was a gender effect. Socially isolated boys were able to engage in more productive collaboration when their partner was an acquaintance than when he was a boy from a friendship pair although, in both cases, dyads were only able to sustain this collaboration with the assistance of an adult. While collaboration between socially isolated girls and their partners was more successful when the partner was from a friendship pair this type of pairing also produced substantial amounts of non-contingent talk and repetition.

As Charlotte's (IS) attempts to collaborate with her partners showed she used repetition as her main way of collaborating. Although, these socially isolated children found it difficult to build on and elaborate each other's ideas it is possible that for children of this age, imitation is one of the ways they use to signal to their partner that they accept his or her contributions as meaningful and legitimate. As Vygotsky (1978) suggests, imitation in the context of collaborative activity allows children to demonstrate behaviours that are in advance of their individual abilities.

There were very few disagreements between children in the context of this study. Except in the few cases where children signalled that they wished to withdraw from the situation, or, (as was the case with boy best friend and girl friend/acquaintance dyads), children created parallel but distinct 'stories', most children accepted each other's contributions with equanimity and humour.

Our attempts to examine how children's pre-existing relationships within their peer group influence their interactions with preferred and non-preferred partners have revealed that the interpersonal processes involved in 'learning to collaborate' are subtle and complex. The study suggests that for very young children, truly effective participation in dyadic collaborative activity only occurs spontaneously when it is situated in an activity setting that is meaningful in the context of their relationship. Where these conditions do not prevail, 'collaborating to learn', or in our case, 'collaborating in active meaning making', requires the support and assistance of an adult. In our study dyadic interaction became triadic interaction for the majority of dyads. For girl friendship dyads the researcher only needed to adopt the role of mediator at the beginning of the story telling session and was able to withdraw once the children had hit upon a story theme that they could share. With most other dyads, however, the researcher had to provide extensive scaffolding and encouragement to enable the children to sustain a successful interaction. Finally, in the least successful dyads, the researcher's role was more that of an instructor than a mediator.

And finally, what of Mo Monkey and Ollie Owl? Even though the creative activity of engaging in joint meaning making was challenging for some dyads, during the course of our study, these two puppet characters enjoyed a rich variety of 'adventures'. These themes were drawn from the children's own experience, their shared cultural knowledge and their understanding of what it means to create stories and dramatic situations. Mo and Ollie went on lots of picnics, ate burgers at McDonalds, visited a cinema in London and went to see an auntie who owned a sweet shop. They went on holiday to Spain, survived car crashes visited the zoo and the beach, climbed mountains and were even attacked by aliens from outer space. They collaborated, they argued, they annoyed each other and at times even threatened to kill each other but, at the end of the day they usually went home for a cup of tea and a nice long sleep.

AUTHORS' NOTE

The authors would like to thank the children and schools that took part in the study, Sally Kynan and Kim Lock for their assistance during the project, and Clare Wood for her insightful suggestions regarding presentation of the qualitative analysis.

REFERENCES

Asher, S. R., & Hymel, S. (1981). Children's social competence in peer relations: Sociometric and behavioral assessment. In J. D. Wine & M. D. Smye (Eds.), *Social competence* (pp.125-157). New York: Guilford.

Azmitia, M., & Hesser, J. (1993). Why siblings are important agents of cognitive development: A comparison of siblings and peers. *Child Development, 64*, 430–444.

Azmitia, M., & Montgomery, R. (1993). Friendship, transactive dialogues, and the development of scientific reasoning. *Social Development, 2*, 202–221.

Dunn, L. M., & Dunn, L. M. (1982). *The British Picture Vocabulary Scale.* Windsor, UK: NFER-Nelson Publishing Co. Ltd.

Engel, S. (1999). *The stories children tell: Making sense of the narratives of childhood.* New York: W. H. Freeman and Company.

Faulkner, D., & Miell, D. (1994, September). *Isolated children's difficulties in developing working relationships during their first year at school.* Paper presented at the International Conference on Group and Interactive Learning, Glasgow.

Gumpel, T., & Frank, R. (1999). An expansion of the peer paradigm: Cross-age peer tutoring of social skills among socially rejected boys. *Journal of Applied Behaviour Analysis, 32*, 115–118.

Hartup, W. W. (1989). Behavioural manifestations of children's friendships. In T. J. Berndt & G. W. Ladd (Eds.), *Peer relationships in child development* (pp.46–70). New York: Wiley.

Hartup, W. W. (1992). Friendships and their developmental significance. In H. McGurk (Ed.), *Childhood social development* (pp.175-205). Hove, UK: Lawrence Erlbaum Associates Ltd.

Hartup, W. W. (1998). The company they keep: Friendships and their developmental significance. In A. Campbell & S. Muncer (Eds.), *The social child* (pp.143–163). Hove, UK: Psychology Press Ltd.

Hayes, D. S., & Casey, D. M. (2002). Dyadic versus individual storytelling by preschool children. *Journal of Genetic Psychology, 163*, pp. 445–459.

Kruger, A. C. (1993), Peer collaboration: conflict, co-operation or both? *Social Development, 2*, 165–182.

Kutnick, P., & Manson, I. (1998). Social life in the primary school: Towards a relational concept of social skills for use in the classroom. In A. Campbell & S. Muncer (Eds.), *The social child* (pp.165–187). Hove, UK: Psychology Press Ltd.

Kutnick, P., & Kington, A. (2003). *Children's friendships and learning in school: Cognitive enhancement through social interaction?* Manuscript submitted for publication.

Middleton, D., & Edwards, D. (Eds.). (1990). *Collective remembering.* London: Sage Publications.

Miell, D., & MacDonald, R. (2000). Children's creative collaborations: The importance of friendship when working together on a musical composition. *Social Development, 9,* 348–369.

Murphy, S., & Faulkner, D. (2000). Learning to collaborate: Can young children develop better communication strategies through collaboration with a more popular peer. *European Journal of the Psychology of Education, XV*(4), 389-404.

Schneider, B. (2000). *Friends and enemies: Peer relations in childhood.* London: Arnold.

Shapiro, L. R., & Hudson, J. A. (1991). Tell me a make-believe story: Coherence and cohesion in young children's picture-elicited narratives. *Developmental Psychology, 27,* 960–974.

Vass, E. (2002). Friendship and collaborative creative writing in the primary school. *Journal of Computer Assisted Learning, 18,* 102–110.

Vygotsky, L. S. (1978). *Mind in society: The development of higher psychological processes.* Cambridge, Mass.: Harvard University Press.

Wells, G. (1986). *The meaning makers.* Portsmouth, NH: Heinemann.

Chapter 3

READING TOGETHER: COMPUTERS AND COLLABORATION

Karen Littleton, Clare Wood and Pav Chera

INTRODUCTION

Recent years have seen computer technologies being used to support children's reading development and a number of studies have evaluated the effectiveness of computer-based reading instruction (for a summary see Chera & Wood, 2003). Much of this work has highlighted the efficacy of computer software packages designed to enhance phonological awareness (e.g. Wise et al., 1989) and word recognition (e.g. Van Daal & Reitsma, 1990) in children experiencing reading difficulties. This emphasis on remediation neglects the potential role that computer technologies might play in supporting typically developing children's early reading. Mindful of this neglect, we have devised a programme of work designed specifically to investigate the use of 'talking books' with beginning readers. Part of this work has focused on the use of talking book software by novice readers working individually (Chera & Wood, 2003). More recently, we have embarked upon a series of studies examining the use of talking books by pairs of young children working together, and largely autonomously, in classroom contexts. Our overall aim is to understand both the processes and products of such peer-based work.

Our study of the collaborative use of talking books is underpinned by our commitment to a socio-cultural approach to understanding development and learning. Socio-cultural theory posits that cognitive processes are inextricably interwoven and enmeshed with social and cultural practices such that cognition and action are inseparable. Seen from this perspective, it is not just the texts (be they electronic or paper-based) that children engage with that are important, it is also:

'...the *ways* (our itals) in which they engage with them that shape reading and writing'
(Wood, submitted).

So from our perspective, understanding literacy and the processes of becoming literate necessitates understanding social practices. It also necessitates the recognition that:

'People read...differently out of different social practices, and these different ways with words are part of different ways of being persons and different ways and facets of doing life.'
(Lankshear & Knobel, 2003, p.8).

In this chapter, we present data from a recently conducted study which was designed to investigate the ways in which beginning readers, 'doing life' in the reception classroom, engage with texts when they work collaboratively with talking books software. Our intention was to study the children's use of such software in a way that emphasized the importance of the learners' talk and joint activity and that did not isolate the collaborators' interactions from the material circumstances and cultural context in which they were embedded.

The investigation reported here offers an initial evaluation of the potential of so-called 'talking books' software as a resource for collaborative literacy activity with children who are beginning to learn to read. Consistent with a socio-cultural approach, this evaluation centred on the processes of learning and meaning making that the children engaged in during their joint activities. Our interest was in how the children made sense of a computer mediated literacy activity where there was minimal adult intervention. As skilled readers, adults recognize the potential of, and the intentions underpinning many of the features of talking books software. As teachers, it is easy to assume that the children will recognize the computer's identity as a 'book' in this context. However, we felt it important to understand the meaning of the task as understood by the children.

THE CONTEXT OF COLLABORATION: THE LITERACY HOUR

At the time of writing, the 'National Literacy Strategy' for England and Wales has a pivotal role to play in shaping schooled literacy practices in English and Welsh primary schools. Introduced in 1998, the centrepiece of this programme for teaching children to read and write is the 'Literacy Hour'. The 'Literacy Hour' is a daily session that consists of thirty minutes of whole class teaching, twenty minutes of small group work with the teacher (referred to as 'guided study') while the rest of the class engages in independent study, followed by a final ten-minute plenary session. It has been adopted in some form by the majority of primary schools in England (Fisher & Singleton, 2000).

Our interest in the collaborative use of talking books software derives partly from a recognition that whilst the guidance associated with the independent study component of the Literacy Hour stresses that:

'Pupils should be trained not to interrupt the teacher and there should be sufficient resources and alternative strategies for them to fall back on if they get stuck. They should also understand the importance of independence for literacy, and how to use their own resources to solve problems and bring tasks to successful conclusion'
(Department for Education and Employment, 1998, p.13)

there is in fact little specific guidance on the form that these resources and alternative strategies might take. We thus began to consider whether the collaborative use of talking books software could represent one alternative strategy – affording an environment in which beginning readers could work together to solve their reading-related problems, independently of the teacher, via discussion and use of the resources and opportunities made available to them through the computer.

THE 'BANGERS AND MASH' TALKING BOOKS

The talking books used in the observational work reported here were identical to those designed and developed by Chera (2000) and evaluated by Chera and Wood (2003). The books were designed in consultation with teachers, children and researchers in literacy, and were simple in nature. They were based on the first series of books in the 'Bangers and Mash' (phonic) reading scheme published by Longman. These books introduce the children to the adventures of two mischievous chimps, Bangers and Mash. The software allowed the children to hear the whole page read aloud when a button at the bottom of the page was clicked, hear individual words spoken when the cursor was moved over the word, and hear and see the word broken down into smaller parts when a word was clicked upon. In each book two pages had an additional 'click me!' button, by which the children could access simple phonic activities based on onset and rime blending. 'Onset' refers to all the initial consonants in a single syllable word, and 'rime' refers to the remaining part, from the first vowel onwards (e.g. str-ing). In the activity pages a featured rime from the book was shown in isolation on the right hand side of the page. On the left were a series of possible onsets. If the children clicked on an onset, they could see the new word that was formed and hear the segments put together to form the new word.

READING 'BANGERS AND MASH' TOGETHER

We observed sixteen pairs of beginning readers working with the 'Bangers and Mash' talking books. These children were recruited from a single reception class in a school in Buckinghamshire. In England all children begin to attend school in the year that they are five, and this is referred to as their reception year. Our sample comprised 14 boys and 18 girls, with a mean age of 4 years 9 months (SD 4.8 months). The children in this sample were allocated to one of a number of different (same gender) pairings that varied the degree to which the children worked with a child of similar, higher or lower reading ability to themselves. As pair type was not observed to affect the children's use of the software, the exact nature of and criteria for pairing are not described here, but a full account of this and related data is presented in Wood, Littleton and Chera (in preparation). The allocation of pairings was undertaken in consultation with the teacher. This meant that pairings could be constructed so as to avoid potentially negative interpersonal conflicts.

The pairs of children were recorded working together once a week for two weeks. At the beginning of each session, the children sat with their partner at a Macintosh Powerbook, and had the features of the software demonstrated to them by a researcher. They were introduced to the functionality of the software and how to navigate forwards, backwards and from the main pages to the activities pages and back again. It was explained to the children that the computer was there to help them read the book if they got stuck, and that they were to read the pages aloud together. The children were also encouraged to help each other if they got stuck and to share and discuss their ideas. It was in this context that the children were talked through a set of 'ground rules' for working together on the computer. These 'ground rules', which are noted below, were also written on an A4 piece of card, along with small pictures to remind the children of the meaning of each sentence. This was placed beside the computer during the session to act as a reminder.

The 'ground rules' were:

- Share the computer.
- Help each other if you get stuck.
- Don't be afraid to have a go – remember that the computer is there to help you.
- Look and listen when the other person is talking.
- Praise each other.

After this introduction, the children were then left to work largely independently under the supervision of the researcher. The researcher was present in case there were any technical difficulties associated with the use of the computer. She was also permitted to offer limited encouragement. On occasion it was necessary for her to intervene directly to diffuse conflictual dynamics between the children, and at other times the children directly appealed to her for praise or support. The children worked at the computer for as long as it took them to complete working with the first of the talking books – 'The Hat Trick'. The children were asked to recap the story briefly at the end of the session to bring it to a close. One week later the same procedure was repeated with the second talking book – 'Eggs'. The second session was video recorded so that the children's interactions with the computer and each other could be analysed in detail. The analyses presented in this chapter are based solely on the video-recordings of the second session of work.

WORKING TOGETHER WITH 'BANGERS AND MASH': MODES OF INTERACTION

The video-recordings of the paired sessions were transcribed in a format that included full details of the children's talk and the contributions made by the computer (for example, when the children 'clicked' with the mouse to hear individual words spoken, or broken down etc.). Details of the children's actions are included in the transcripts only where they are integral to the interpretation being made. We undertook a detailed qualitative analysis of the transcripts, focusing our analytic efforts on the ways in which the pairs engaged with and constructed the meaning of the computer task – mindful throughout that:

> 'We shall be able to interpret meanings and meaning making in a principled manner only in the degree to which we are able to specify the structure and coherence of the larger contexts in which specific meanings are created and transmitted.'
> *(Bruner, 1991, pp. 64–65)*

At the heart of our analysis lay a concern with the cultural context and dynamic processes of meaning making, in particular the learners' engagement with and constructions of the meaning of the educational task they were working on. Our analytic work has revealed several distinctive 'modes of interaction' – where a mode of interaction is defined as:

'a certain type of interaction, a genre, with a typical dynamic. It is the framework giving meaning to the overall activity of the participants.'
(Hoogsteder, Maier & Elbers, 1998, p. 181)

By identifying the modes of interaction that characterized the children's activity, we gain some understanding of their expectations, understandings and constructions of the task. Such modes are not trivial observations of actions; they reveal how the children are characterizing the task, and therefore set parameters on the children's actions and, by implication, the scope for collaboration.

'....modes of interaction – classified globally and characterized locally – can be powerful frameworks for participants, although they not be aware in which mode they interact and how this affects their (inter)actions.'
(Hoogsteder, et al., 1998, p. 184)

Our analyses revealed that when engaged in joint reading of a talking book, the pairs of beginning readers adopted diverse modes of interaction, sometimes within a single session. The extracts that follow illustrate the different modes observed overall. However, it should be noted that whereas some pairs adopted a single mode that dominated their interactions on the task, others were more dynamic – shifting their mode, for example, in response to their changing conception of the task or as their interest in it increased or decreased.

Some of the children we observed clearly adopted a 'reading' mode of interaction, where they followed the instructions they had been given at the outset and attempted to read the text together. These children usually only accessed the computer feedback if they got stuck or wanted to check that they had read a page or word correctly. Extract 1, which illustrates this, is taken from Becky and Julie's session – at the point in the story when Bangers puts the egg in his hat (NB. All names used are fictitious).

Extract 1: Becky and Julie

Julie:	He puts
Computer:	/ he / puts / puts /
Julie:	[Julie points to each word and looks at Becky as she slowly says each one]. He puts ⌈the egg in the hat
Becky:	⌊the egg in the hat
Researcher:	Well done
Computer:	/ puts /
Researcher:	Well done, Becky
Computer:	/ the / egg /

[Julie whispers to Becky who nods and turns the page]

Julie:	[Looking at the screen] Its
Becky:	He
Julie:	⌈[Points to each word and looks at Becky as she speaks, as before]. It's fun to throw the egg and catch it
Becky:	⌊It's fun to throw the egg

Julie:	Now let's go onto the next bit
Becky:	( ) [Becky turns the page]

Julie: [points at words as she speaks] ⎡Bangers throws the egg up 1...2...3 times.
Becky: ⎣Bangers throws the egg up 1...2...3 times.

[Becky turns the page]

Julie: [points at screen] ⎡Mash runs in he has no hat on
Becky: ⎣Mash runs in he has no hat on. Now we go to the next bit. Let's go to the next bit.

Julie:	Lets go to the next bit.

[Becky turns the page]

Here we can see that in this extract Becky and Julie check, by using the computer, that they have read 'He puts' and 'the egg' correctly and then they continue their joint reading of the text until they become unsure of the section that describes Mash running into Bangers. Julie appears to adopt the 'teacher like' role of directing her less able partner's activity on the task. Her attention is fixed on Becky rather than the computer screen as she reads: note the way that the one time that her attention falls on the screen instead of on Becky, Becky makes her first mistake, and Julie immediately responds by restarting their reading of the line and re-establishing the 'point and read' procedure. She points to each word to cue Becky that they are to read together, and allows Becky full control of the mouse, much like an adult does with a child they are supporting. Throughout their session of joint work both children are concerned to mark when it is appropriate to move on 'to the next bit' and they keep focused and pre-dominantly on-task for the duration of their work. This extract is thus illustrative of a mode of interaction where the framework giving meaning to the overall activity is derived from the instructions given to the children by the researcher.

There was, however, considerable evidence of other modes of interaction, some of which had a clear correspondence with literacy practices developed in other contexts. As active learners, interpreting the meaning and use of an instructional activity they had not previously encountered, the children frequently recast the reading task so it complied with their own understandings and past experiences. A good example of this recasting and 'bridging' from the known to the new is the mode of interaction we termed 'listening'.

In this mode there was little, if anything, in the way of overt verbal interaction between the children. Their engagement with the talking book was achieved primarily through listening to the story being 'read' by the computer, whilst their engagement with each other was sustained via eye contact, gesture and positive affect, for example, laughing together. Extract 2 illustrates some of the characteristics typifying this 'listening' mode.

Extract 2: Tina and Sharon

Computer:	It's Bangers. He is big. He has a red hat on. / it's / Bang / Bangers / Bangers / is / hat / big / Bangers / Bangers / Bangers / Bangers / Bangers / B- / angers / Bangers / Bangers / Bangers /
Tina:	( ) [Tina turns the page]
Computer:	/ gets / egg / Bangers / egg / the / gets / the / the / table / from / (...) Bangers gets an egg from the box on the table.
Tina:	( ) [Tina turns the page twice]
Sharon:	( ) [Sharon takes over control of the mouse]

Computer:	It's fun to throw the egg and catch it. [Tina points to the screen and Sharon turns the page]
Sharon:	Yes. Bangers throws.
Computer:	Bangers throws the egg up 1…2…3 times. [Sharon turns the page]
Sharon:	( )
Tina:	( ) [Tina points to the screen]
Computer:	Mash runs in. He has no hat on.
Sharon:	( )
Tina:	( ) [Sharon turns the page]
Computer:	He runs into Bangers
Sharon:	( )
Tina:	( ) [Tina points to the screen. Sharon turns the page]
Sharon:	( )
Tina:	( )
Computer:	Can you see the egg? Will it hit Mash?
Tina:	[points] ( ) …egg. [Sharon turns the page] ( )
Computer:	It did! Bang on top of his head! [Tina and Sharon both laugh. Sharon turns the page. Tina laughs].
Computer:	Mash cries as egg runs in his eyes. [Tina and Sharon both laugh. Sharon turns the page].
Tina:	( ) [Tina points at the screen and laughs].
Computer:	Mum runs in. She rubs the egg off. [Sharon turns the page] She is cross with Bangers. She tells him off. [Sharon turns the page] But she gives Mash a big hug. [Sharon turns the page] Bangers cries. He has to have a hug as well. [Sharon turns the page] Then they have eggs for tea.

As can be seen from the extract, Tina and Sharon typically access speech feedback from the computer without speaking, or reading aloud from the screen. So, apart from the comment 'Yes. Bangers throws.' and the repetition of the word 'egg', the children's session of work with the talking book largely consists of listening to the speech feedback generated by the computer – typically on a whole word or whole page basis. The adoption of a 'listening' mode is done with no explicit negotiation on the part of Tina and Sharon, and despite the instruction to read aloud together, these learners seem to share the presupposition that the computer is the 'teller' of the story and they are the 'told'. Whilst they evidently use pointing to establish joint reference and to progress through the story, the framework giving meaning to these children's work with the talking book appears to be one derived from our culture's broader repertoire of literacy related practices – and is one in which children listen to stories being read. So Tina and Sharon do not work with the talking book in the manner requested by the adult and their response to the task is one in which they have brought to bear their previous experiences and encounters in order to make sense of the new.

The use of listening as a basis for engaging with the talking book was also evident in a mode of interaction we called 'listen and repeat'. Here the children listened to the speech feedback, typically whole page feedback, from the computer, but then went on to repeat what was said, either in parallel or one after the other before moving onto the next page. In Extract 3, taken from Hayley and Monica's session of work with the computer, we can see the girls adopting such a mode of interaction, taking turns to repeat what the computer has just said.

Extract 3: Hayley and Monica

Computer: Mum runs in. She rubs the egg off.
Monica: Mum runs in. She rubs the egg off.
Hayley: She rubs the egg off.
[Monica turns the page]
Computer: She is cross with Bangers. She tells him off.
Hayley: She is cross with Bangers she tells him off
Monica: She tells him off. She is cross with Bangers she
            tells him off. [Monica turns the page]
Computer: But she gives Mash a big hug.
Monica: But she gives Mash a hug.
Hayley: But she gives Mash a big hug. [Monica turns the page]
Computer: Bangers cries. He has to have a hug as well.
Monica: Bangers cries he has to have a hug as well. [Monica turns the page]
Computer: Then they have eggs for tea.
Monica: Then they have eggs for tea.
Hayley: Then they have eggs for tea.

In this extract it is the use of speech feedback from the computer, and not Hayley and Monica's own attempts at reading the text, which initiates each phase of the work with the talking book. Other children, however, rather than listening and repeating would 'listen and elaborate.'

In the 'listen and elaborate' mode the children would listen to the computer 'tell' part of the story but would then go on to embellish that aspect of the story – elaborating and commenting on the text they had just heard, often empathizing with the characters. In Extract 4 we see Peter who is working with Tim doing just this. The boys are part way through their session of work and they have just reached the point in the story when Bangers puts the egg in his hat.

Extract 4: Peter and Tim

Peter: [Peter takes control of the mouse]. I'll do this one.
Computer: He puts the egg in his hat.
Peter: [To the researcher] It'll get smashed in that.
Computer: / puts / puts / puts /
Peter: [To the researcher] Click on here?
Computer: He puts the egg in his hat.
Peter: ( ) [turns the page] Oh.
Tim: My turn. [Peter turns back a page] My turn [Tim turns the page]
Computer: It's fun to throw the egg and catch it.
Peter: [To the researcher] And it gets squished and smashed.
Researcher: Does it?
Peter: ( ) and click on [Tim turns the page] those numbers.
Computer: Bangers throws the egg up one, two / two / two / two / three / three / three/
Peter: Oh! [To the researcher] He clicked on number three he did.
Computer: / throws / Bang- / one / one / [Tim turns the page] / hat / Mash runs in. He
             has no hat on. [Tim turns the page]

Peter: Uh oh
Computer: He runs into Bangers. [Tim turns the page]
Peter: [To the screen]. Run then. Watch out there's an egg.
Computer: Can you see the egg? ⌈Will it hit Mash?
Peter: ⌊There it is! [leans across the desk to point at the
          screen. Tim turns the page].
Peter: Get Mash! Oh no! [Peter covers his mouth with his hand. Tim smiles at
          Peter and then at the researcher]. It's happened [to the researcher] done the
          eggs crashed on each (tower).
          The⌈ Mash is cracked now.
Computer: ⌊It did! Bang on top of his head!
Peter   Yeah.
[Peter goes to turn the page using the trackpad on the front of the laptop, but Tim brushes
his hand away and turns the page with the mouse]
Computer: Mash cries as egg runs in his eyes. [Tim turns the page]
Peter: In his eyes? Ergh.

As with Extract 2, there is evidence that engagement with this software can be strongly
mediated by the users' prior experience of literacy-related activities. In this exchange, Peter's
way of interacting with the talking book dominates and he repeatedly elaborates and
comments on the text – devices which are frequently used in storytelling to promote and
sustain children's involvement and joint engagement with stories or texts. Such devices are
used as ways of contextualizing or explicating key words, information or ideas and as a
means of 'modelling' or moderating affective responses to the unfolding narrative. In this
instance, however, Peter elaborates and comments on the story himself. His emotional
engagement with the story is clearly evident as he warns Mash to 'Run' and 'Watch out'
because 'there's an egg' and in his exclamation of 'Ergh' as he realizes that the egg is running
in Mash's eyes.

Peter's is a creative response to the challenge of working with an unfamiliar piece of
technology. It is one that suggests that as part of a process of meaning-making he is
attempting to situate his experience of using the talking book in an appropriate cultural
context in order to make sense of it. This is additionally illustrated by the way that he directs
his comments towards the adult rather than to his partner. He 'recognizes' that this is a
reading task that has been set by an adult in a school context, rather that one that has been
initiated by the boys as a result of some form of genuine shared activity. He therefore expects
his efforts to be aimed towards, and noted by, the adult concerned. Thus he seems to be
adopting a way of interacting with the talking book which parallels school-related practices
he has encountered in other contexts.

An empathic response to the characters was also evident in a mode of interaction we
termed 'acting'. Here the emotional engagement with the story was evidenced not only by the
use of elaboration, but also by non-verbal articulation and gesture, which can be seen in
Extract 5. In this extract, Olga and Susie are working with the software at the point in the
story when the egg has hit Mash.

Extract 5: Olga and Susie

Olga: [Olga laughs, points at the screen and rubs her eyes like Mash.] Ah, he's crying.

Susie: Bangers, Bangers, Bangers.

Computer: / Mash / Mash /

Susie: Banger Banger

Computer: / Mash /

[Susie pretends to cry and rub her eyes then Olga also pretends to cry and both girls rub their eyes in an exaggerated style]

Olga: ( )

Computer: / -ash / egg / egg / e- /

Suzie: ( )

Computer   / -gg / egg / [turns the page]

Suzie: ( )

Olga: [Olga laughs] There's his mummy isn't it?

Suzie: ( ) [Suzie is looking at the computer]

Computer: / r- / r- / r- / -uns / the / the /   / egg / she / egg / e- /-gg / egg / is / in /
Suzie: Apple apple   There's an apple

Suzie: Let me try.

Computer: /i-/[Suzie and Olga both try to click the mouse button at the same time]

Olga: Suzie! [Olga takes over control of the mouse]

Computer: /-n/ / in / [Olga turns the page]

Olga: Your turn

Suzie: ( )

[Olga pretends to be Banger's mother telling him off and wags her finger at the image on the screen.]

Suzie: Shall we see what happens next?

Olga: Yeah.

Olga's laughter in response to the egg hitting Mash, is rapidly followed by the recognition that Mash is crying and she begins to rub her eyes like Mash noting: 'Ah, he's crying'. A little later Susie begins to make crying noises and rub her eyes too. Olga then joins in, both girls 'crying' and rubbing their eyes in a similar, exaggerated style. This acting out of the story is also evident when the girls reach the point in the story when Bangers' mum is telling him off and Olga makes 'telling off' noises and wags her finger at the image on the computer screen, pointing her finger in a similar manner to the illustration of Bangers' mum. Once again this is not a way of interacting around the computer that had been encouraged by the researcher, but it is a way of working with the software which is indicative of the girls' awareness of and sensitivity to the characters' emotional states and active engagement with the storyline of the talking book, something that is positively promoted and encouraged when reading in other contexts.

In addition to the modes of interaction discussed previously, we also found evidence of a mode of interaction in which the children engaged with the story, but the framework giving meaning to the overall activity was one involving playful use of the computer and specific features of the software. This is evident in Extract 6 below.

Extract 6: Ruth and Carol

[Ruth has been in control of the computer, but has just shown Carol how to click on the words and Carol is now temporarily in control].

Computer: / his / he / h- / -ee / he / hat / h- / at / hat / egg / he / in / in / in / his / puts / puts / the / the / hat /

Carol: ( ) (.) [Ruth takes over the mouse]

Computer: / his / his / he / put / p- / -uts / puts / the / the / egg / e- / -gg / egg / hat / h- / -at / his / he / he / at / in / i-/ -n / in / [Ruth turns the page]

Carol: [To the researcher] What's he doing?

Computer: / it / it / is / fun / f- / -un / to /

Carol: ( )

Computer: / throw /

Carol: ( )

Computer: / catch /

Carol: ( )

Computer: / a / [Ruth turns the page] /B- / -ang / Bangers / throws / egg / e- / -gg / egg /

Carol: [To the researcher] Not a very good thing to do. [Ruth turns the page]

Computer: / on / on / on / Ma- / g- / a / run / r- / is / hat h- / at / h- / at / on / [Carol sighs and Ruth turns the page]

Carol: ( )

Computer: / ee / h / ee / h / ee / ee / h / ee / h / ee / h / ee / h / ee / h / ee / h / ee / h / ee / h / ee / h / ee / h / ee / h / ee / ( ) / ee / h / ee / h / ee / h / ee / h / ee / h / ee / h / ee / h /

In this extract Ruth and Carol have reached the point in the story where Bangers puts the egg in his hat. They move the cursor over the words to hear them read aloud or click on them to hear and see the word broken down into smaller parts and then turn to the next page. They work quickly through the next three pages, not reading aloud but moving the cursor over some of the words whilst omitting others, with Carol questioning what Bangers is doing and commenting that throwing an egg is 'Not a very good thing to do'. When they reach the point in the story that reads 'He runs into Bangers' Ruth repeatedly clicks on the word 'he'. This goes beyond the degree of repetition required to confirm the sound of the sub-components of the word 'he' and the girls appear to play with the software, rapidly clicking so that the sub-components of the word are read again and again. Thus the relatively fleeting exploration of some pages of the book, taken together with the repetition of 'h' and 'e', indicated that the girls appeared to be treating the talking book like a computer game, and the task of reading together was not a central concern. For some children, then, the framework giving meaning to the activity was not one that had its roots solely in prior experiences of reading, but was one that was also mediated by prior use of computers and the playing of computer games.

Our analyses also remind us that when learners work together on a school task the business of building and sustaining mutually satisfying social relationships occurs in tandem with classroom activities. In Extract 7 we see Laura and Jill working together on the talking book. Laura's focus is on working through the story, despite the fact that her partner Jill is in a more playful frame of mind, being excited about the impending school disco. The extract reveals Laura to be skilled in managing the potentially problematic conflict between her partner's off task behaviour and her own desire to complete the activity they were set.

Extract 7: Laura and Jill

[The girls are whispering. Laura points, both nod and Laura clicks]

Computer:	/ on / It's Bangers. He is big. He has a red hat on.
Jill:	You know, you know what? You know what?
Laura:	What?
Jill:	Tomorrow I'm going to the disco.
Laura:	( )
Researcher:	You reading the story both of you?
Computer:	/ he / he /
Jill:	( )
Laura:	( )
Computer:	/ he / [Jill turns the page]
Jill:	( ) egg
Laura:	What? [Jill turns the page] (Oh you) [Laura reaches across to regain control of the mouse]
Jill:	I like doing that [smiles].
Laura:	( ) like that. ( ) [Laura turns the page]
Jill:	( )
Laura:	( )
Computer:	/ gets / Bangers / -angers / Bangers / gets / the / Bangers gets an egg from the box on the table. [Laura turns the page while Jill's attention wanders]
Researcher:	Jill
Computer:	He puts the egg in his hat. [Laura laughs]
Jill:	Mine. [Jill takes over control of the mouse]
Computer:	/ he / puts /
Laura:	I'll do it. ( ) [Laura points and turns the page]
Jill:	You know what [Laura turns the page] When I go to the disco today I'm going to get ready right now after school.
Laura:	I don't know why ( ) it's a bit dumb.

In Extract 7 the girls' interaction is mediated by and negotiated within the framework of routines and expectations concerning what it is and is not appropriate to talk about in classroom settings. Laura's management of her partners' off-task talk about the disco indicates her sensitivity to the researcher's concerns that they should be reading and the interaction is shaped by her understandings of 'the values, rules and common representations of school' (Murphy, 2000, p.140). Laura is not overtly dismissive of her friend's interest in the disco, but does not engage with it. Notable in this is the fact that Jill recognizes that it is acceptable for her partner not to pick up on her conversation: she does not get irritated, she instead recognizes that she should also be engaged with the task, and increases her activity on it, albeit temporarily. Both children show understanding of each other's immediate interests, and each tolerates limited participation in each other's preferred activity (Jill shows token efforts at engaging with the task, while Laura offers some limited contributions to Jill's conversation about the disco). The mode of interaction is one that is oriented towards sustaining an on-going friendly relationship without compromising Laura's desire to 'get the job done'.

Before bringing our discussion of modes of interaction to a close, it is important to note that whilst the vast majority of the children worked in pairs to complete the session of work together, there were pairs whose work was characterized by a 'disputational' mode of interaction. These pairs were overtly conflictual and had difficulties working together independent of adult support. They engaged in heated disputes about control of the mouse and whose turn it was, appealing to the researcher to intervene. These children were also frequently distracted, glancing around the classroom. Extract 8, taken from Darren and Philip's session of work illustrates this mode of interacting.

Extract 8: Darren and Philip

[Darren is using the mouse]

Computer:	Bangers gets an egg from the box on the table. [Philip reaches across and takes control of the mouse]
Darren:	No don't push me off
Computer:	/an/
Darren:	( ) [Darren turns to the side, with his back to Philip]
Computer:	/an / /an/ /an/ /an/
Researcher:	Darren, I'm going to ask you some questions at the end
Computer:	/Bang-/ /Bangers/
Researcher:	Darren, can you watch Philip, I'm going to ask you some questions at the end. [Darren turns to look at the screen]
Computer:	/box/ /b/ /ox/
Philip:	( )
Computer:	/box/
Darren:	( ) [Darren turns page. Philip takes Darren's hand off of the mouse]
Philip:	( )
Darren:	( )
Computer:	He puts the egg in his hat.
Darren:	( ) [Darren looks away. Philip points and takes over the mouse]
Computer:	/hat/ /hat/ /the/ /his/ /his/ /the/
Darren:	[To the researcher]. What's he doing? [Picks up sheet of ground rules and turns away from Philip again]
Computer:	/his/ /hat/ /hat/ /hat/
Researcher:	Its reading the story Darren
Computer:	/he/ /he/ /puts/ /the /egg/
Researcher:	Darren
Darren:	He won't let me have a turn. [Philip sits back from the computer]
Researcher:	It's your go now – he's letting you have a go. [Darren takes control of the mouse]
Computer:	/the/ [Darren turns page]
Philip:	[points] (do you like these)
Computer:	/its/ / fun/
Darren:	fun
Computer:	/the/ /and/ /fun/ /it/ /the/ /the/
Philip:	( ) [Philip takes over the mouse again]
Computer:	/throw/ [Darren becomes distracted]

At the beginning of the extract we see Philip trying to access the machine by out-manoeuvring his partner (e.g. the moment when he removes his partner's hand from the mouse, or takes control while Darren is distracted) rather than by mutual consent or asking. Darren looks at the sheet detailing the ground rules on a number of occasions but doesn't point them out to his domineering partner, whom he turns his back on when he does not have control of the computer. The boys seem unwilling to talk directly to each other, and this is illustrated elsewhere in their session where almost all their dialogue is directed at the adult. It should be noted, as mentioned earlier, that all the pairs were constructed in consultation with the teacher, and were identified as children who would normally 'get on' with each other during a shared task. It would thus seem that these children do not recognize the task as affording the opportunity for collaboration. Their behaviour around the computer suggests that their understanding of either reading activities and / or many computer-based tasks is that they are individual activities rather than tasks that can or should be shared. Thus, their culturally influenced reading of the task results in the adoption of an overarching mode of interaction that is *individualized*. It is in these instances that we see the children adopting behaviours that exclude the scope for shared meaning making.

SUMMARY AND CONCLUSIONS

The evidence that we have presented in this chapter demonstrates that the talking books software 'Bangers and Mash', when introduced into the life of a reception classroom, can resource many diverse modes of interaction. The modes of interaction we have discussed can be seen as constituting different computer-text mediated social practices, some of which echo or seem to involve the application or adaptation of practices encountered in other literacy-related contexts, such as hearing a story read aloud to them by an adult (illustrated by the 'listening' and the 'elaborating' modes of interaction). Other modes are more reminiscent of direct transfer of past computer use, such as in the 'playing' mode.

The diverse ways of engaging with the talking-books software observed can be seen as embodying culturally-based processes of meaning making, in which beginning readers are making sense of the social situation afforded by the availability of a partner and a novel piece of software. As the extracts illustrate, at times this process of sense making and the interpretation of the situation differed between peers, and was at odds with that intended by the researchers and the teacher. The learners were thus building and applying interpretative frameworks, adapting: 'classroom activities such that they complied with their own understandings and past experiences' (Jackson, 1987, p.86). The meaning of the reading activity the children had been set was not a fixed or tangible commodity, rather, it was contextually constituted and fundamentally situated.

Whilst in many cases the children's modes of interacting embodied creative engagement with the collaborative reading task, it is important to recognize that effective participation in classroom-based reading activities demands the recognition and production of: 'the 'right' situated meanings...– that is those shared by the community of practice to which ...(the learners) are being 'apprenticed' (Gee, 2000, p. 200). Beginning readers are expected to conform to expected behaviour patterns and particular ways of relating and interacting, both with texts and others. The implication here is that practitioners wishing to use talking books in the context of collaborative work will need to give careful consideration to how best to enable effective participation in these classroom-based reading activities – such that children come to recognize and produce the 'right' situated meanings, discerning and complying with the accepted learning patterns of their classroom (Jackson, 1987, p.85).

Whilst we acknowledge that the modes of interaction we observed may reflect particular cultural practices in the specific context studied, we feel that our work has important implications for the design of evaluation studies in relation to computer-based resources for learning to read. Such resources are seldom evaluated (Chera & Wood, 2003; Hodges & Sasnett, 1993), and the evaluations that do exist tend to focus on the products of learning – how much the children's reading attainment has improved as a result of introducing this new resource (e.g. Olson, Wise, Ring & Johnson, 1997; Van Daal & Reitsma, 1990). This inevitably means that the evaluations tend to be controlled investigations in which the software is seldom taken up and used as part of regular classroom-based work. As a consequence we have no understanding of what children bring to the use of such computer-based resources.

Such an approach to evaluation risks construing the process of teaching literacy to early readers as a one-sided affair: the children, seemingly, having little to contribute to the situation that is relevant, being novices not just in reading, but in the educated discourse that surrounds learning about reading. This characterisation, which implies a somewhat passive role on the part of the children, over-simplifies the complex nature of their learning interactions and neglects their participation in learning activities as active 'meaning-makers'. Our observations thus point to the importance of exploring children's understanding of the literacy resources we provide them with – rather than designing evaluation studies in such a way as to deny that children's understanding of the task will impact on their potential to learn from the software, or in ways that simply assume that children will recognize the learning agenda that is implicit in the nature of the software's interactive features. We need to understand how the situations in which children are working and the meanings they ascribe to tasks support or constrain their activity and performance, mindful throughout that we never experience artefacts, such as computers and associated-software, in isolation but only in connection with a contextual whole. An object … 'is always a special part, phase or aspect of an environing experienced world' (Dewey, 1938, p.67). Children's reactions to and performance on a computer-supported reading task may thus be crucially determined by the context of activity within which the task is encountered. When studying and evaluating the efficacy of such computer-supported collaborative activity it is vital that we attempt to understand participants' goals and frames of reference, as opposed to working with our own assumptions concerning what these are or may be. Our studies of beginning readers thus need to treat children as people with concerns, not just objects of concern (Prout, 1998).

These observations offer an important insight into both 'learning to collaborate' and 'collaborating to learn' using computer based approaches to supporting literacy. Firstly, children have to recognize learning situations as offering an appropriate opportunity for collaboration. That is, some children may view computer-based literacy activities as a context in which shared working is inappropriate (perhaps because of the emphasis in UK classrooms on assessment of literacy at an individual level), or even undesirable at a personal level, because they perceive computer use as something sufficiently attractive that they are unwilling to share the experience if it means that their own contact with the computer will be limited in some way. The first barrier to collaboration is not always to do with interpersonal factors such as age, gender or ability. Often, as our work illustrates, collaboration fails because the children see no opportunity or need for it.

When the children were observed to work together, their collaboration was not always directed towards the educational goal that we had in mind. This reminds us that collaborative activity is 'creative' in that it broadens the repertoire of experiences from which children can interpret the potential of the task they are presented with. While desirable, such diversity is at odds with the prescriptive nature of literacy tuition in the UK at the present time. In this way 'collaborating to learn' is fraught with potential pitfalls for both teacher and student who have to negotiate shared understandings of each other's expectations and needs.

Amongst this age group we see evidence of children working together, making sense of the task collectively. The children are collaborating to learn, but their interpretations of what the intended lesson might be (e.g. listening to a story, telling their own stories, reading independently, playing a game) can conflict with those that we have as educators. Developing a range of activities that can recast many of these modes of interaction as potentially productive forms of literacy learning, is the next challenge for those seeking to develop collaborative learning practices in the classroom.

AUTHORS' NOTE

The authors would like to thank the children and school that took part in the study, Yvette Evans and John Burns for their assistance during the project, and Katherine Rowbotham for her help with the data transcription.

REFERENCES

Bruner, J. (1991). *Actual minds, possible worlds*. Cambridge, MA: Harvard University Press.

Chera, P.D.K. (2000). *Multimedia CAL and Early Reading: Iterative Design, Development and Evaluation*. Unpublished Doctoral Thesis, University of Bristol, UK.

Chera, P., & Wood, C. (2003). Animated multimedia 'talking books' can promote phonological awareness in children beginning to read. *Learning and Instruction, 13*, 33–52.

Department for Education and Employment (1998). *The National Literacy Strategy – Framework for Teaching*. London: DfEE.

Dewey, J. (1938). *Experience and education*. New York: Macmillan.

Fisher, R., & Singleton, C. (2000). Symposium: the national literacy strategy – introduction. *Journal of Research in Reading, 23*, 242–244.

Gee, J. (2000). Discourse and socio-cultural studies in reading. In M. Kamil, B. Mosenthal, P. Pearson, & R. Barr (Eds.), *Handbook of reading research, Volume III*. London: Lawrence Erlbaum Associates.

Hodges, M.E., & Sasnett, R.M. (1993). Multimedia Computing – Case Studies from MIT Project Athena. London: Addison-Wesley.

Hoogsteder, M., Maier, R., & Elbers, E. (1998). Adult-child interaction, joint problem solving and the structure of co-operation. In M. Woodhead, D. Faulkner, & K. Littleton (Eds.), *Cultural worlds of early childhood*. London: Routledge.

Jackson, M. (1987). Making sense of school. In A. Pollard (Ed.), *Children and their primary schools: A new perspective*. London: The Falmer Press.

Lankshear, C. & Knobel, M. (2003). *New literacies: Changing knowledge and classroom learning*. Buckingham: Open University Press.

Murphy, P. (2000). Understanding the process of negotiation in social interaction. In R. Joiner, K. Littleton, D. Faulkner & D. Miell (Eds.), *Rethinking collaborative learning*. London: Free Association Books.

Olson, R.K., Wise, B., Ring, J., & Johnson, M. (1997). Computer-based remedial training in phoneme awareness and phonological decoding: effects on the posttraining development of word recognition. *Scientific Studies of Reading, 1,* 235–253.

Prout, A. (1998) *Concluding remarks*, Conference on Children and Social Exclusion, Centre for the Social Study of Childhood, Hull University.

Van Daal, V.H.P., & Reitsma, P. (1990). Effects of independent word practice with segmented and whole word sound feedback in disabled readers. *Journal of Research in Reading, 13,* 133–148.

Wood, C., Littleton, K., & Chera, P. (Submitted). *Beginning readers' use of talking books: Styles of working*.

Wood, E. (Submitted). Progression and continuity in early childhood literacy.

Wise, D., Olson, R., Ansett, M., Andrews, L., Terjak, M., Schnieder, V., Kostuch, J., & Kriho, L. (1989). Implementing a long term computerised remedial reading program with synthetic speech feedback: hardware, software and real-world issues. *Behaviour Research Methods, Instruments and Computers, 21,* 173–181.

Chapter 4

PEER COLLABORATION AND INDIVIDUAL LEARNING: INCUBATION, CONTRADICTION AND COLLECTIVE INSIGHT

Christine Howe, Donna McWilliam and Gillian Cross

INTRODUCTION

There is now considerable evidence that peer collaboration can facilitate learning, especially when the topic has a strong conceptual element (Damon & Phelps, 1989; Howe, Tolmie, Duchak-Tanner & Rattray, 2000; Rogoff, 1990). The evidence stemmed originally from research using Piagetian constructs, particularly conservation and visual perspective-taking (e.g. Ames & Murray, 1982; Bearison, Magzamen & Filardo, 1986; Doise & Mugny, 1984). It was supplemented by work with a social focus, introduced to redress the 'logico-mathematical' emphasis of the Piagetian approach (e.g. Damon & Killen, 1982; Kruger, 1992; Roy & Howe, 1990). Finally, it has been endorsed via standard curricular subjects, e.g. mathematics (Damon & Phelps, 1989; Davenport, Howe & Noble, 2000; Webb, 1989), the humanities (Miell & MacDonald, 2000; Morgan, Hargreaves & Joiner, 2000; Pontecorvo, Paoletti & Orsolini, 1989), and, of particular relevance here, elementary science (Azmitia & Montgomery, 1993; Howe, Tolmie & Mackenzie, 1995b; Howe & Tolmie, 1998).

In many cases, the facilitating effects of peer collaboration can be assumed to operate through the straightforward process described by Doise and Mugny (1984): the collaborating peers achieve collective insights that surpass what they can manage independently, and then bring their individual knowledge into line. One illustration within the first author's previous work is the study by Howe, Tolmie, Anderson and Mackenzie (1992a), where undergraduates worked in pairs to determine the relative speeds of computer-simulated trains. Individual understanding of how speed can be calculated using distance-time information was assessed by change between pre-tests prior to peer collaboration and post-tests three weeks afterwards. Pre- to post-test change was strongly correlated with the collective understanding displayed during collaboration, with the latter being on average considerably in advance of the understanding revealed at pre-test. Similar results were obtained by Howe, Tolmie, Greer and Mackenzie (1995a), in research where eight- to twelve-year-old children tried in foursomes to ascertain the determinants of heating and cooling. The pivotal factor as regards pre- to post-test advance was the achievement during collaboration of greater understanding of the processes by which heat is transferred.

Nevertheless, despite the above, there are also instances where collective insights cannot be the source of collaboratively induced learning. Referring once more to the first author's work, Howe, Rodgers and Tolmie (1990) found that peer collaboration in foursomes could assist eight- to twelve-year-olds' understanding of floating and sinking, as indexed by change between individual pre-tests prior to collaboration and individual post-tests a few weeks afterwards. However, in one of the two studies that Howe et al. report, pre- to post-test change was unrelated to performance while collaborating. In the second, there was a relation between change and performance during the collaborative task, but the relation was just as strong when the children asserted their own views in opposition to the rest of the group as when they constructed ideas jointly. Similarly, in a further study with eight- to twelve-year-olds that addressed motion down an inclined plane, Howe, Tolmie and Rodgers (1992b) found that collaborative performance was typically worse than pre-test, and also unrelated to pre- to post-test change. Nevertheless, pre- to post-test change was both progressive, and contingent upon the wider collaborative experience.

Howe et al. (2000) unearthed a similar dissociation between collaboratively induced learning and collective insights in the domain of shadow formation, and Wegerif, Mercer and Dawes (1999) reported the same phenomenon with Raven's Progressive Matrices. Yet, despite this wealth of evidence, there has not, until recently, been any attempt to explain why the dissociation occurs. Theorizing around peer collaboration has taken Doise and Mugny's (1984) approach for granted. It has therefore focused on how the assimilation of collective insights occurs, whether, for instance, it involves the 'internalisation' of cognitive structures as Vygotsky (e.g. 1978) suggested (see also Tomasello, Kruger & Ratner, 1993), or whether it is best viewed as the 'appropriation' of social practices (Brown et al., 1993; Rogoff, 1990). In recognition of the imbalance, we have spent the past few years upon a programme of research that tries to redress matters, and in the present chapter we shall summarise what we have found. We shall conclude that the results not only clarify the conditions under which dissociation from collective insights occurs; they may also have implications for conceptualisations of learning when such insights are definitely involved. In particular, we shall suggest that the adoption of one learning process rather than the other may depend upon the form that collaborative dialogue takes, specifically the degree to which it includes unresolved contradiction. However, the form taken by dialogue is only important because of the nature of the underlying cognitive processes, necessitating a socio-cognitive approach to the book's central issue, of what it means to 'collaborate to learn'.

INCUBATION IN COLLABORATIVE CONTEXTS

The starting point for our research was evidence that when peer collaboration triggers learning that is independent of collective insights, the effects are not usually apparent until some time has elapsed. For instance, in their study of motion down an incline, Howe et al. (1992b) found that performance on an immediate post-test, administered within twenty-four hours of peer collaboration, was no better than at pre-test. This was despite the fact that, as noted above, there were clear signs of progress a few weeks later. Similar results have been obtained by Draper et al. (1992), Scanlon, Issroff and Murphy (1998), and Tolmie, Howe, Mackenzie and Greer (1993), the latter observing progress between post-tests held four and eleven weeks after peer collaboration in research concerned with floating and sinking. Faced with such evidence, it seems reasonable to assume that, when collaboratively induced learning is dissociated from collective insights, the learning takes place during the post-collaborative interval. Thus, the thrust of our research was to ask what the interval can supply that is not obtainable from peer collaboration itself.

Our thinking was guided by the fact that, even though the post-collaborative interval provides opportunities for follow-up consultation with parents, teachers, peers or books, such consultation is unlikely to be critical for the phenomenon we were exploring. Howe et al. (1992b) found that follow-up consultation was rare, and when it occurred, it was not associated with pre- to post-test growth. As a result, we assumed that the post-collaborative activity did not involve overt, socially apparent processes, but rather depended upon implicit cognitive mechanisms. This led us to accept that post-collaborative progress could be encompassed within a concept that has exercised cognitive psychologists for some considerable period of time (see, e.g., Wallas, 1926), the notion of 'incubation'. No matter what its everyday connotations might be, 'incubation' is used in cognitive psychology (Yaniv & Meyer, 1987) to refer to any advance that takes place after a period during which discernible activity has ceased, and this of course is precisely what happened in the work we are concerned with. Renewed interest in incubation within cognitive psychology (see Dorfman, Shames & Kihlstrom, 1996) has led to detailed explanations of why it occurs, and we looked to see whether these explanations were potentially applicable to peer collaboration. Our conclusion was that, based on the explanations, the post-collaborative interval might be providing any or all of three opportunities for growth.

First (paralleling incubation research by, e.g., Anderson, 2000; Smith & Blankenship, 1989, 1991), the post-collaborative interval might allow for the breaking of unhelpful mental sets that collaboration induces. There is no evidence at present that peer collaboration creates such sets. On the other hand if sets occur, their breaking presupposes that individuals have alternative perspectives to call upon. Thus, their potential relevance is endorsed by the fact that exposure during collaboration to a *range* of perspectives has been shown to optimize outcomes (Doise & Mugny, 1984; Howe et al., 1995b). Second (stemming this time from incubation research by, e.g., Campbell, 1960; Dorfman et al., 1996; Yaniv & Meyer, 1987), the post-collaborative interval might permit benefits to be obtained from reflective appraisal of candidate ideas. As with set breaking, there is no direct evidence that appraisal takes place, let alone proves helpful. Nevertheless (perhaps in contrast to set breaking), it is consistent with Howe et al. (1992b) and Tolmie et al.'s (1993) detection of a mixture of relevant *and* irrelevant ideas during their first post-tests, even though performance at this stage was sub-optimal. Change between first and second post-tests was primarily a shift in balance towards relevancies. Finally (related particularly to the incubation research of Dorfman et al., 1996; Perkins, 1981; Seifert, Meyer, Davidson, Patalano & Yaniv, 1995), it is possible that peer collaboration primes individuals to make productive use of external events, and the interval provides the opportunity to have the relevant experiences. Like reflective appraisal, this explanation can deal with the gradual prioritising of relevant ideas over irrelevant, except that this time the impetus would come from the 'biasing' effects of collaboration rather than from subsequent reflection.

GENERAL APPROACH

Recognizing the above possibilities, we conducted three studies to establish whether the post-collaborative interval allows: a) the breaking of 'mental sets' that peer collaboration induces (Study 1); b) the obtaining of assistance from 'reflective appraisal' of collaboratively triggered ideas (Study 2); c) the experiencing of 'external events' that, thanks to collaboration, can be used productively (Study 3). The studies were conducted with nine- to twelve-year-old children attending state primary schools in or around the City of Glasgow, and were concerned with mastery of the factors relevant to floating and sinking. They will be presented here in summary form, with a full report to appear in Howe, McWilliam and Cross (Forthcoming).

The studies were all embellishments of a basic pre-test – intervention – post-test design as outlined in Table 1. The pre-tests were administered to all participating children on a class-by-class basis, with the children responding individually in writing. Six pre-test problems involved physically present objects, e.g. a school eraser, a bottle of washing up liquid, with the children asked whether (and why) each object would float or sink in a tank of water. Six problems involved descriptions of real-world scenarios, e.g. icebergs floating, pebbles sinking, with the children asked why these occur. We hoped to include about 36 children in each research 'condition' (i.e. 1A, 1B, 2A etc as detailed in Table 1), and the pre-test sample for each study was set with this in mind. The older children performed better than the younger at pre-test in all three studies, and the girls performed better than the boys in two. However, there were few age or sex differences in learning gain, and the effects of age and sex never interacted with the effects of condition. As a result, age and sex will be ignored, for brevity, in what follows.

Depending on the design of the study (see Table 1), some or all of the pre-tested children worked through a collaborative task about one week after the pre-test, and were audio-taped while they did this. The task was administered via a workbook to (in general) foursomes, membership of each foursome being restricted to children from the same school class, but otherwise decided at random. The task was closely modelled on Tolmie et al. (1993), and involved: a) presentation of six sets of randomly assorted objects, e.g. block, ball and key, or curved shape, rubber ring and die; b) individual predictions in writing for each set in turn of which objects would float or sink; c) invitations to discuss predictions and reach agreement, to test predictions empirically by immersion, and to interpret outcomes jointly. Eight weeks after the collaborative task (and, in Study 1, immediately afterwards in addition), post-tests were presented. Post-testing followed the same procedures as pre-testing, repeating some problems, but also introducing new ones. Like the pre-test, the post-tests contained six problems relating to physically present objects, and six relating to real-world scenarios.

Table 1: Design of the three studies

	Individual Pre-test	Collaborative Task		Immediate Post-test	Post Collaborative Intervention		Delayed Post-test
		Standard	Plus Fixation Trigger		Reflective Exercises	Demonstrations	
Study 1	1A, 1B	1A	1B	1A, 1B	-	-	1A, 1B
Study 2	2A, 2B, 2C, 2D	2A, 2C	-	-	2A, 2B	-	2A, 2B, 2C, 2D
Study 3	3A, 3B, 3C, 3D	3A, 3C	-	-	-	3A, 3B	3A, 3B, 3C, 3D

Scoring of the pre- and post-tests focused on the factors mentioned by the children when giving reasons for the predicted outcomes (physically present objects) and described events (real-world scenarios). Each factor was scored on the five-point scale used by Howe et al. (1990) and Tolmie et al. (1993): 0 = No physical factor mentioned, e.g. 'Don't know', 'It's meant to float'; 1 = Irrelevant physical factor or relevant factor in the wrong direction, e.g. 'It sinks because it's metal', 'It floats because it's heavy'; 2 = Unco-ordinated relevant factor, e.g. 'It floats because it's light', 'It sinks because it's small'; 3 = Co-ordinated relevant factor, e.g. 'It floats because it's light for its size', 'It sinks because it's too heavy for the water to hold'; 4 = Co-ordinated object and fluid density, e.g. 'It's heavier than the same amount of water'.

Thereafter three composite measures were derived, the first being a measure of productivity and the others being measures of understanding:

- Factor Total (FT) – The total number of distinct factors mentioned for each problem, e.g. 'It sinks because it's metal and heavy' produces FT = 2 (metal, heavy);
- Total Relevant (TR) – The total number of factors for each problem scoring 2 or more, e.g. 'It sinks because it's metal and heavy' produces TR = 1 (heavy);
- Conceptual Level (CL) – The score given to the best scoring factor, e.g. 'It sinks because it's metal and heavy' produces CL = 2 (heavy).

For purposes of analysis, each child was awarded FT, TR and CL scores for their pre-and post-test performances, obtained by summing across responses to the twelve test problems. Across the three studies, inter-judge agreement over scoring of 25% to 33% samples averaged 96% for FT score, 99% for TR score, and 96% for CL score. As will become apparent, analysis of audio-tapes in Studies 1 and 3 and of post-collaborative interventions in Studies 2 and 3 introduced further dimensions of scoring. With these dimensions too, inter-judge agreement was high, ranging from 96% to 100%.

STUDY 1: SET BREAKING

The first study was concerned with the possibility that peer collaboration can create unhelpful mental sets, which require an interval to be broken. Subsequent to pre-testing, half of the children (Condition 1A – see Table 1, N = 30) engaged in what might be called the 'standard' collaborative task as described above, i.e. individual predictions and then six cycles of joint prediction, testing and interpretation under direction from a workbook. The other half (Condition 1B, N = 31) worked with a task that contained all the standard features, but included additional steps at the end of each cycle. These steps were modelled on Howe et al. (1995a) and Tolmie et al. (1993), and were expected to trigger fixation upon a relatively small number of causal factors, when compared with the standard task. In other words, they were expected to generate stronger mental sets. The steps involved the groups first looking at all the objects known up to that point to be 'floaters', deciding together 'what are the most important things for floating' and writing their answers on cards. They involved them then repeating the process for the objects identified as 'sinkers'.

Analysis of the audio-taped interactions relating to the first, third and fifth cycles of prediction, testing and interpretation (i.e. with the additional 1B steps excluded for comparability) revealed that the task manipulation worked as anticipated. Nine groups experienced the 1A task and nine the 1B task, and at the end of the first cycle of activity, they were more or less equivalent, over both the total number of factors mentioned (t (16) = 1.19, ns) and the number of distinct factors within the total (t (16) = .18, ns). By the third cycle, there were signs of differentiation, with the 1B children producing about 75% of the total factors generated by the 1A children (t (16) = 2.33, p < .05), and an equivalent percentage of the distinct factors (t (16) = 1.89, ns). By the fifth cycle, the differentiation was marked with the 1B children producing only 50% of the total factors generated by the 1A children (t (16) = 3.34, p < .01), and 50% of the distinct factors (t (16) = 4.49, p < .001).

The differences between the conditions had implications for performance on the immediate post-test, which was administered within one hour of the collaborative task. In the 1A condition, there were strong positive correlations between immediate post-test FT scores and both the total number of factors mentioned across the task cycles (r (28) = .53, p < .01) and the number of distinct factors within the total (r (28) = .43, p < .05). The equivalent correlations for the 1B condition were, respectively, r (29) = .14, ns and r (29) = .26, ns. This suggests that, with a minimal (or non-existent) mental set, the ideas expressed during collaboration were carried forwards to immediate post-test more-or-less intact, whereas with a stronger set this did not happen. However, it need not mean that in the latter circumstance, the ideas carried forwards were the sub-sample that had become the mental set, and there were in fact good reasons for thinking that this did not happen. FT scores at immediate post-test in the 1B condition showed a strong *negative* correlation (r (29) = -.54, p < .01) with FT scores awarded to the factors written on cards. Far from suggesting the operation at immediate post-test of a strong mental set, this indicates swift rejection and remedial action.

a) Pre-test to Immediate Post-test Change

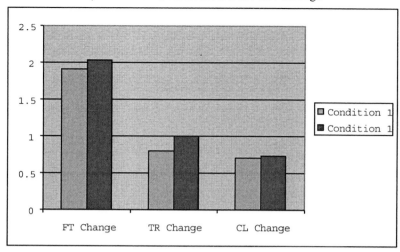

b) Immediate Post-test to Delayed Post-test Change

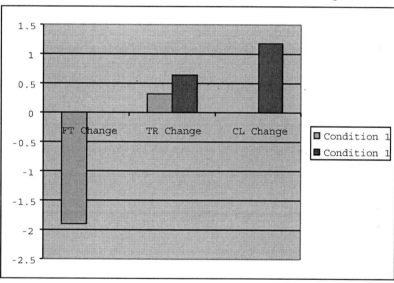

Figure 1: Differences between Conditions over Mean Change in Scores (Study 1)

If mental sets can be broken within minutes of peer collaboration, they are unlikely to be material factors in post-collaborative progress, and this was confirmed by patterns of change between pre-test and immediate post-test, and between immediate post-test and delayed post-test. If set breaking is important, there should have been less progress in Condition 1B than in Condition 1A in the first case, and more progress in the second. After ascertaining that the conditions were equivalent at pre-test, the relevant indices were obtained by subtracting each child's pre-test scores from their immediate post-test scores, and each child's immediate post-test scores from their delayed post-test scores. As Figure 1 shows, change between pre-test and immediate post-test was, if anything, greater in Condition 1B than in Condition 1A rather than the hypothesized less, although none of the differences were statistically significant.

Although change between immediate and delayed post-test was in the predicted direction, here too the differences were statistically non-significant. In view of these results, a generally negative conclusion was drawn from Study 1. In essence, this was that although peer collaboration can produce mental sets (and can vary in its propensity to do this depending on task design), these sets are short-lived phenomena. They do not require intervals to be broken, and therefore opportunities to break mental sets cannot be the 'added value' that intervals supply.

STUDY 2: REFLECTIVE APPRAISAL

In addition to suggesting that set breaking plays a minimal role, the results of Study 1 indicate that knowledge is actively constructed during the post-collaborative period. Earlier, two further interpretations of post-collaborative activity were acknowledged, both of which presume active construction. Study 2 investigated the first of these interpretations, that construction proceeds by reflective appraisal. After being pre-tested, children were assigned at random to engage or not engage in the 'standard' collaborative task, i.e. the one used in Study 1's Condition 1A. 50% of the children who engaged in the collaborative task, i.e. a randomly selected pair from each foursome (Condition 2A – see Table 1, N = 36), and a similar number of the children who did not engage (Condition 2B, N = 34) went through reflective exercises two, four and six weeks afterwards. These exercises required the children, working independently, to write down all the ideas they had ever encountered as to why each of four objects (e.g. empty plastic bottle, metal key, sponge, anchor) floated or sank, and to evaluate each idea as 'good', 'bad' or 'in-between' by ticking an appropriate box. The objects varied between exercises, and the order of exercises varied between children. The remaining 50% of children who engaged in the collaborative task, i.e. the other pair from each foursome (Condition 2C, N = 36), and the same number of children who did not engage (Condition 2D, N = 36) simply took the post-test along with Conditions 2A and 2B. Scheduled eight weeks after the collaborative task, the post-test took place two weeks after the final reflective exercise.

If reflective appraisal is the mechanism by which children who engage in peer collaboration are assisted during the post-collaborative interval, this should have been apparent through superior performance during the reflective exercises. Specifically, the 2A children who experienced peer collaboration should, when compared with the 2B children who did not experience collaboration, have produced a greater number of relevant factors during the reflective exercises and/or shown superior insight into the relevance of the factors that they did produce. To check the first possibility, TR scores were assigned for each object within an exercise, with FT scores also assigned as a control. To check the second possibility, evaluation scores were assigned for each object according to the manner in which the ideas were appraised. For instance, rating 'the key floats because it wants to' as 'good' would have resulted in a low score; rating the idea as 'bad' would have resulted in a high score. In fact, there were no differences whatsoever between Conditions 2A and 2B over mean TR scores or mean evaluation scores. The only sign of variation was over FT scores, but even here the differences were statistically significant on one occasion only. There was then no evidence of superior performance after collaboration than in its absence.

If reflective appraisal is the mechanism by which children who engage in peer collaboration are assisted, the reflective exercises should have been of value to such children in their own right, by providing structure and/or additional opportunities for the ongoing process. As a consequence, pre- to post-test change in the 2A children who experienced peer collaboration plus the reflective exercises should have been superior to pre- to post-test change in the 2C children who only experienced collaboration or in the 2B children who only experienced the reflective exercises, as well as in the 2D children who did not experience either of these. The conditions were equivalent at pre-test, and therefore as with Study 1, it was legitimate to consider change via post-test scores with pre-test subtracted. The results of comparing the conditions over change scores are shown in Figure 2. Statistical analysis revealed that in terms of productivity (as indexed by FT scores), Condition 2A outstripped Conditions 2C and 2D, but was equivalent to Condition 2B ($\underline{F}$ (3, 138) = 12.75, $\underline{p}$ < .001). In terms of understanding (as indexed by TR and CL scores), Condition 2A was no better than Condition 2C, although both outstripped Conditions 2B and 2D ($\underline{F}$ (3, 138) = 2.95, $\underline{p}$ < .06 for TR; $\underline{F}$ (3, 138) = 5.04, $\underline{p}$ < .01 for CL). The implication is that the reflective exercises added no value as regards understanding beyond that obtainable from peer collaboration itself. All they did was keep a higher number of candidate factors on the agenda. This, coupled with the undistinguished performance of the 2A children during the reflective exercises themselves, suggests very strongly that reflective appraisal does not play a critical role in post-collaborative growth.

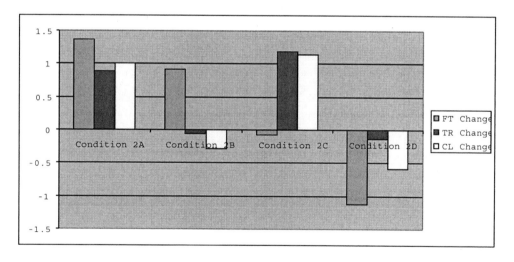

Figure 2: Differences between Conditions over Mean Change in Scores (Study 2)

STUDY 3: EXTERNAL EVENTS

By their very nature, the reflective exercises directed attention backwards to what had already been encountered. As a result, they achieved something that is inimical to the third possible interpretation of post-collaborative progress, that peer collaboration primes children to make productive use of subsequent events. This interpretation was addressed in Study 3. As with Study 2, children were assigned at random after being pre-tested to engage or not engage in the standard collaborative task. 50% of the children who engaged in the task

(Condition 3A -see Table 1, $\underline{N}$ = 35, two from each foursome, with the subsequent loss of one child due to absence from school) and a randomly selected sample of children who did not engage in the task (Condition 3B, $\underline{N}$ = 36) experienced demonstrations two, four and six weeks after the task. The demonstrations focused on the propensity to float or sink of: a) pairs of objects that were identical in all relevant respects except weight; b) pairs of objects that were identical in all relevant respects except size; c) triads of objects that were identical in all relevant respects except weight and size. In each case, children working independently and writing in booklets, predicted and then recorded the outcomes of immersion in water. The children in Conditions 3A and 3B were post-tested two weeks after the final demonstration, together with the remaining 50% of children who engaged in the collaborative task, i.e. the other two from each foursome (Condition 3C, $\underline{N}$ = 36), and a randomly selected sample of pre-tested children who did not experience the collaborative task or the demonstrations (Condition 3D, $\underline{N}$ = 36).

If peer collaboration primes children to make productive use of subsequent events, the demonstrations should have had a more positive impact on the 3A children who experienced peer collaboration than the 3B children who did not have this experience. This should perhaps have been especially likely for the second and third demonstrations which addressed size: there is considerable evidence (Howe, 1998) that nine- to twelve-year-olds have difficulties with the role of size, while in general understanding the role of weight, which was the subject of the first demonstration. To explore the matter in depth, responses to each set of objects in the demonstrations were awarded FT, TR and CL scores, using the standard scoring scheme, and were further coded for correct vs. incorrect use of weight (W) and size (S). As anticipated, the conditions were more or less equivalent over the first demonstration. However, by the second demonstration, matters had changed dramatically, with the 3A children obtaining significantly higher TR, CL and S scores than the 3B. The same pattern was discernible with the third demonstration, although this time none of the differences were statistically significant.

In addition, there was a very strong association between performance during the third demonstration in Condition 3A and performance at post-test. Post-test FT scores were predicted by third demonstration FT, TR, CL and S scores ($\underline{r}$ (33) = .45 to .62, $\underline{p}$ < .01), post-test TR scores were predicted by third demonstration TR and S scores ($\underline{r}$ (33) = .35 and .39, $\underline{p}$ < .05), and post-test CL scores were predicted by third demonstration FT, TR, CL and S scores ($\underline{r}$ (33) = .36 to .42, $\underline{p}$ < .05). In Condition 3B, only post-test FT scores were predicted by performance during the third demonstration. Overall then, there was a substantial boost in Condition 3A's performance during the second demonstration that was preserved through to post-test. The boost was not observed in Condition 3B, and insofar as the 3B children performed well at post-test it was less strongly influenced by the demonstrations. More importantly perhaps, the boost in Condition 3A's performance was not only carried through to post-test, but also resulted in pre- to post-test advances in understanding that were in excess of those observed in any other condition. The relevant values are shown in Figure 3, with equivalence at pre-test once more warranting simple post-test less pre-test measures of change. One way ANOVAs revealed no differences between the conditions over FT change ($\underline{F}$ (3, 129) = .42, $\underline{ns}$), but significant differences over TR and CL change ($\underline{F}$ (3, 129) = 3.18, $\underline{p}$ < .05 for TR; $\underline{F}$ (3, 139) = 4.33, $\underline{p}$ < .01 for CL). Post hoc tests (Scheffé $\underline{p}$ < .05) showed that change in Condition 3A was greater than in all other conditions.

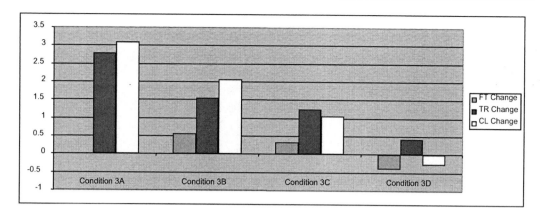

Figure 3: Differences between Conditions over Mean Change in Scores (Study 3)

CONTRADICTION AND COLLECTIVE INSIGHT

The results of our research suggest, then, that of the three opportunities identified for the post-collaborative interval, only one is relevant to collaboratively induced learning. The opportunity for breaking mental sets seems irrelevant, insofar as when strong sets were created in Study 1, they were broken within minutes of the collaborative task. They did not require a significant interval. Moreover, strength of mental set was unrelated to progress from pre-test to immediate post-test, or from immediate post-test to delayed. The opportunity for post-collaborative appraisal can also be discounted. Performance during the reflective exercises in Study 2 was no better after peer collaboration than in its absence, suggesting no special advantages when appraisal occurs in collaborative contexts. Furthermore, the structure provided by the exercises added no value to peer collaboration as regards growth of understanding over the collaborative experience itself. On the other hand, experiences of relevant events do seem helpful when these follow peer collaboration, suggesting that this may be the key opportunity provided by the post-collaborative interval. In particular, responses to the Study 3 demonstrations were superior after peer collaboration than in its absence, and they were more robustly predictive of pre- to post-test change. Pre- to post-test change after peer collaboration followed by demonstrations was superior to pre- to post-test change after collaboration alone or demonstrations alone.

As intimated already, the value of external events could only have been boosted by peer collaboration, if collaboration has the power to prime individuals to use their experiences productively. We felt therefore that it was crucial to clarify the priming process, and we wondered whether the differential responses to weight and size during the Study 3 demonstrations might provide a clue. It will be recalled that responses to the first demonstration, which focused upon weight, did not vary as a function of engagement or non-engagement in peer collaboration, but responses to the second demonstration, which focused upon size, did vary. Without suggesting that the priming was specific to size (since many factors were mentioned during the collaborative task apart from weight and size), the difference indicates that something took place that sensitized the children to the effects of size. Recognizing this, we analysed the audio-taped recordings ($\underline{N}$ = 18 foursomes) that were made during Study 3 for references to size. With six recordings, size was never mentioned. With the other twelve, it was mentioned between two and thirteen times ($\underline{M}$ = 6.00), but always in a fashion that included unresolved contradiction. In other words, bigness was associated with floating at one point and with sinking at another, and the inconsistency was not sorted out. Comparison of the 3A children who experienced the two types of discussion revealed no significant differences over FT change, but massive differences over TR and CL change. The children who experienced the contradictory discussions made nine times the TR progress observed in the children who failed to discuss size, and thirteen times the CL progress.

Any conclusions must be tentative given the post-hoc nature of the analysis, but the results strongly suggest that contradiction was what primed the 3A children to respond productively to the demonstrations. As a consequence, an answer can be proposed not simply to the question of what takes place during the post-collaborative interval, but also to the more fundamental issue of how peer collaboration can trigger learning independently of collective insights. The answer is that when collaboration gives rise to unresolved contradiction, participants are sensitized to the information relevant to resolution that can be gained from subsequent experiences. It is, without doubt, an answer that could apply to other reports of independence from collective insights. Of the ones mentioned earlier that occurred in the first author's work, two (Howe et al., 1990; Tolmie et al., 1993) related to floating and sinking, and therefore were as likely to have depended upon unresolved contradiction as the results described here. The others (Howe et al., 1992b; Howe et al., 2000) were concerned with motion down an inclined plane and shadow size. As it happens, children in the relevant age range have been shown to hold conflicting ideas over whether light or heavy balls roll fastest down slopes (Howe, 1998), and over whether shadow size is directly or inversely proportional to lamp-object and object-screen distance (Howe, Tolmie & Sofroniou, 1999). Therefore, here too there will have been scope for contradictory opinions. More generally, the proposed answer is also consistent with the evidence, mentioned earlier, that learning gains from peer collaboration are optimized when participants are exposed to a range of ideas (Doise & Mugny, 1984; Howe et al., 1995b). After all, the greater the number of ideas, the more likely it is that some will conflict and, as a consequence, trigger the post-collaborative process that is under discussion.

Nevertheless, judging by the collaborative interactions that took place during Study 3, differences of opinion do not have to be juxtaposed in explicit disagreement. Such juxtaposition did occur, e.g. 'I think it will float because it's small and light'; 'But the QE2's not small, and it floats'. However, juxtaposition was rare. In the vast majority of cases, the contradictory ideas were associated with different task items. For instance, having predicted that the plastic die would float because it is small, the children frequently asserted, many minutes later, that icebergs float because they are big. This suggests that, to the extent that contradiction operates as a prime, its priming function is a consequence of children's efforts to represent interactions to themselves. These efforts may involve post-collaborative 'sorting' of collaboratively generated ideas: the immediate post-test results in Study 1 suggest that in certain circumstances children have reasonably good recollection of what transpires during collaborative tasks. Nevertheless, the negative picture regarding reflective appraisal that emerged from Study 2 indicates that the sorting route should be followed with caution. A more parsimonious explanation is that construction occurs because of failure to achieve coherence during on-task storage in memory. For instance, taking a semantic network approach to memory (Collins & Loftus, 1975) for illustration, a 'schema' for, e.g., 'floating objects' can be envisaged that is associated with 'slots' like 'weight' and 'material', and 'values of slots' like 'light' and 'wooden'. Given evidence that the values of the 'size' slot are both 'big' and 'small', coherence would be precluded, and the slot should remain 'activated' until clarification is obtained. There are of course many other approaches to memory within cognitive psychology, but although the details of application to the present context would differ, the basic point would remain the same.

From certain perspectives, the issue of how representation is achieved would be unimportant. What would be crucial is the fact that, because represented contradiction must involve co-ordination *across* dialogue rather than extrapolation *from* dialogue, it necessitates some contribution from cognitive processes. Postulating a role for cognition has sometimes been regarded as problematic, when developing theories of collaborative learning (e.g. Rogoff, 1990 – but see Brown et al., 1993, for a more qualified stance). Nevertheless, if the role can be accepted, other matters fall into place. For example, the investigations that the led to the present research did not merely show learning in the absence of collective insights (as in Howe et al., 1992b), they also (e.g. Howe et al., 1990) showed learning that was independent of collective insights even when these occurred. However, once cognitive processes that effect co-ordination across dialogue are acknowledged, it becomes possible to anticipate that what constitute collective insights at one moment in time could become sources of unresolved contradiction as the discussion unfolds, making independence entirely comprehensible. Continuing with the previous example, a (hypothetical) discussion of the form 'Icebergs float because they're big'; 'Yeah, big things usually float – look at the QE2'; 'So we all agree – it's being big that matters' would amount to a collective insight since, all other things being equal, big things are more likely to float than small. Yet such a discussion would also be a source of unresolved contradiction, if it occurred despite (and without immediate recognition of) an earlier statement (possibly also agreed across the group) that a die will float because it is small. Indeed if the contradiction was spotted during collaboration and addressed, the outcome could once more be a collective insight. However, given that children in the nine- to twelve-year age group seldom refer to earlier task items during collaborative interactions (Howe et al., 1995a, 2000), such 'second-order' collective insights are likely to be rare

The general implication is that learning from collective insights and learning from external events may be two sides of the same coin, with the balance depending on the degree of contradiction. However, if that can be accepted, albeit tentatively, other consequences follow. The first is the need to take a holistic approach to collaborative interaction when predicting or interpreting its outcomes. This does not mean looking at every remark that is made: our work suggests that to understand the responses to the size demonstration, only references to size had to be considered. However, it was necessary to consider all references to size and, more importantly, their relationships (contradictory or not) to each other. The need to acknowledge relationships has not typically been recognized in research concerned with peer collaboration, which may be why statistical associations between features of interaction and learning outcomes are typically rather weak (see e.g. Howe & Tolmie, 1998). Nevertheless, once the point is accepted, it has important consequences, both for practitioners monitoring classroom interaction to ensure productive behaviour and for theoreticians. For instance, the notion, alluded to earlier, that individuals 'appropriate' social practices (see

Brown et al., 1993; Rogoff, 1990) implies a focus upon the practices per se rather than their location within the broader context of meanings. This may prove a limitation.

A further implication from the above is that work is needed to establish when collective insights are or are not likely to be contradicted. It is probable that both the achievement of collective insights and their contradiction depend on participants having differing opinions, since differences have been shown to predict collaboratively induced gain across a wide range of contexts (Howe et al., 1990, 1992a, 1992b, 1995b; Williams & Tolmie, 2000). However, differences are possible without incompatibility when, for instance, participants subscribe to different parts of the full story, or show different degrees of understanding along a continuum. Perhaps, it is in these circumstances that collective insights will prove robust against contradiction, and become the trigger to learning. Certainly, this suggestion concurs with the two studies mentioned earlier (Howe et al., 1992a, 1995a) that found a close tie-up between insights and post-collaborative gain. In both studies the main difference between participants was over degrees of mastery of the basic constructs; there was no contradiction. The proposal is also compatible with work by Williams and Tolmie (2000), which showed that the understanding of inheritance that eight- to twelve-year-olds achieved during peer collaboration was strongly predictive of their pre- to post-test gain. Again, variation between participants prior to interaction was primarily in terms of how much or how little grasp they had of the scientific concept.

The general conclusion from all of this is that to make further progress as regards the issue of 'collaborating to learn', greater attention needs to be paid to the relationships at stake. The critical relationships include those between the claims that are made during interaction (whether these are contradictory or not), and those between the beliefs of the participating individuals (whether contrasts are or are not associated with incompatibility). One reason why the centrality of relationships is seldom recognized at present may be the continuing fascination with collective insights at the expense of all other possibilities, for as intimated above taking insights as the focus tends to direct attention towards salient (and essentially decontextualized) moments. Collective insights *are* important, and it is crucial to continue the debate, referred to already, over the mechanisms by which they achieve their importance. The central point of the chapter is, however, that collective insights are not the only processes at play. Once this is recognized not only should the field move on; understanding of how collective insights themselves operate should also be broadened.

AUTHORS' NOTE

Funding for Studies 1, 2 and 3 was provided by ESRC award R000239092. Thanks are due to the ESRC for their support, to Andy Tolmie for comments on methodology, to Crystal Haskell for help with data coding, to Norie Sharp & Pat Gallagher for technical and secretarial assistance, and to the pupils and teachers from the participating schools. Address for correspondence: Professor Christine Howe, Department of Psychology, University of Strathclyde, 40 George Street, Glasgow G1 1QE, UK (email: c.j.howe@strath.ac.uk).

REFERENCES

Ames, G. J., & Murray, F. B. (1982). When two wrongs make a right: promoting cognitive change by social conflict. *Developmental Psychology, 18*, 894–897.

Anderson, J. R. (2000). *Cognitive psychology and its implications.* 5th edition. New York: Worth.

Azmitia, M., & Montgomery, R. (1993). Friendship, transactive dialogues and development of scientific reasoning. *Social Development, 2*, 202–221.

Bearison, D. J., Magzamen, S., & Filardo, E. K. (1986). Socio-cognitive conflict and cognitive growth in young children. *Merrill-Palmer Quarterly, 32*, 51–72.

Brown, A.L., Ash, D., Rutherford, M., Nakagawa, K., Gordon, A., & Campione, J.C. (1993). Distributed expertise in the classroom. In G. Salomon (Ed.), *Distributed cognitions: Psychological and educational considerations* (pp. 188–228). Cambridge: Cambridge University Press.

Campbell, D. T. (1960). Blind variation and selective retention in creative thought. *Psychological Review, 67*, 380–400.

Collins, A. M., & Loftus, E. F. (1975). A spreading-activation theory of semantic processing. *Psychological Review, 82*, 407–428.

Damon, W., & Killen, M. (1982). Peer interaction and the process of change in children's moral reasoning. *Merrill-Palmer Quarterly, 28*, 347–367.

Damon, W., & Phelps, E. (1989). Critical distinctions among three approaches to peer education. *International Journal of Educational Research, 5*, 331–343.

Davenport, P., Howe, C., & Noble, A. (2000). Peer interaction in the teaching of mathematics: explanation and the co-ordination of knowledge. *Revue Suisse des Sciences de l'Education, 3*, 481–507.

Doise, W., & Mugny, G. (1984). *The social development of the intellect.* Oxford: Pergamon.

Dorfman, J., Shames, V.A., & Kihlstrom, J.F. (1996). Intuition, incubation and insight: Implicit cognition in problem solving. In G. Underwood (Ed.), *Implicit cognition* (pp. 257–296). Oxford: Oxford University Press.

Draper, S., Mohamed, R., Byard, M., Driver, R., Hartley, R., Mallen, C., Twigger, D., O'Malley, C., Hennessy, S., O'Shea, T., Scanlon, E., & Spensley, F. (1992). *Conceptual change in science.* Final Report to ESRC.

Howe, C. J., Rodgers, C., & Tolmie, A. (1990). Physics in the primary school: Peer interaction and the understanding of floating and sinking. *European Journal of Psychology of Education, V*, 459–475.

Howe, C. J., Tolmie, A., Anderson, A., & Mackenzie, M. (1992a). Conceptual knowledge in physics: The role of group interaction in computer-supported teaching. *Learning and Instruction, 2*, 161–183.

Howe, C. J., Tolmie, A., & Rodgers, C. (1992b). The acquisition of conceptual knowledge in science by primary school children: Group interaction and the understanding of motion down an inclined plane. *British Journal of Developmental Psychology, 10*, 113–130.

Howe, C.J., Tolmie, A., Greer, K., & Mackenzie, M. (1995a). Peer collaboration and conceptual growth in physics: Task influences on children's understanding of heating and cooling. *Cognition and Instruction, 13*, 483–503.

Howe, C., Tolmie, A., & Mackenzie, M. (1995b). Computer support for the collaborative learning of physics concepts. In C. O'Malley (Ed.), *Computer-supported collaborative learning* (pp. 51–68). Berlin: Springer.

Howe, C.J. (1998). *Conceptual structure in childhood and adolescence: The case of everyday physics.* London: Routledge.

Howe, C., & Tolmie, A. (1998). Productive interaction in the context of computer-supported collaborative learning in science. In K. Littleton & P. Light (Eds.), *Learning with computers: Analysing productive interaction* (pp. 24–45). London: Routledge.

Howe, C.J., Tolmie, A., & Sofroniou, N. (1999). Experimental appraisal of personal beliefs in science: constraints on performance in the 9 to 14 age group. *British Journal of Educational Psychology, 69*, 243–274.

Howe, C.J., Tolmie, A., Duchak-Tanner, V., & Rattray, C. (2000). Hypothesis testing in science: Group consensus and the acquisition of conceptual and procedural knowledge. *Learning and Instruction, 10*, 361–391.

Howe, C.J., McWilliam, D. & Cross, G. (Forthcoming). *Chance favours only the prepared mind: Incubation and the delayed effects of peer collaboration.*

Kruger, A.C. (1992). The effect of peer and adult-child transactive discussions on moral reasoning. *Merrill-Palmer Quarterly, 38*, 191–211.

Miell, D., & MacDonald, R. (2000). Children's creative collaborations: the importance of friendship when working together on a musical composition. *Social Development, 9*, 348–369.

Morgan, L., Hargreaves, D., & Joiner, R. (2000). Children's collaborative music composition: communication through music. In R. Joiner, K. Littleton, D. Faulkner, & D. Miell (Eds.), *Rethinking collaborative learning* (pp. 52–64). London: Free Association.

Perkins, D. N. (1981). *The mind's best work.* Boston, MA: Harvard University Press.

Pontecorvo, C., Paoletti, G., & Orsolini, M. (1989). Use of the computer and social interaction in a language curriculum. *Golem, 5*, 12–14.

Rogoff, B. (1990). *Apprenticeship in thinking: Cognitive development in social context.* Oxford: Oxford University Press.

Roy, A. W. N., & Howe, C. J. (1990). Effects of cognitive conflict, socio-cognitive conflict and imitation on children's socio-legal thinking. *European Journal of Social Psychology, 20*, 241–252.

Scanlon, E., Issroff, K., & Murphy, P. (1998). Collaborations in a primary classroom. In K. Littleton & P. Light (Eds.), *Learning with computers: Analysing productive interaction* (pp. 62–78). London: Routledge.

Seifert, C.M., Meyer, D.E., Davidson, N., Patalano, A.L., & Yaniv, I. (1995). Demystification of cognitive insight: Opportunistic assimilation and the prepared-mind perspective. In R.J. Sternberg & J.E. Davidson (Eds.), *The nature of insight* (pp. 65–124). Boston, MA: Bradford Books.

Smith, S. M. & Blankenship, S. E. (1989). Incubation effects. *Bulletin of the Psychonomic Society, 27*, 311–314.

Smith, S.M. & Blankenship, S. E. (1991). Incubation and the persistence of fixation in problem solving. *American Journal of Psychology, 104*, 61–87.

Tolmie, A., Howe, C.J., Mackenzie, M., & Greer, K. (1993). Task design as an influence on dialogue and learning: Primary school group work with object flotation. *Social Development, 2*, 183–201.

Tomasello, M., Kruger, A. C., & Ratner, H. H. (1993). Cultural learning. *Behavioral and Brain Sciences, 16*, 495–552.

Vygotsky, L. S. (1978). *Mind in society.* Cambridge, MA: Harvard University Press.

Wallas, G. (1926). *The art of thought.* New York: Franklin Watts.

Webb, N. (1989). Peer interaction and learning in small groups. *International Journal of Educational Research, 13*, 21–39.

Wegerif, R., Mercer, N., & Dawes, L. (1999). From social interaction to individual reasoning: An empirical investigation of a possible socio-cultural model of cognitive development. *Learning and Instruction, 9*, 493–516.

Williams, J., & Tolmie, A. (2000). Conceptual change in biology: Group interaction and the understanding of inheritance. *British Journal of Developmental Psychology, 18*, 625–649.

Yaniv, I., & Meyer, D. E. (1987). Activation and metacognition of inaccessible stored information: Potential bases for incubation effects in problem solving. *Journal of Experimental Psychology: Learning, Memory and Cognition, 13*, 187–205.

Chapter 5

"You Can See It As You Wish!" Negotiating a Shared Understanding in Collaborative Problem Solving Dyads

Kristiina Kumpulainen and Sinikka Kaartinen

INTRODUCTION

In this chapter we discuss a detailed case study which investigated interactive processes among two peer dyads and the relationship of these processes to the establishment of a shared understanding between dyad members. The goal of the case study was to deepen our understanding of the interactive processes that take place among collaborating peer dyads and to explore the part these processes play in shared meaning-making. In the analysis of interactive processes, we devote special attention to the nature of students' communicative processes, problem solving strategies and mathematical language and how they shape collaborative problem solving. We draw on the micro-analysis of two contrasting case dyads that illuminate the type of interaction processes that support (Case dyad 1) or challenge (Case dyad 2) shared meaning-making during collaborative problem solving. Our findings suggest that the practice of collaborating to learn is tightly interwoven with the practice of learning to collaborate. That is, students' cognitive, interactional and social skills are all highly relevant for meaningful and productive collaborative learning activity. We hope to demonstrate the potential of micro-level, process analyses for mapping out the interactional resources that mediate collaborative problem solving among dyads. We shall argue that understanding these resources has important pedagogic implications relating to the type of assessment and support practices that should guide collaborative working modes in the classroom.

In the following extract, a female dyad, Anu and Kati are working together on a geometric design task during an elementary mathematics lesson. The students are constructing a three-dimensional geometrical object from a picture on a work sheet with the help of cutouts, two-dimensional geometric shapes available to them on their desk.

Kati:	Hey, but it goes like this. So, how can you put these here like this?
Anu:	Just to make my working easier.
Kati:	It goes like this.
Anu:	Pardon.
Kati:	Yeah. It must be a wide triangle which goes like this and..
Anu:	I see it as a kind of triangle.
Kati:	You can see it as you wish!
Anu:	Like this. It isn't like that.
Kati:	No.
Anu:	Well, one cannot argue against opinions but..
Kati:	But...
Anu:	But you are still arguing.
Kati:	Well, I cannot argue alone.

From this extract we can see that the collaborative design task appears to engage the students in rich dialogue in which different views and perspectives are negotiated in order to establish a shared understanding of the task and its possible solutions. In this extract, both students share and explain their personal perspectives of the nature of the object to be built. In addition, they propose strategies, advance speculations and evaluate their way of working and their problem solving. Although the interactive practices of this dyad signal deep engagement and commitment to joint problem solving, they also reveal some of the challenges inherent in working in a collaborative mode. Take for example the middle of the interaction episode and Kati's frustrated comment *"You can see it as you wish!"* This brief extract shows that negotiating a shared understanding of the situation during collaborative problem solving is not always easy or even self-evident. Yet, the establishment of a common ground, or shared understanding, is widely recognized as one of the most important prerequisites for a successful collaborative learning activity (Gibbs & Mueller, 1990; Moschkovich, 1996; Phelps & Damon, 1989; Roschelle & Teasley, 1995).

We wanted to investigate in detail how profitable and/or disadvantageous consequences of peer collaboration develop in the moment-by-moment interactions that take place between students in problem solving dyads. The focus of our attention was on the students' communication processes, problem solving strategies and mathematical language and on the dynamics involved in the construction of a shared understanding. Before describing the empirical study, we shall briefly review existing research on collaborative learning. We shall also clarify the meaning of shared understanding for socially shared learning activities.

Prior Research on Collaborative Interaction and Learning

The contribution of peer collaboration on students' social and academic learning has been widely documented (e.g. Azmitia, 1996; Cowie & van der Aalsvoort, 2000; Cohen, 1994; Forman & Cazden, 1985; Sharan, Shachar, & Levine, 1999; Littleton & Light, 1999; Stevens & Slavin, 1995; Webb & Palincsar, 1996). Peer collaboration can be defined as a coordinated activity during which participants collectively process and solve problems in order to achieve a joint outcome. This requires a large degree of mutual engagement in joint negotiation and, most importantly, the establishment of shared understanding with regard to the problem solving in question. The definition of peer collaboration that we adopt here is one that sees students working jointly on the same task in order to negotiate shared meanings that may challenge the subjective understandings of participants, or that go beyond what they already know individually (Dillenbourg, 1999).

Although peer collaboration can provide a large resource base for knowledge co-construction and self-reflection, previous research has shown that not all peer interaction creates productive learning opportunities (Forman, 1989; Teasley, 1995). The quality of learning in peer groups is closely associated with the nature of the collaboration and the interactions that learners engage in while working on academic tasks (Chan, 2001; Chi & Bassock, 1989; King, 1992; Mercer, 1996; Wegerif & Mercer, 1997; Webb, 1991; Webb, Troper, & Fall, 1995).

Moreover, collaborative interactions do not take place in a vacuum. They are closely embedded in the sociocultural context of the activity (Rogoff & Toma, 1997). When considering the nature of activity settings designed for collaborative learning, instructional conditions have been shown to shape the nature of peer collaboration, interaction and learning as have features of group composition (Cohen, 1994; Fuchs, Fuchs, Kazdan, Karns, Calhoon, Hamlet, & Hewlett, 2000; O'Donnell, & Dansereau, 1992; Sharan, Schachar, & Levine, 1999). For example, instructional situations requiring rote learning within the context of closed tasks, such as mathematical problems with one correct answer, can easily lead to mechanistic and product-oriented interactions. Open-ended and unstructured tasks, on the other hand, have been found to create conditions for exploratory and heuristic interactions and problem solving processes that pose new opportunities and challenges for successful collaborative learning (Damon & Phelps, 1989; Hogan, Nastasi, & Pressley, 2000). Open learning tasks change the expected roles and activity patterns that students with different characteristics are likely to adopt in joint problem solving situations. These activity patterns and roles include, among others, tutoring, domination and freeloading behavior as well as the equitable division of labor between collaborating peers (Cohen, 1994).

A review of research on collaborative learning processes (e.g. Azmitia, 1996; Cohen 1994; Webb & Palincsar, 1996) demonstrates, on the whole, that previous studies have relied to a large extent on the measurement of individual contributions and outcomes. More recent studies, however, have shifted the unit of analysis to a consideration of collective action in which individuals and social context are treated as interdependent (Greeno, Collins, & Resnick, 1996; Lave, 1998). These more recent approaches stress the role of interaction and discourse in conceptual development and define learning as participation in discourse communities. These studies are framed by situative or sociocultural theories of learning, and take the interaction and discourse processes constructed during collaborative activity as primary sources of data to be analyzed using methods and perspectives from sociolinguistics, anthropology, sociology and psychology. Detailed analyses of interaction and discourse processes among collaborating partners are conducted in order to investigate the ways in which meanings are constructed and realized through social activity (Gee, 1996; Goodwin & Heritage, 1990). Discourse analysts regard interactions as dynamic and transactional and define context as a co-construction by participants that emerges on a moment-by-moment basis in a social situation. As participants interact during socially-shared activities they are regarded as creating an 'ecology' of social and cognitive relations that mutually and continuously influence each other (Erickson, 1996).

Constructing a Shared Understanding in Peer Collaboration

In the study we describe below, we adopt Roschelle and Teasley's (1995) proposal that collaborative problem solving can be described as taking place in a negotiated and shared conceptual space or 'Joint Problem Space' constructed and maintained via shared language, situation and activity. Consequently we maintain that collaboration can not be considered to take place automatically just because individuals are co-present. Nor do we hold to the explanation that the learning gains achieved through collaboration result solely from the individual effort that occurs on exposure to alternative views, explanations and arguments. Instead, we see collaborative learning and problem solving as a social meaning-making activities where cognition and social relations are interdependent and where participants must make deliberate efforts to co-ordinate their language and activity to arrive at a shared understanding. Accordingly, the benefits of peer collaboration can be seen in the co-construction of knowledge realized by the collective sharing and negotiation of views and perspectives (Damon & Phelps, 1989; Wegerif & Mercer, 1996; Mercer, 2000; Tudge, 1992; Tudge & Rogoff, 1989). From this standpoint, social and verbal interaction and other semiotic tools embedded in the learning situation are regarded as important resources for the construction of shared understanding (Vygotsky, 1978; Wertsch, 1991). It is these resources that regulate the nature of collaborative learning activity during joint problem solving (Moschkovich, 1996; Roschelle & Teasley, 1995).

Findings on the advantages and disadvantages of heterogeneous dyads over homogeneous ones (e.g. Shaw, 1976; Webb, & Kenderski, 1984) or mixed ability versus same ability dyads for promoting successful collaborative activity have been somewhat inconsistent (see e.g. Perret-Clermont, 1980; Tudge, 1992; Webb, 1991). Existing research, however, has shown consistently that to understand the benefits and outcomes of peer collaboration, attention must be given to the nature of shared understanding and constructive activity constructed during the process of collaboration (Roschelle & Teasley, 1995; Webb, et al., 1995). Tudge (1992) has gone so far as to suggest that participants' relative degrees of competence may not be readily apparent to partners in a peer interactive dyad. He has shown that the less competent partner in a pair may well persuade the other partner to adopt his/her approach to the matter in question even though this is not necessarily the optimum approach. Findings such as this indicate that the negotiation of a shared meaning during collaborative peer problem solving can have deleterious as well as beneficial consequences.

Although prior research on collaborative learning processes has greatly contributed to our knowledge about individual contributions and outcomes, it has paid less attention to the ecology of communication, including turn taking, coherency and the conversational properties that support shared meaning-making between the participants. To understand the variability in collaborative outcomes and learning gains better, therefore, there is a need for thick descriptions of the interaction processes that take place during collaborative problem solving, with a specific focus on the interactional resources that support and/or challenge the practice of collaborative meaning-making (Pea, 1993). In the study discussed below, we focus on the processes of peer collaboration in heterogeneous dyads and show how micro-level analyses can illuminate how students co-construct a shared conceptual space through the mediational framework of communication, problem solving strategies and shared language.

THE STUDY

The Case Dyads

In this chapter we present a detailed microanalysis of the interaction processes of two male dyads selected from a larger data set of 20, twelve-year-old students from a Finnish elementary mathematics classroom. These students were observed whilst working in self-selected, same gender dyads during a design task. Prior to working in pairs, students attempted to carry out the design task individually. The outcome scores and subsequent working processes resulting from students' individual activity on the design task were used to identify existing differences in the problem solving skills of members of different dyads. The two case dyads selected for detailed analysis were composed of heterogeneous pairs representing different levels of competence in solving the design tasks. They were selected also on the basis that they showed contrasting differences their interaction processes during collaborative problem solving. Case dyad 1 illuminates interactional processes found to support the construction of a shared understanding, whereas Case dyad 2 highlights interaction processes which challenge joint meaning-making among peer dyads within the context of the design task. These dyads also showed differences the outcome scores for the design activity: Case dyad 1 had scores that indicated successful problem solving whereas Case dyad 2's scores showed mediocre results (see Table 1).

Table 1: Outcome scores from the design task

Students	Session 1 (Solo)	Session 2 (Dyadic)	Session 3 (Dyadic)	Session 4 (Solo)
Teemu	10	11	12	10
Sami	6	11	12	11
Joni	10	7	5	10
Kimmo	5	7	5	10
M (10 dyads)	8.1	10.0	11.1	10.7

Note. The maximum score students could attain in any session was 12 points.

Description of the Learning Situation

The task was located in the students' mathematics curriculum and consisted of a socially shared learning activity which required geometrical explanations to be constructed and evaluated by negotiation and experimentation. Tools provided in the activity setting, such as geometrical sketches and cards representing different faces of geometrical objects, were available to support the students' joint problem solving.

Dyads were provided with a work sheet showing sketches of three-dimensional objects and were asked to construct these with the help of two-dimensional objects or shapes. The two-dimensional shapes were cutouts of polygons such as pentagons, quadrilaterals and triangles. The sketches of the geometrical objects could be visualized in different ways, and hence there were many solutions to the tasks. The students had more cutouts on their desks than they needed. During the actual collaborative problem solving sessions, the student dyads sat around a desk on which all the materials needed for the task were provided. These included six sketches of geometrical objects, 30 to 50 cutout shapes, sellotape, and writing tools. The teacher-researcher was present in the classroom to support students' problem solving. The teacher did not, however, intervene in the students' work unless requested to do so. At the beginning of each session the teacher gave students oral instructions that clarified the nature of the design task and encouraged them to work collaboratively. Students were not given any specific instructions on how to solve the design tasks or on how to collaborate effectively. Figure 1 presents a photograph of students' working on the design task.

Figure 1: Dyadic problem solving on the design task

Data Collection

During the study, the students' participated in four, problem solving sessions altogether. Each session lasted between 25 and 45 minutes and each involved six different but equally difficult design tasks. Data collection covered all four sessions. Each student participated in all four sessions. The first and the fourth sessions were carried out as an individual activity, whereas the second and third sessions were conducted with students working in dyads. The composition of the dyads remained the same in both sessions. Each of the four sessions was videotaped as a whole and supplemented with the researcher's field notes. The videotapes were fully transcribed and analyzed according to the analysis framework described below. The present chapter uses the data from students' problem solving across both dyadic sessions.

Coding and Analyses

Each of the four sessions consisted of six design tasks. The maximum score for each task was two points. The total score for each session was 12 points. The general evaluation criteria used to score the students' task productions were: *exactly corresponding design* (2 points); *partly corresponding design* (1 point); *non-corresponding design* (0 points).

The analysis of the interaction processes that occurred within peer dyads focused on the communicative functions of the interaction and on the nature of the social activity emerging in joint activity. In addition, specific attention was given to the students' problem solving strategies and to the mathematical language they used during the design process. The categories for each analytic focus emerged from and were grounded in the interaction data from the study.

Analysis of Communicative Functions

A functional analysis of peer interaction focuses on the purposes for which verbal language is used in a given context and is designed to investigate and highlight the communicative functions of the linguistic strategies used by individual students during interaction (Gumperz, 1982; Halliday & Hasan, 1989). The identification of communicative functions in peer interaction relies on taking account of 'implicature'; that is to say, acknowledging that what a speaker implies, suggests or means may be different from what he or she literally says. As a consequence, the communicative functions of utterances can not be identified on the basis of linguistic form alone. Rather, they must be identified within the context of an utterance's retrospective and prospective effects on the actual discourse in terms of both content and form.

The categories describing the communicative functions of the case dyads identified in this study were as follows: informative, argumentative, reasoning, evaluative, organizational, interrogative, responsive, repetitive, agrees/disagrees, dictation, reading aloud and affective. Each function in the framework reflects participants' social-cognitive-discursive actions as they verbally interact during the course of their social activity (Kumpulainen & Mutanen, 1999). Definitions and examples of the communicative functions describing students' verbal interaction are summarized in Table 2.

Table 2: Categories describing the communicative functions of students' discourse

Category	Description	Example
Informative	Provides information	*we are supposed to use faces that are of different size*
Argumentative	Justifies information, opinions or actions	*but they're not attached to each other..look because a kind of flap should be used there*
Reasoning	Reasons in language	*here we have three triangles of equal size*
Evaluative	Evaluates work or action	*now for the first time we have a real problem*
Organizational	Organizes or controls behavior	*let's go through all the triangles*
Interrogative	Poses questions	*look..what do you think this shape is*
Responsive	Replies to questions	*- what about that one* *- it is also too big*

Category	Description	Example
Repetitive	Repeats spoken language	*- here they are probably* *- yeah, probably* *- probably*
Agrees	Expresses agreement	*yeah..it is the triangle*
Disagrees	Expresses disagreement	*it cannot be*
Dictation	Dictates text	*write three, twenty-five, nine, twenty-one and thirty-five*
Reading aloud	Reads text aloud	*twenty-two..thirty..six..okay*
Affective	Expresses feelings and emotions	*I feel a bit ashamed..this is a crazy idea*

Analysis of Social Activity

The analysis of the students' social activity was designed to characterize the nature of social relationships established within the dyads. The analysis is realized at an episodic level, defined by the mode of interaction. The categories that characterized the different modes of social activity in peer dyads were: *collaborative, tutoring, argumentative, conflict, dominative* and *confusion modes*. Definitions, (with examples), of these categories are given in Table 3. It should be noted that the *argumentative* and *tutoring* modes describe the nature of collaboration between the participants and in this sense can be regarded as sub-modes of collaborative activity. The argumentative mode implies constructive interaction in which students negotiate their differing understandings in a rational way by giving judgments and justifications. This often leads to a shared understanding of the situation. The tutoring mode shows students helping and explaining for the purpose of assisting the other to understand the matter at hand. The collaborative mode includes interaction in which the participants attempt to achieve a mutual understanding of the situation, ideas are jointly negotiated, the reasoning is transactive, and the discourse is coherent. In collaborative interaction participants often assist one another and hence create bi-directional zones of proximal development (Forman, 1989).

Analysis of Problem Solving Strategies

The primary unit of analysis of the students' problem solving strategies used was the utterance. As the data from this study show, sometimes semantically connected utterances form distinct episodes that characterize a particular type of problem solving strategy. Not all utterances were found to reflect problem-solving strategies, however, and consequently not all were coded.

The analysis of the students' problem-solving strategies fell into six categories. These were *measuring, visualizing, constructing, testing, excluding* and *evaluating*. These categories are summarized in Table 4 and describe the various types of cognitive processes associated with the different problem- solving strategies students used to carry out the task.

Table 3: Categories describing the nature of social activity between peers

Category	Description	Example
Collaborative	Joint activity characterized by equal participation and shared meaning-making	- *shall I measure these sides ..so they are again three and let's say twenty-eight, is it so?* - *yeah* - *then..we still need these two ones* - *and the top here*
Tutoring	Student helping and assisting another student	- *no look these one..look we could then use squares which are of equal size..look for squares of this size..two more..that third one and where..twenty this one here..look Sami..this goes here and this goes here and in summary, it goes like this*
Argumentative	Students are faced with social or cognitive conflicts which are resolved by rational argumentation and demonstration	- *no it is not that one..it should be narrower* - *yes it is..look (shows by demonstration)* - *oh yes it is* - *and now the bottom..it must be a triangle*
Conflict	Students are faced with cognitive and social conflicts which are left Unresolved	- *which side face?* - *this one* - *no it isn't...this is slanting this line here. this is not..these are the only ones here in which the line is slanting and this is longer* - *well does it fit then?* - *wait* - *no don't do it now* - *yes..yes..*
Domination	Student dominating the work which leads to unequal participation in joint reasoning	- *where is the large triangle?* - *oh, yeah.. (confused)* - *take those away* - *haha..what are we looking for?*
Confusion	Characterized by the lack of shared understanding	- *no..it is not like that..this is the same* - *well does it really go like that..no it does not* - *well all the same let's do it wrongly but I think it should be done differently* - *well you think so..you always think you are correct and that's why you say it* - *no I don't..well you say then how it could go* - *this could be shorter* *(silence)* - *are you getting anywhere* - *yes*

Table 4: Categories describing students' problem-solving strategies

Category	Description	Example
Measuring	Investigates the size and shape of a solid by measuring	- *this is a slightly different length but* - *no it isn't*
Visualizing	Uses visualization and sketching in joint reasoning of the nature of a solid	- *look it goes like this if one views it from above* - *true and then..*
Constructing	Builds a solid with the help of cards representing different faces	- *take those small ones* - *I took them there already..wait, I'll look for them from there..okay now I found them...now it is ready..* - *yeah exactly that one* - *yeah and then here* - *the base* - *it doesn't quite..*
Testing	Investigates the structure of a solid by testing and matching faces to those shown in the picture	- *okay..it should be this kind of a triangle* - *here..it is this one* - *wait, we must see..wait..no* - *no* - *or then we should take a smaller triangle* -*what about this smaller triangle..no..*
Excluding	Organizes and selects faces on the table in order to exclude those ones that do not fit with the solid to be constructed	- *hey..let's move these* - *yeah yeah let's move these they do not belong..wait..where did that other triangle fit* - *or then wait* - *hey hey.. what if one of these triangles is the best*
Evaluating	Critically examines joint problem-solving processes and task-productions	- *this may be destroyed..this is so difficult* - *yes it is..but it is easier for us than the other one ...okay let's continue to search for the pieces*

Analysis of Mathematical Language

Two categories were used for the analysis of the mathematical language students were observed to use during the joint problem solving episodes: *informal language* and *formal language*. Informal language is defined as the use of referents such as pronouns, adjectives, number cards or metaphors whereas formal language is defined as the use of formal concepts from the field of geometry in joint problem solving (see Table 5 for examples).

Table 5: Categories describing students' mathematical language

Category	Description	Example
Informal language	Uses referents such as pronouns, adjectives, number cards or metaphors in joint reasoning and problem-solving	*- then it could be this thick one..another one like this..or this seems to go straight..yes it does..yes*
Formal language	Uses the formal concepts of geometry in joint reasoning and problem-solving	*- it isn't that one..it's this triangle look* *- it isn't possible..look since this is equilateral*

Analysis Procedure

The interaction data of the study were analyzed in several phases. In the first phase, the video material of the students' interaction processes was examined together with the field notes written during observations. Next, the verbal interaction of the dyads was transcribed. After that, the interaction and behaviors apparent in the videotapes were analyzed on a moment-by-moment basis by following the written transcripts. Particular attention was paid to the nature of the students' social interaction, problem solving strategies and mathematical language. Other features observed and analyzed involved the students' use of the tools available in the problem solving situations, and the students' construction of time within their activity. The analyses resulted in micro-analytical maps. The micro-analytical maps describe the sequential evolution of peer interaction as constructed by students interacting with, and acting on, each other's messages. In addition, the maps show the construction of time in the students' activity as well as contextual information necessary for the interpretation of the social activity in question. Horizontal lines mark the beginnings and closures of thematically connected episodes in the analytical maps.

Two researchers analyzed the interaction data. Disagreements concerning the analyses were negotiated until joint agreement was established. Due to the interpretative and contextual nature of the analyses, this procedure was deemed the most suitable. The results of these analyses are presented next.

RESULTS OF THE ANALYSES

Case 1: Constructing a Shared Understanding

The Nature of Social Interaction

Case 1 describes the interactive dynamics of a dyad, Sami and Teemu. The social interaction of this dyad reveals interactive strategies and mechanisms that appear to support collaborative reasoning.

The functional analysis of the dyad's social interaction across the two sessions reveals that the students' social interaction was mostly characterized by the reasoning, organizational, agreeing, and argumentative functions. In the flow of the students' interaction, the use of these functions often formed reasoning, argumentative and organizational episodes. Figure 2 below highlights the communicative functions used by Teemu and Sami in their social interaction.

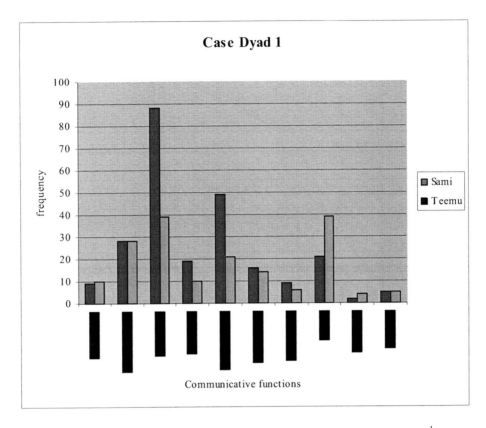

Figure 2: The distribution of communicative functions among Case dyad 1[1]

This figure shows that the students participated rather equally in social interaction. The data analysis also reveals slight differences between the students' communicative strategies. Whereas Teemu agreed more often with the ideas and suggestions created *(Teemu N:39/60, Sami N:21/60)*, Sami was more involved in reasoning *(Sami N:88/127, Teemu N:39/127)* and organizing *(Sami N:49/70, Teemu N:21/70)* the students' problem solving activity. These features highlight further the richness in these two students' collaboration modes and indicate that each played somewhat different participatory roles in their joint problem solving.

As the extract shown in Table 6 indicates, the social interaction of this dyad is coherent and highly collaborative, reflecting mutual understanding and equal participation in problem solving. The students' social interaction includes tutoring and argumentative episodes, during which they help one another to grasp their way of thinking and understanding by explicating their point of view through verbal and non-verbal interaction, as well as with the help of the tools they are using.

---

[1] The frequencies of communicative functions describing repetition, dictation and reading aloud are not included in the figures due to their extremely low occurrence.

Table 6: The nature of social interaction in case dyad 1

				Communicative Functions	Social Activity	Contextual Notes

| SESSION: 1.1.2 Mathematics |
| PUPILS: Sami and Teemu |
| WORKING TIME: 09:09 – 09:23 |

Time	Participation		Transcribed Peer Interaction	Communicative Functions	Social Activity	Contextual Notes
09:18	125	TEEMU	bottom....how come	argumentative question	collaborative	
09:19	126	SAMI	no..but that's the bottom .. that's that sort of a triangle and the lid is that sort of a triangle...they are connected...it shows there how they are connected	answering by demonstration	collaborative tutoring	
	127	TEEMU	no..look..this is	argumentation		
	128	SAMI	yeah..its connected	argumentation		
	129	TEEMU	Wait	organizing		
	130	SAMI	that could be created by side triangles in a way	reasoning		
	131	TEEMU	a triangle comes here..a triangle comes here..a triangle comes here and here comes a rectangle	reasoning by demonstration		outlining the geometrical object
	132	SAMI	yeah..exactly and here for the roof as well	agrees and reasons		
	133	TEEMU	could it go here	reasons		Sami tries to speak at the same time
	134	SAMI	this one..this one yeah..wait a minute...yeah this is the rectangle	reasons		
	135	TEEMU	and this belongs there too	reasons		
	136	SAMI	should we find another one similar to that	makes a reasoning question		
	137	TEEMU	like this	answering by demonstration		
	138	SAMI	no it's smaller	argumentation		
	139	TEEMU	it's smaller..there..no it isn't	agrees and reasons		
09:20	140	SAMI	no it isn't...what if that bottom is different....let's take these bigger ones you suggested.. since these are of equal size here at the back..now I found another one ....the little triangles go there...the little long ones go...	agrees, organizes and reasons	collaborative	

At the beginning of the episode in Table 6, Teemu poses an argumentative question to Sami, *"bottom...how come?"* (turn 125). Although his utterance indicates disagreement, it also seems to work as an attempt at creating a joint meaning with his peer about the sketch of the solid to be constructed. Sami answers Teemu in turn 126, *"no..but that's the bottom..that's that sort of a triangle and the lid is that sort of a triangle...they are connected...it shows there how they are connected"*, by demonstrating and explaining his perception of the solid sketched on the work sheet. In his following turn (127) Teemu again questions Sami's idea of the structure of the solid by argumentation, *"no..look..this is"*, and indicates that they are not sharing a joint understanding of the situation. In turn 128, *"yeah..it's connected"*, Sami still argues against Teemu's conceptualization. In this argumentative episode (turns 125-128) the drawing of the object appears to work as an important tool for the dyad's argumentative interaction, despite the fact that it is not explicitly articulated in the students' verbal interaction. Teemu's following utterance *"wait"* (turn 129) appears to close the argumentative episode and to start a new one, in which a joint meaning about the sketch of the object is created. This interaction episode is characterized by chains of reasoning utterances and seems to be stimulated further by Sami's utterance, *"that could be created by side triangles in a way"* (turn 130). Here he starts to reason verbally about the forms of the side faces of the solid to be constructed. In his following utterance, *" a triangle comes here...a triangle comes here...a triangle comes here and here comes a rectangle"* (turn 131), Teemu leads their joint problem solving further by demonstration and explanation. The interaction episode is followed by connected utterances (turns 132-135) during which the students in turn speculate and test appropriate side faces for their construction.

Metaphorically, in this interaction episode the students have become one social entity in that they build or "weave" their joint thinking and problem solving. Turns 136 to 140 can be considered to belong to the same interaction episode since they deal with the same problem-solving topic and also show high-level collaboration. It is worth giving particular emphasis, however, to the strategies and signs that the students implicitly use to sustain a shared focus and understanding. In turn 136, Sami's utterance, *"should we find another one similar to that"*, the willingness to sustain collaboration is indicated by his proposal of strategies for proceeding in their task. Teemu replies to Sami's proposition in turn 137, *"like this"*, by giving his suggestion in a tentative format. The following turns (138-140) are characterized by repetition, which is used in the students' problem solving to indicate agreement.

Interestingly, both students appear to take up each other's words and use them in their follow-up utterances, as can be seen from the extract. Sami's utterance in turn 140 again gives evidence of the dyad's joint exploratory activity when he makes his thinking and reasoning visible by means of his verbal language and gestures, as well as by his use of the cards and sketches of the solids. The collaborative nature of their activity is also witnessed in his utterance, *"let's take these bigger ones **you suggested**"*. Here he explicitly shows himself to value his partner's ideas and suggestions and shows that he considers Teemu as a legitimate participant in their collaborative endeavor.

Problem Solving Strategies and Mathematical Language

Table 7 models Sami's and Teemu's reasoning processes and use of mathematical language and further illustrates how their social interaction reflects the construction of a shared understanding in joint activity. The data analysis shows that these students' problem solving strategies included measuring, visualizing, constructing, and excluding activities.

Particularly, measuring, visualizing and constructing activities appeared to form larger episodes in the students' social interaction, reflecting joint reasoning in the design task. Noteworthy in the students' problem solving activity is also the fact that they seemed to approach the design task from a holistic viewpoint by visualizing the structure of the object in question.

Table 7: The nature of mathematical reasoning in case dyad 1

SESSION: 1.1.2 Mathematics
PUPILS: Sami and Teemu
WORKING TIME: 09.09 - 09.23

Time	Participation		Transcribed Peer Interaction	Mathematical Problem-Solving		
				STRATEGIES	*LANGUAGE*	
					Informal	*Formal*
09:09	1	SAMI	*let's write Kalle and Erkki*			
	2	TEEMU	*write my name also*			
09:10	3	SAMI	*well ..okay.. we should first start with those side triangles*	constructing		side triangles as parts of a solid
	4	TEEMU	*Yeah*			
	5	SAMI	*take this*			
	6	TEEMU	*pardon me..but they aren't..oh well*			
	7	SAMI	*these here..they're of equal size..then we should find the sides*	measuring		sides as parts of a solid
	8	TEEMU	*are they these ones*		a pronoun as a referent	
	9	SAMI	*aren't they right angles*			right angles as parts of a triangle
	10	TEEMU	*well no..so are they*			
	11	SAMI	*wait..there should be three pieces since..wait a minute..the base should be of different size*			base as a part of a solid
	12	TEEMU	*it should be a triangle..the base..the base is a triangle*	visualizing		triangle as a base of a solid
	13	SAMI	*no..it is..look this..look*			
	14	TEEMU	*yeah..and then we need this above*		a pronoun as a referent	
	15	SAMI	*yeah these sides exactly*			sides as parts of a solid
	16	TEEMU	*look the gable is this one*	constructing	a metaphor (gable)	
	17	SAMI	*this one..now another like this..do we have another similar one*		pronouns as referents	
	18	TEEMU	*Here*			
	19	SAMI	*here..now we need a little bit bigger base..would that be suitable*	measuring		base as a part of a solid
09:11	20	TEEMU	*no but it is a triangle that base*	visualizing		triangle and base as parts of a solid
	21	SAMI	*no it isn't it is a square*			square as a part of a solid
	22	TEEMU	*so it is..I was just visualizing it in a funny way*			

SESSION: 1.1.2 Mathematics
PUPILS: Sami and Teemu
WORKING TIME: 09.09 - 09.23

Time	Participation		Transcribed Peer Interaction	Mathematical Problem-Solving		
				STRATEGIES	LANGUAGE	
					Informal	Formal
	23	SAMI	yeah..but now we have again a problem..this is too long this system..so what if..could it	measuring	a metaphor (system)	
	24	TEEMU	hey..shall we move these	excluding		
	25	SAMI	yeah..yeah..let's move these..now these don't belong..wait..where could that triangle fit..oh			triangle as a face of a solid
	26	TEEMU	wait..hey			
	27	SAMI	hey..hey..what if one of these triangles is the best	visualizing		triangle as a face of a solid
	28	TEEMU	you mean one of these ones		a pronoun as a referent	
	29	SAMI	no but these..look then we could use the squares which are all of equal size..could you..find two more squares of this size..that thirty-three..well..where..twenty this here..look Teemu..when this goes here and this one goes like this..		number cards and pronouns as referents	square as a part of a solid
	30	TEEMU	Yeah			
	31	SAMI	so it should be formed with these		a pronoun as a referent	
	32	TEEMU	wait..like this	constructing		
	33	SAMI	look..this is going to be like this..		pronouns as referents	
09:12	34	TEEMU	yeah it is			
	35	SAMI	it should be formed up with these		a pronoun as a referent	
	36	TEEMU	yeah it should			
	37	SAMI	write them down			

The analysis of these students' mathematical language reveals that they actively conceptualized the task through both formal and informal language. Formal language used in joint reasoning included specific concepts such as a triangle and a square, as well as general geometrical concepts, such as a side and a base. The students' informal language consisted of referents, such as pronouns and adjectives. The number cards provided by the activity setting were also used to support joint problem solving. In summary, the analysis of the students' mathematical language shows that informal and formal reasoning was rich and lively and that both were actively contributing to the collaborative interaction.

Case 2: Missing the Opportunity to Establish a Shared Understanding

The Nature of Social Interaction

Case 2 describes the social interaction of another dyad, Joni and Kimmo, working on the design task. The social interaction of this dyad highlights elements in the students' interaction that indicate a lack of shared understanding.

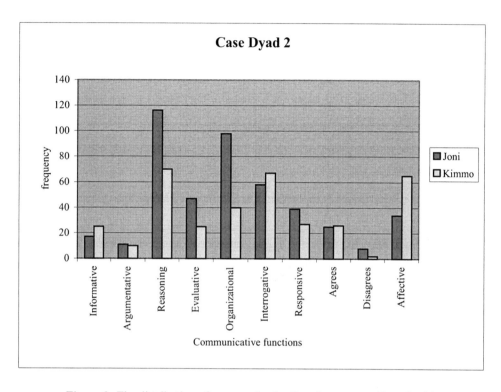

Figure 3: The distribution of communicative functions among Case dyad 2

The functional analysis of the students' verbal communication collected from the two dyadic working sessions (see Figure 3) shows that the students' interaction was mostly characterized by the reasoning, organizational, questioning, and affective functions. As with the other dyad, reasoning and organizational episodes reflect the nature of the design task, which seemed to encourage exploratory activity. The high occurrence of the affective functions signals the students' emotional engagement in their problem solving. The analysis also reveals distinct differences in each students' communicative strategies. The data show that Kimmo produced more affective statements than Joni *(Kimmo N:65/99, Joni N:34/99)*. Joni, on the other hand, organized the activity *(Joni N:98/138, Kimmo N:40/138)* and reasoned *(Joni N:116/186, Kimmo N:70/186)* more frequently than Kimmo. The differences in the students' communicative strategies and types of participation are evidence of the imbalance in their social interaction, Joni being the active and dominant problem-solver and Kimmo fading into the background showing signs of slight frustration.

The analysis of the interactive dynamics of Joni and Kimmo's social interaction shows that at the beginning the students were task-oriented and interested in the design task. Both students started the activity eagerly. Soon, however, Joni started to dominate the task, for example, by handling the cards and giving orders, and did not give Kimmo much space. Kimmo did not seem to notice this at first, but gradually started to be a bit restless since Joni did not take up his suggestions or ideas. Interestingly, Kimmo soon accepted his role and started to withdraw from the activity, letting Joni do most of the problem solving. From the data it appears that Joni was thinking aloud rather than trying to solve the design task collaboratively. Only in those instances when Joni regarded the task as difficult to solve did he start to seek confirmation of his ideas from Kimmo. The interaction episode in Table 8 highlights the nature of these students' social interaction.

This extract (see Table 8) starts with Joni's question, *"where is the large triangle?"* (turn 147), in which he indirectly asks Kimmo to find a large triangle for the solid to be constructed. In his reply, Kimmo answers with an affective statement, *"oh..yeah"*, although the video-analysis shows his attention is directed to holding the cards the students have already constructed. In turn 149 Joni continues his orders, *"take those away"*, but does not explain what he is actually trying to do. In his following utterance, *"haha..what are you looking for?"* (turn 150), Kimmo tries to ask Joni to clarify his thinking and strategies. Joni replies to Kimmo in turn 151 by saying, *"a kind of a triangle to the center"*, but this reply and the tone in which it is uttered implies that Joni is thinking aloud rather than aiming at joint problem solving. The lack of a shared understanding between the students is further evidenced in the forthcoming discourse (turns 152–155, 158–161), which shows an incoherence between the conversational turns in that the students, particularly Kimmo, seem not to be responding to each other but rather to be solving the task individually.

In turn 155 Joni also signals that he is a bit restless and wants to move on to another problem-solving task even though they have not yet solved the earlier one. In the same turn he also speculates, *"hey..could it be these?"* which leads Kimmo to ask him to clarify his reasoning *"do you mean these small ones?"* (turn 156). In his following turn 157 Joni confirms by saying, *"these"*. In turn 158 Kimmo attempts to strengthen their collaboration by saying, *"what about these big ones..I think they look big..like this"*. Joni's following turn 159 indicates that he is still thinking by himself, *"I think"*, which leads Kimmo to be confused, *"I don't know"* (turn 160). The confusion between the students at this stage appears to lead Kimmo to withdraw from active problem solving. This is evidenced by his turn, *"I don't want to"* (turn 166), when Joni asks him to hold the cards.

Problem Solving Strategies and Mathematical Language

Table 9 models the Joni and Kimmo's mathematical problem solving strategies and language during collaborative activity. The analysis of social interaction of this dyad indicates asymmetric interaction in which one of the students occasionally dominated the activity. The data analysis of the students' mathematical reasoning further indicates lack of a shared understanding within the dyad, as is evidenced by the fragmented nature of the students' problem solving strategies and mathematical language. The students' problem solving strategies seem to have been mostly grounded in measuring the size and shape of a solid and constructing activity. A few conversational turns focused on testing (turns 1 and 2) and visualizing (turn 3). As the data analysis shows, joint reasoning was infrequent in this dyad. What is also noteworthy within this dyad is the fact that Joni mainly initiated the dyad's problem solving strategies.

Table 8: The nature of social interaction in case dyad 2

SESSION: 1.1.2 Mathematics PUPILS: Kimmo and Joni WORKING TIME: 11:05 – 11:30					
Time	**Participation**		**Transcribed Peer Interaction**	**Communicative Functions**	**Social Activity**	**Contextual Notes**

Time		**Participation**	**Transcribed Peer Interaction**	**Communicative Functions**	**Social Activity**	**Contextual Notes**
11:16	147	JONI	where is the large triangle	asking for information	slight domination from Joni's side	looking for a face
	148	KIMMO	oh, yeah...	affective utterance		Kimmo is holding the construction students have already made
	149	JONI	take those away	organizing		
	150	KIMMO	hahah...what are you looking for	affective utterance and asking for information	Kimmo initiates collaboration	
	151	JONI	a kind of a triangle to the center...these tasks are a bit too difficult..	answering and evaluating		
	152	KIMMO	how about this one then	reasoning in a question form		
	153	JONI	it might be...perhaps two of these there...	reasoning		
	154	KIMMO	basically no	reasoning		
11:17	155	JONI	show me ...hmm...let's turn to the next exercise..let's solve that one since it is easier...it is what one sees...hey, could it be these..	organizing, evaluating and reasoning	slight domination from Joni's side	
	156	KIMMO	do you mean these small ones	reasoning in a question form	Kimmo initiates collaboration	
	157	JONI	these	answering		
	158	KIMMO	what about these big ones, I think they look big..like this...	reasoning		
	159	JONI	I think...(indistinct)	-		
	160	KIMMO	I don't know..	informing	signs of "a free rider effect" starting to appear	
	161	JONI	that's a bit too thick that one there..that's there...rather small..	reasoning		comparing cards
	162	KIMMO	that's not it..heheheh...	reasoning		
	163	JONI	its all the same really	reasoning		
	164	KIMMO	let's try both	organizing		
	165	JONI	let's take...this is there below, isn't it?..bigger one..hold it	organizing, reasoning and organizing		organizing working
	166	KIMMO	no, I don't want to	disagrees	social conflict	

Table 9: The nature of mathematical reasoning in case dyad 2

SESSION: 1.1.2 Mathematics
PUPILS: Kimmo and Joni
WORKING TIME: 11:05 - 11:30

Time	Participation		Transcribed Peer Interaction	Mathematical Problem-Solving		
				STRATEGIES	LANGUAGE Informal	Formal
11:05	1	JONI	okay..that kind of a triangle..this one	testing		triangle as a part of a solid
	2	KIMMO	this kind..is it this kind		pronouns as referents	
	3	JONI	wait…we should look..wait..no			
	4	KIMMO	no			
	5	JONI	or then..we should take a smaller triangle	measuring		triangle as a part of a solid
	6	KIMMO	what about this one..is this a bit shorter..not at least		pronouns as referents	
	7	JONI	wait wait wait			
	8	KIMMO	this one		a pronoun as a referent	
11:06	9	JONI	wait..could these go together..they could go like this..couldn't they	constructing	pronouns as referents	
	10	KIMMO	they fit			
	11	JONI	then it could be this thick one..another one like this..or this seems to go straight..yes it does..yes		adjectives and pronouns as referents	
	12	KIMMO	genius			
	13	JONI	and one more of those ones..there and then another one of these triangles		pronouns as referents	triangle as a part of a solid
	14	KIMMO	is it this one		a pronoun as a referent	
	15	JONI	a kind of a long one..no..here..okay..here it is	measuring	adjectives and pronouns as referents	
	16	KIMMO	for the time being			
	17	JONI	mmm			
	18	KIMMO	three..forty-seven	constructing	number cards as referents	
	19	JONI	thirty-nine was..twenty..ouh yeah..juuh..here above is this		number cards and pronouns as referents	
	20	KIMMO	and underneath			
	21	JONI	yeah and underneath..well..well like..and then that one which is of this length	measuring	pronouns as referents	
	22	KIMMO	it is			
	23	JONI	this one		a pronouns as a referent	
	24	KIMMO	no it's not quite..two of those		pronouns as referents	
11:07	25	JONI	okay..then..we should find those two..these may be a bit difficult	constructing	pronouns as referents	
	26	KIMMO	let's see..these could		a pronoun as a referent	
	27	JONI	well wait..these are shaped as squares			square as a face
	28	KIMMO	they are a kind of			
	29	JONI	too long..about the shape of a square..now this kind..could it be here	measuring	pronouns as referents	square as a face
	30	KIMMO	yeah			

This analysis of the students' mathematical language in joint problem solving shows that their verbal interaction mainly rested on informal reasoning. The students' informal language consisted of the use of pronouns, adjectives and the use number cards as referents. The students' formal language consisted of concepts such as a triangle, a small triangle and a square. Only one of the two students, Joni, was found to use formal language when verbalizing his reasoning.

Contrasts in Interaction Processes between Case Dyads: A Summary

In this study, collaborative problem solving was reflected by equal participation in social interaction, including joint reasoning of problem solving strategies and active conceptualization and visualization of the situation. Collaboration between peers seemed to be supported by reciprocal attempts to create a joint meaning when making problem solving visible via explanation and demonstration. The students' appreciation of each other's contribution to problem solving and its explicit communication to their partner was also seen to support joint reasoning and to promote the students' sense of being legitimate participants in their collaborative endeavour. From the standpoint of mathematical reasoning, interactions which supported collaborative problem solving were those where students operated on their partners' reasoning and those where students co-ordinated their perspectives and explanations into a global view in order to apply and test them. In addition, symmetric interaction was evidenced in representational interactions where students paraphrased their partner's reasoning as well as in interactions in which ideas and suggestions were challenged by opposing views (see also Azmitia & Montgomery, 1993; Berkowitz, Oser, & Althof, 1987; Kruger, 1993; Tolmie, Howe, Mackenzie, & Greer, 1993). Yet, in order to establish and maintain a shared focus even in conflict situations, it was found to be important that the partners stayed in a task-focused mode and kept their personal views in check.

Collaborative problem solving among heterogeneous dyads was also found to pose challenges for joint meaning-making. Particularly for dyads who repeatedly faced cognitive or social conflicts, the outcome was often asymmetric interaction and problem solving, with diminished potential for shared meaning-making. On the other hand, in some cases conflict situations resulted in peer tutoring episodes or argumentative episodes during which one member of the dyad scaffolded his/her partner towards a joint understanding. This mode of peer interaction was found to require a shared focus and explicit attempts to maintain collaboration.

In this study, problems with collaboration were evidenced by incoherent transactions in which divergent strategies and verbal conceptualizations were introduced without the resulting construction of a shared meaning. The emergence of incoherent interaction often resulted from a conflict or because one or other student dominated the interaction. In cases such as this students were unable or sometimes unwilling to negotiate a joint understanding of the situation. A closer look at the students' mathematical reasoning showed that the problem solving activity of these dyads rested mainly on unintegrated strategies, which focused on local measuring and constructing activity with little global visualization. The data analysis also highlighted imbalances in the nature of the students' participation in providing strategies and conceptualizing the problem solving activity. This imbalance was evident, for example, where one student was more involved in problem solving and mathematizing the situation, or where both students in the dyad imposed their own perspectives and approaches into the interaction with little attempt at negotiating a joint meaning. The analysis of the two contrasting case dyads draws attention to the necessity of taking into account students' social and cognitive skills and habits in maintaining productive, task-focused interaction when studying the nature of peer collaboration.

GENERAL DISCUSSION

Today, collaborative working modes are being explicitly capitalized on in many classroom settings. Collaborative problem solving around interesting tasks is widely considered to foster deep engagement in the subject matter and to provide students with a sense of agency of their working and learning at school (Cohen, 1994; Webb & Palincsar, 1996). The present study provides further evidence of the potential power of collaborative working modes. Here, the collaborating dyads were found to engage in exploratory activity including reasoning, problem posing and solving. The strategies used to solve the design problems included versatile approaches that involved constructing, measuring, visualizing, testing, excluding and evaluating. The students' verbal interactions included reasoning, hypothesizing, argumentation, organizing, and questioning. All of these are important features of inquiry-based interaction that have been shown to provide opportunities for the co-construction of knowledge (Cohen, 1994; Hogan, et al., 2000; Moschkovich, 1996). All in all, the opportunity to approach and conceptualize the task using a variety of problem solving strategies and through informal and formal language seemed to support the students' active participation in joint problem solving.

In addition to domain specific learning opportunities, collaboration with peers creates a social context in which learners can practice their social and interactional skills. This includes practicing the ways in which to engage in constructive dialogue (Barron, 2000). Our study shows that when students are asked to solve a problem together they are confronted with a number of challenges. These challenges include negotiating different views and perspectives, resolving conflicts and discrepancies in understanding as well as establishing common frames of reference (Miyake, 1986; Roschelle, 1992). Although in some other conversational contexts, such as mother-child interactions, the establishment of mutual knowledge is often a natural reciprocal process guided by mutual interests (Bruner, 1978; Gibbs & Mueller, 1990; Stern, 1977), open-ended problem solving situations in school contexts set forth distinct challenges for shared meaning-making. Here, the domain and nature of the task as well as participants' expertise, goals and orientations to the actual task and to collaborative working modes may be in stark opposition. Consequently, the ability of collaborators to establish of a common frame of reference can not be taken as self-evident (Forman & Larreamendy-Joerns, 1995; Schwartz, 1995). In fact, as shown above for Joni and Kimmo, the emerging patterns of interaction can impede rather than create conditions for shared meaning-making and joint action (Tudge, 1992).

The present study confirms earlier research on collaborative learning by demonstrating that the social and cognitive processes inherent in peer problem solving are highly dynamic in nature, shaping collaborative activity on a moment-by-moment basis (Erickson, 1996; Moschkovich, 1996). Vion (1992), when characterizing the dynamic nature of interaction situations introduces the concept of heterogeneous interactive space (cf. Grossen, 1994). This refers to the social, cognitive and interactive roles and contexts which interacting partners have to negotiate in order to achieve a joint understanding. Similarly Stern (1977), when discussing the processes of shared meaning-making in early infancy between caregiver and child, characterizes the ongoing interaction as a "dance". Using this metaphor, he portrays the myriad of interactional spaces through which interacting partners move in their attempts to adjust to each other's topics, emotions, and tempos in order to establish shared meaning.

Interaction Markers for Shared Meaning-Making

Barron (2000) claims that three distinct aspects of collaborative problem solving interaction mark the nature of shared understanding among interacting groups. These are (a) the degree of mutuality in interaction, (b) joint focus of attention, (c) shared task alignment. These aspects appear to provide a useful interpretative framework for the present study and its findings.

Mutuality refers to the nature of the opportunities for equal participation and meaning making that is created during ongoing interactions. In this study, the analyses clearly show that the interaction processes of Case dyad 1 were marked by dialogue indicating that processes involved in reciprocity and mutuality were operating. This was reflected in the turn-taking and participation profiles of the students as well as by those interaction episodes that illustrated the occurrence of genuine transactional dialogue (Berkowitz, Oser, & Althof, 1987). By contrast, the interactions of Case dyad 2 showed unbalanced participation profiles and frequent failures to respond appropriately to contributions posed by the other partner in the dyad. This type of unbalanced interaction highlights the challenges to mutuality that can occur during social interaction. These challenges were also reflected in the incoherent strategies and mathematical language the students in Case dyad 2 used during problem solving.

The degree of joint attention to problem solving was also found to vary between the case dyads in this study. Case dyad 1 continuously monitored the level of their joint attention and immediately repaired instances where there was a danger of loosing a joint frame of reference. This was reflected in the students' communicative functions and by the nature of their social relationships that ranged from mutual co-construction to reciprocal tutoring. Furthermore, this dyad maintained shared attention by joint evaluation and monitoring of problem solving processes. This dyad also collaborated by sharing the physical materials of the design task and this too supported the development of shared meaning. In Case dyad 2, the interaction processes reflected more individualized working modes. This was demonstrated both in the nature of interactions the students engaged in during problem solving as well as in the ways they utilized the tools available to them for shared meaning-making. One partner in this dyad appeared to be unwilling to explain his views and perspectives to his partner, nor did he want to share the materials, rather he preferred to construct the design tasks quite independently. Consequently, possibilities for joint attention were minimal despite the efforts of the other student.

The problems faced by Case dyad 2 in constructing joint attention lead us to another yet related aspect of collaborative interaction, the establishment of a collaborative orientation toward problem solving, i.e. shared task alignment. Clearly, in Case dyad 2 one student had a preference for solving problems independently and for prioritising his own ideas. In Case dyad 1, on the other hand, both students showed a distinct interest in co-constructing solutions as evidenced by the explicit comments they used when making reference to each other's ideas.

Are the challenges identified in the interaction processes of Case dyad 2 unique? Unfortunately, the answer to this question is likely to be negative. Learning practices reflecting individual decision-making and social domination within collaborative interactions are not that rare. The existence of these patterns of interaction reflects in part a culture of traditional instruction and assessment that emphasizes individual performance, competition and comparison (Barron, 2000). Within this culture, frequently too little value is placed on the qualities of shared meaning-making. Thus, attention is mostly devoted to the *individual* practice of collaborating to learn and not so much on the *social* practice of collaborative learning or on the practice of learning to collaborate.

In addition to developing new assessment methods for collaborative peer learning that concentrate on the social dimensions of collaborative learning, in the future it will be important to direct more attention to helping students to engage in meta-reflection during collaborative problem solving. In this way they can become aware of the attentional engagement of themselves and their interacting partners whilst solving problems together. Moreover, there seems to be a need to help students develop strategies for establishing a shared understanding during joint problem solving particularly during moments of confusion, domination and/or conflict. Alternative assessment tools for shared meaning-making as well as instructional practices aiming at helping students to develop strategies for establishing a shared understanding, are likely to be informed by scientific research studies and well-developed analytic tools for studying interaction. These tools and instructional practices are also likely to be informed, however, by paying attention to participants' self-reflections on the nature and success of their own attempts to engage in collaborative problem solving.

REFERENCES

Azmitia, M. (1996). Peer interactive minds: developmental, theoretical, and methodological issues. In P.B. Baltes, & U.M. Staudinger (Eds.), *Interactive minds. Life-span perspectives on the social foundation of cognition* (pp. 133-162). Cambridge: Cambridge University Press.

Azmitia, M., & Montgomery, R. (1993). Friendship, transactive dialogues, and the development of scientific reasoning. *Social Development, 2*, 202-221.

Barron, B. (2000). Achieving coordination in collaborative problem solving groups. *The Journal of the Learning Sciences, 9*(4), 403-436.

Berkowitz, M.W., Oser, F., & Althof, W. (1987). The development of sociomoral discourse. In W.M. Kurtines & J.L. Gewirtz (Eds.), *Moral development through social interaction* (pp. 322-352). New York: Wiley.

Bruner, J. (1978). The role of dialogue in language acquisition. In A. Sinclair, R.J. Jarvella, & J.M. Levelt (Eds.), *The child's conception of language* (pp. 241-256). Berlin: Springer-Verlag.

Chan, C.K.K. (2001). Peer collaboration and discourse patterns in learning from incompatible information. *Instructional Science 29*, 443-479.

Chi, M.T.H., & Bassock, M. (1989). Learning from examples via self-explanations. In L.B. Resnick (Ed.), *Knowing, learning, and instruction: Essays in honour of Robert Glaser* (pp. 251-282). Hillsdale, NJ: Erlbaum.

Cohen, E. (1994). Restructuring the classroom: Conditions for productive small groups. *Review of Educational Research, 64*(1), 1-35.

Cowie, H., & van der Aalsvoort, G. (Eds.), (2000). *Social interaction in learning and instruction. The meaning of discourse for the construction of knowledge*. Amsterdam: Pergamon Press.

Damon, W., & Phelps, E. (1989). Critical distinctions among three approaches to peer education. *International Journal of Educational Research, 13*, 9-19.

Dillenbourg, P. (Eds.). (1999). *Collaborative learning: Cognitive and computational approaches*. Oxford: Pergamon.

Erickson, F. (1996). Going for the zone: The social and cognitive ecology of teacher-student interactions in classroom settings. In D. Hicks (Ed.), *Discourse, learning and schooling* (pp. 29-62). Cambridge, MA: Cambridge University Press.

Forman, E. A., & Cazden, C. (1985). Exploring Vygotskian perspectives in education: The cognitive value of peer interaction. In J. Wertsch (Ed.), *Culture, communication and cognition: Vygotskian perspectives* (pp. 323-347). Cambridge, MA: Cambridge University Press.

Forman, E. A. (1989). The role of peer interaction in the social construction of mathematical knowledge. *International Journal of Educational Research, 13,* 55-70.

Forman, E., & Larreamendy-Joerns, J. (1995). Learning in the context of peer collaboration: A pluralistic perspective on goals and expertise. Processes and products of collaborative problem solving: Some interdisciplinary perspectives [Special issue]. *Cognition and Instruction, 13*, 549-564.

Fuchs, L.S., Fuchs, D., Kazdan, S., Karns, K. Calhoon, M., Hamlett, C., & Hewlett, S. (2000). Effects of workgroup structure and size on student productivity during collaborative work on complex tasks. *The Elementary School Journal, 100*, 183-212.

Gee, J. (1996). Introduction to discourse analysis: Theory and method. London: Routledge & Kegan Paul.

Gibbs, R.W., Jr., & Mueller, R.A.G. (1990). Conversation as coordinated, cooperative interaction. In S.P. Robertson, W.Z. Zachary, & J.B. Black (Eds.), Cognition, computing, and cooperation. Norwood, NJ: Ablex.

Goodwin, C., & Heritage, J. (1990). Conversation analysis. Annual Review of Anthropology, 19, 283-307.

Greeno, J.G., Collins, A., & Resnick, L.B. (1996). Cognition and learning. In D.C. Berliner, & R.C. Calfee (Eds.), Handbook of educational psychology (pp. 15-46). New York: Macmillan.

Grossen, M. (1994). Theoretical and methodological consequences of a change in the unit of analysis for the study of peer interactions in a problem solving situation. *European Journal of Psychology of Education, 11*(1), 159-173.

Gumperz, J.J. (1982). Discourse strategies. Cambridge: Cambridge University Press.

Halliday, M.A.K. & Hasan, R. (1989). *Language, context, and text*. London: Oxford University Press.

Hogan, K., Nastasi, B.K., & Pressley, M. (2000). Discourse patterns and collaborative scientific reasoning in peer and teacher-guided discussions. *Cognition and Instruction, 17,* 379-432.

King, A. (1992). Facilitating elaborative learning through guided student-generated questioning. *Educational Psychologist, 27,* 111-126.

Kruger, A.C. (1993). Peer collaboration: Conflict, cooperation, or both? *Social Development, 2,* 165-183.

Kumpulainen, K., & Mutanen, M. (1999). The situated dynamics of peer group interaction: An introduction to an analytic framework. *Learning and Instruction, 9,* 449-474.

Lave, J. (1988). *Cognition in practice: Mind, mathematics, and culture in everyday life.* Cambridge: Cambridge University Press.

Littleton, K., & Light, P. (1999). *Learning with computers: Analyzing productive interaction.* London: Routledge.

Mercer, N. (1996). The quality of talk in children's collaborative activity in the classroom. *Learning and Instruction, 6,* 359-377.

Mercer, N. (2000). *Words and minds: How we use language to think together.* London: Routledge.

Miyake, N. (1986). Constructive interaction and the iterative process of understanding. *Cognitive Science, 10,* 151-177.

Moschkovich, J.N. (1996). Moving up and getting steeper: Negotiating shared descriptions of linear graphs. *The Journal of the Learning Sciences, 5*(3), 239-277.

O'Donnell, A.M., & Dansereau, D.F. (1992). Scripted cooperation in student dyads: A method for analysing and enhancing academic learning and performance. In R. Hertz-Lazarowitz, & N. Miller (Eds.), *Interaction in cooperative groups: The theoretical anatomy of group learning* (pp.120-141). Cambridge: University Press.

Pea, R.D. (1993). Learning scientific concepts through material and social activities: Conversation analysis meets conceptual change. *Educational Psychologist, 28,* 265-277.

Perret-Clermont, A. N. (1980). *Social interaction and cognitive development in children.* London: Academic Press.

Phelps, E., & Damon, W. (1989). Problem solving with equals: Peer collaboration as a context for learning mathematics and spatial concepts. *Journal of Educational Psychology, 81,* 639-646.

Rogoff, B., & Toma, C. (1997). Shared thinking: Community and institutional variations. *Discourse Processes, 23,* 471-497.

Roschelle, J. (1992). Learning by collaborating: Convergent conceptual change. *Journal of the Learning Sciences, 2,* 235-276.

Roschelle, J., & Teasley, S.D. (1995). The construction of shared knowledge in collaborative problem solving. In C. O'Malley (Ed.), Computer supported collaborative learning. NATO ASI Series F: Computer and system sciences (Vol. 128, pp. 69-97). Berlin: Springer-Verlag.

Schwartz, D.L. (1995). The emergence of abstract representations in dyad problem solving. *Journal of the Learning Science, 4,* 321-354.

Sharan, S., Shachar, H., & Levine, T. (1999). *The innovative school: Organization and instruction.* Westport, CT: Bergin and Garvey (Greenwood).

Shaw, M. (1976). *Group dynamics. The psychology of small group behaviour.* New York: McGraw-Hill.

Stern, D. (1977). *The first relationship*. Cambridge, MA: Harvard University Press.

Stevens, R., & Slavin, R. (1995). The cooperative elementary school: Effects on students' achievement, attitudes and social relations. *American Educational Research Journal, 32*, 321-351.

Teasley, S. (1995). The role of talk in children's peer collaborations. *Developmental Psychology, 31,* 207-220.

Tolmie, A., Howe, C., MacKenzie, M., & Greer, K. (1993). Task design as an influence on dialogue and learning: Primary school work with object flotation. *Social Development, 2*, 183-201.

Tudge, J.R.H. (1992). Processes and consequences of peer collaboration: A Vygotskian analysis. *Child Development, 63*, 1364-1379.

Tudge, J.R.H., & Rogoff, B. (1989). Peer influences on cognitive development: Piagetian and Vygotsskian perspectives. In M.H. Bornstein & J.S. Bruner (Eds.), *Interaction in human development* (pp. 17-40). Hillsdale, NJ: Erlbaum.

Vion, R. (1992). *La communication verbale. Analyse des interactions*. Paris: Hachette.

Vygotsky, L.S. (1978). *Mind in Society* (M. Cole, V. John-Steiner, S. Scribner, & E. Souberman, Eds.). Cambridge, MA: Harvard University Press.

Webb, N.M. (1991). Task-related verbal interaction and mathematics learning in small groups. *Journal for Research in Mathematics Education, 22,* 366-389.

Webb, N., & Kenderski, C. (1984). Student interaction and learning in small-group and whole class settings. In P. Peterson, L. Wilnkinson, & M. Hallinan (Eds.), *The social context of instruction. Group organization and group processes* (pp. 153-170). London: Academic Press

Webb, N., & Palincsar, A.S. (1996). Group processes in the classroom. In R. Calfee & C. Berliner (Eds.), *Handbook of Educational Psychology* (pp. 841-873). New York: Prentice Hall.

Webb, N.M., Troper, J., & Fall, J.R. (1995). Constructive activity and learning in collaborative small groups. *Journal of Educational Psychology, 87,* 406-423.

Wegerif, R. & Mercer, N. (1997). A dialogical framework for researching peer talk. In R. Wegerif & P. Scrimshaw (Eds.), *Computers and talk in the primary classroom* (pp. 49-61). Clevedon: Multilingual Matters.

Wertsch, J. (1991). *Voices of the mind: A sociocultural approach to mediated action.* Cambridge, MA: Harvard University Press.

Chapter 6

DEVELOPING THE CAPACITY TO COLLABORATE

Lyn Dawes and Claire Sams

INTRODUCTION

Collaboration in the classroom can occur as a consequence of asking groups of children to work on a joint task. Teachers often seat children in groups and provide them with shared activities in the expectation that mutual support will increase motivation and help to raise achievement. In this chapter we will describe some of the advantages of group work, highlight some problems that occur, and go on to explain how the Thinking Together approach has addressed the element of chance involved in asking children to work together. We suggest that direct teaching of speaking and listening skills can help children to understand the purposes of group work and provide them with the means to collaborate with one another. We also present our findings relating to teacher strategies which have been shown to help children as they develop effective discussion skills and begin to apply them.

GROUP WORK IN THE CLASSROOM

Teachers have grouped children to work together in UK primary schools since the early 1970s. This is not simply a classroom management strategy. The Bullock report (1975) pointed out that in the primary years especially, a child's ability to speak and listen is nearly always more developed than their ability to read and write. Sharing their work with others through talk can benefit children by helping them to develop their thinking in any curriculum area. The nature of such sharing will depend on the context, but might include children:

- directly asking for help;
- questioning;
- discussing a joint problem;
- observing one another;
- guided activity;

- inviting feedback;
- jointly creating (for example) a picture or document;
- pooling information or understanding.

All of these joint activities are undertaken through a mixture of demonstration, writing and speaking and listening. Of these, speaking and listening provides the main medium through which questioning, answering, discussion, dialogue, information provision and explanation take place.

However, despite there being good educational reasons to put children into groups, observers of group activity in classrooms have reported that talk was often off-task, uncooperative and of little educational value (Galton, Simon & Croll, 1980; Bennett & Cass, 1989). OFSTED evidence has indicated that grouping pupils to work together may have classroom management as its purpose and that group tasks will not necessarily entail collaboration (Kutnick & Rogers 1994). Why might this be so? Observational research provides one explanation (Fisher, 1993; Mercer, 1996). It seems that some ways of talking in group activity can be of special educational value, but that such discussions are relatively uncommon in classrooms. That is, children in classroom groups may talk with one another in ways that do not engage them in any prolonged or profound thinking about ideas or questioning of reasons, evidence or information. There seems to be a low natural incidence of the kind of discussion which has been called 'Exploratory Talk', a way of using language for reasoning which was first identified by the pioneering British educational researcher Douglas Barnes (Barnes & Todd, 1995; Mercer 2000). In Exploratory Talk participants engage critically but constructively with each other's ideas. Relevant knowledge is shared and suggestions are actively sought by questioning and challenge. Contributions are treated with respect. Opinions, ideas and suggestions offered for joint consideration should be supported by reasons. In Exploratory Talk, *knowledge is made publicly accountable* and *reasoning is visible in the talk.*

There are good reasons for wanting children to use this kind of talk in group activities, because it embodies a valuable kind of 'co-reasoning', with speakers sharing knowledge, challenging ideas, evaluating evidence and considering options in a reasonable and equitable way. Exploratory Talk represents an effective way of using language to think collectively which is embodied in some powerful genres, such as those used in science, law and business, and it is reasonable to expect that education should help every child to become aware of its value and become able to use it effectively. Yet it is very unusual for children to be given direct teaching which helps them to work, and more specifically talk, together productively with other children. But asking children to work in a group without teaching them how to do so may mean that the cognitive load of the task is just too great. Some children may be fortunate enough to collaborate very well together, and some may have had home experiences of ways of using language which encourage the use of talk of an exploratory kind; but others may struggle so much with the social demand of the task that their learning is affected. In some situations group work may often amount to little more than a rather puzzling seating arrangement. Galton and Williamson (1992) reported that even though the seating pattern of many classrooms was to group tables and children, children were actually working individually.

It is difficult to decide what to do about this effect. Believing it to be important, many teachers have organized and encouraged group work. The National Oracy Project (Norman,

1987) with its emphasis on learning through talk strongly influenced not only a generation of teachers but also the structure of the English orders of the National Curriculum. The development of speaking and listening skills was considered equally important to developing reading or writing. However, the more recent introduction of a rigid curriculum and an emphasis on 'standards', target setting and testing have meant that the space and time for learning conversations has diminished. The implementation of the National Literacy Strategy seems to have provided the mixed message of emphasizing links between children's talk, writing and cognitive development while placing much less emphasis on providing opportunities for children to develop oral skills (Grugeon et. al 2001 p 19).

So grouping children as an organisational strategy for teaching and learning may be common, but its effectiveness for promoting understanding cannot be taken for granted. But group work can begin to promote collaboration when attention is given to the quality of children's joint activity. As Light and Littleton (1994) point out:

'To the question of whether group work leads to better cognitive outcomes, the answer will always be, 'it depends' (p.101). It is important to identify the complex range of conditions on which learning and development depends; once these are clarified, the element of chance can be reduced. When organizing children into groups with an educational purpose, teachers take into account a variety of factors ranging from the mundane to the very subtle; these include the number of children, their personalities, friendships, gender and ability, which children are present on any given day, and aspects of the children's histories only available to the teacher who knows them well. We suggest that a further factor makes just as much difference to how well learning goes on in groups: each individual learner's *capacity to collaborate*. Ding and Flynn (2000) emphasize the idea that for effective collaboration to occur there must be a shared understanding of task and goals coupled with the facility to collaborate embedded in a wider set of underlying skills. We argue that it is crucial that the uses of such skills, which can be directly taught, are made explicit to learners. If not, collaboration is much less likely to be effective. The capacity to collaborate is fortunately not an innate quality. It can be developed through a variety of experiences and is enhanced by direct teaching and learning in classroom situations. This capacity involves two particular aspects:

- an understanding of the purpose of collaboration;
- the facility to engage in productive discussion of the kind we have described as Exploratory Talk.

THE CAPACITY TO COLLABORATE

The Open University's Thinking Together research team has conducted a series of classroom research projects into group work with a focus on the talk that occurs as children work together. The research has established that unless children understand precisely what we (as teachers) mean when we ask them to discuss their work, their talk together may not allow an interchange of ideas and opinions. In the Thinking Together approach (see Dawes et al 2000) children were made aware that their aims for any group activity must be as much to do with high quality, educationally effective talk and joint reasoning as with curriculum learning. They were taught a programme of lessons which raised awareness of how to use language to generate Exploratory Talk. Illustrative transcripts of the classroom talk of children aged nine and ten years in this chapter are taken from the project data. Further information about the approach can be found at www.thinkingtogether.org.uk.

GROUND RULES FOR EXPLORATORY TALK

If a group of people is to work well together, for example on resolving a dilemma or solving a problem, the contributions of all participants must have the same status within the group. All must be aware that sharing their thoughts and knowledge is not just important but essential. Everyone must accept that they should be able to describe the reasoning behind ideas they put forward. The group should be aware that offering a rational challenge to the ideas of others is an essential contribution to the discussion. Discussions conducted along these lines are adhering to a set of ground rules which, as long as they are mutually understood and recognized, may never be made explicit. Problems arise for groups when participants have different ideas of what ground rules operate. Such talk may end with people feeling that others have been dominant, assertive, unreasonable, or that individuals have been too quiet, and have not contributed. These things happen in groups in many settings – not just classrooms. The Thinking Together approach rests on raising awareness of the importance of joint ground rules and then helping groups to work within rules decided by the whole class.

Key features of the Thinking Together programme are:

1   Children are taught a series of talk lessons. Aims for group talk are made explicit in the whole class introduction. During plenary sessions, groups reflect on the quality of their talk.
2   In the talk lessons, the class are directly taught speaking and listening skills (such as challenging with respect, reasoning, negotiating ideas) and are provided with contexts for collaboration in which they can apply such skills.
3   Classes create and agree on a shared set of ground rules for Exploratory Talk to use when working with one another in groups.

The ground rules for talk operate in the same way as rules for sport or a board game. They reduce the degrees of freedom of individuals in a way that ensures that the whole group can benefit from joint enterprise. This may seem a little prescriptive or cumbersome; but in practice the rules are simple enough to understand and assimilate. The precise form of the ground rules is negotiated by each teacher with their class, so that they are expressed in words contributed by the children. The rules are generated from children's own reflective comments on what they think makes a good discussion. A set of ground rules from a class of 9 – 10 year olds is given here.

Ground rules for exploratory talk:

1   We will share what we know with each other.
2   We will ask everyone to say what they think.
3   Everyone should listen to others.
4   We will think about what to do together.
5   We will give reasons for what we say.
6   We will decide what to do only when everyone has said all they want.

The children in the study rapidly learned to apply the ground rules during group work. They seemed to appreciate that the rules provided a common, agreed understanding of how things should proceed. We noted that when children were using spoken language in this way, their reasoning became 'visible' in the talk – shown for example in their increased use of words like 'I think...' 'because...' and 'why...?'. These words can be thought of as *indicator words* of Exploratory Talk. Children in the study were observed to begin to use more Exploratory Talk (compared with children of similar backgrounds in matched 'control' schools) and became significantly better at working together to solve the non-verbal reasoning problems of the Raven's Progressive Matrices Test (Mercer, Wegerif & Dawes, 1999). Learners who were under-achieving in areas of curriculum learning when they started the lessons benefited most from the consistent use of the ground rules. It appears that this approach, the opportunity to experience structured dialogue with their classmates helps to develop their facility to reason things through. Working in mixed ability groups of three helped those with a range of special needs in education to become better integrated into the class and to gain increased confidence in communicating with others.

The effect of group activity on individual development can be related to the claims made by the psychologist L.S. Vygotsky (1978) that intermental or *social* activity can promote intramental or *individual psychological* development. That is, helping children to become more effective in using language for thinking together can contribute to the development of personal ways of thinking. The importance of ensuring that children have the opportunity to collaborate through talking together cannot be overstated. In our Thinking Together groups, the children have been taught to use spoken language as a tool for thinking together.

'The greatest change in children's capacity to use language as a problem solving tool takes place [...] when socialized speech is *turned inward*; [...] language takes on an intrapersonal function in addition to its interpersonal use' (Vygotsky 1978 p 27).

The 'socialized speech' of the talk groups had been turned inward to help develop a facility to think (using language) when working alone. So it seems that developing the capacity to collaborate can support both social and individual achievement. Compared to the children in the control schools, children who had studied the Thinking Together lessons improved their joint problem solving skills. More than this, individual children showed an increased capacity to reason when asked to complete Raven's puzzles (Raven's Progressive Matrices) alone. We believe that our data shows that given the skills and opportunity to undertake rational discussion with groups of their peers, children can develop a way of internal questioning and reflection which enables them to think through their ideas and come to more reasoned conclusions when working individually.

During their talk lessons and group discussions, the children were learning new combinations of words, new structures and new purposes for their talk. By doing this they seemed to assimilate a model for reasoning which they could use in situations where they had to puzzle something out for themselves. Having practised with their classmates, they were better able to generate an inner dialogue in which they weighed up alternatives and considered reasons before taking a decision. We measured the effect of this dialogic reflection when we asked the children to undertake the Raven's reasoning tests: they did better, having applied the structure for reasoning provided by their new capacity to collaborate. The tests are described by their originators as tests of clear thinking and deductive ability which is an aspect of problem solving.

We have talked about raised achievement which is an important aim in classroom contexts. But from the child's point of view, there are additional benefits to learning talk skills and agreeing to joint ground rules for talk. Relationships shape talk and relationships are shaped by talk (Maybin, 1996). The ground rules allow children an opportunity to escape, for a while, some of the most constraining or stifling aspects of their relationships with their peers. Children using the approach do not have to compete too hard for attention, or be constantly careful about what they reveal of their thoughts or feelings in case they are criticized, rejected or simply ignored. Video evidence of children discussing their work using their class ground rules shows a marked increase in tolerance of one another's views, a constructive response to suggestions and a positive style of interaction. Children are engaged with the subject of the discussion in a way that reduces the drive to comment on, or react to, one another's personal manner. All can expect to be asked what they think. To be a valued participant in an active discussion is to be in an interesting situation. For the duration of the activity, at least, the difficult and often dismaying negotiation of the social hierarchy of the classroom (playground, school, housing estate, part of town...) is for a time suspended. From a wider perspective, perhaps we might even consider talk as a tool for re-defining larger contexts. That is, *how* the child speaks and listens to those around them may have a more profound impact on their circumstances than the acquisition of a better understanding of (for example) mathematics or science. The brief suspension of the most negative aspects of group interaction could be extended as the child learns strategies to negotiate with a wider group of others, to gain confidence in their own voice, and to make things happen through talk (Littleton *pers. comm.)* There is some evidence to support this assertion in the interviews conducted with both pupils and adults involved in the Thinking Together study. Participants commented that they were now more able to use talk as a tool for negotiating to resolve issues and to get things done in contexts beyond the classroom and these particular lessons.

COLLABORATIVE CONTROVERSY

Helping learners to collaborate in order that all might benefit is not just a matter of ensuring that everyone is placidly amenable or that disagreement is quickly stifled or avoided. The essence of Exploratory Talk is that it encourages contribution of a range of opinions and a variety of reasons for ideas. By the nature of things, some of these are going to conflict. Indeed Johnson and Johnson (1997) advocate building collaboration and co-operation through encouraging controversy and argument. They note that ensuring groups tackle problems through presenting opposing arguments helps learners to generate discussion and sharing of differing view points. If the mixture of competitive and co-operative elements within group work can be balanced, the ensuing discussion can move the group towards deeper understanding. Whilst learning to collaborate, children can be made aware that there will be differences between their ideas, conclusions, theories, information, perspectives, opinions and preferences, which they can usefully state and rationalize. So, while everyone may offer competing ideas, intellectual development depends on co-operation with one another to examine these ideas and make meaning of one another's claims.

There is an interesting relation between the work of Johnson and Johnson and that of the Thinking Together approach.

'Although controversies can operate in a beneficial way they will not do so under all conditions. [...] Whether there are positive or negative consequences depends on the conditions under which controversy occurs and the way in which it is managed' (Johnson & Johnson 1997).

This is confirmation of Light and Littleton's 'it depends' – the cognitive outcomes of group work are very dependent on context. The conditions or **key elements** which Johnson and Johnson specify for ensuring the co-operative harnessing of controversy to educational ends are:

1 a co-operative context: open minded listening to the opposing position;
2 heterogeneous participants: heterogeneity leads to diverse interaction and resources for achievement and problem solving;
3 relevant information shared among participants;
4 social skills: disagreeing with ideas while acknowledging each other's personal competence: seeing the issue from a number of perspectives;
5 rational argument: generating ideas, making tentative conclusions based on current understanding.
(adapted from Johnson & Johnson 1997).

Johnson and Johnson do not say how to enable teachers and learners to control these crucial contextual elements. We suggest that the Thinking Together approach offers ways of addressing all of them, starting with ensuring a co-operative context for heterogeneous groups of children. The ground rules for talk ensure that information is shared and provide a structure in which children can generate rational argument without adult intervention. Direct teaching of talk skills establishes active listening and facilitates social interaction. The positive gains for children undertaking Thinking Together may be a result of providing a classroom environment which meets all of the conditions for collaborative controversy.

TEACHING TALK

When considering types of group talk it is important to take account the wider classroom context in which these occur. Groups do not work in isolation, but within the scope of the lessons designed and taught by the teacher. Evidence from the Thinking Together study has highlighted two critical factors that affect children's learning of the skills they need to use talk as a tool for co-reasoning or *interthinking* (Mercer 2000):

- the way the lesson is structured;
- the strategies the teacher employs to engage children in the process of learning to use dialogue effectively.

The management of both of these factors lies with the teacher. Planning the effective structuring of lessons involving a range of teaching strategies can support the development of a collaborative approach within groups. The Thinking Together lessons are designed in the three-part structure that has become increasingly familiar in classrooms following the introduction of the National Literacy Strategy and the numeracy framework. This format involves a whole class introduction, a group work session, and a whole class plenary. The next section of this chapter describes teacher strategies which emphasize, teach and sustain collaboration during each of these sections of the lesson.

TEACHER STRATEGIES 1: WHOLE CLASS INTRODUCTION

A whole class introduction provides an opportunity for the teacher to link the lesson with previous learning and to recall the ground rules for talk once these have been generated. It draws on the shared memory of the class (Wertsch, 2002), allows the teacher to make the ground rules an important focus for the lesson, set the curricular context and explain the activity. A key part of the introduction is to set clear objectives for the lesson so that the children know what they are going to learn. Learning objectives include aims for the kind of talk that is to be used (which sometimes might include specific vocabulary) and aims for the curriculum content of the lesson. As well as sharing these objectives with the children, it is very important to set *criteria for success* that relate to both of these objectives (Clarke, 2001). In this way the children know what they need to do to achieve the objectives, and the teacher establishes a clear framework within which to assess children's learning. Employing this existing good practice, the teacher is able to introduce a new element to the lessons – that is, groups using talk as a tool for thinking together.

How can the teacher ensure that the whole class introduction is effective in setting the scene for collaborative learning? It is essential to capture the children's interest right from the start. Teachers use strategies which help the entire class to move along the same line of thinking, generating common understanding of the lesson content and purpose. In Thinking Together lessons, the way in which the joint recall of the ground rules is undertaken is important in motivating the children's engagement with group work. In Transcript 1: *Revising the Ground Rules*, which has a mathematics context, a teacher elicits this previous shared experience in a stimulating and effective way. As she questions the class, the teacher records the rules in speech bubbles on the whiteboard for visible reference.

Transcript 1: Revising the Ground Rules

Teacher:	How are your Thinking Together skills going to help you with that? Why do you need to do that in your Thinking Together group? Kelly?
Kelly:	We need to talk about it.
Teacher:	Why do you think we need to talk about it?
Kelly:	To get more ideas.
Teacher:	Excellent. If we talk about it we might have a few more ideas than just working on our own.
Paula:	And because you can't just think that it's the answer when somebody else has got another idea – you have to check with the group – see what they think.
Teacher:	Excellent. OK. So if I walk around the classroom while everybody is talking together in their groups I wonder what kind of things might I hear people saying?
Asif:	"What do you think?"

Teacher:	That's a good one. Why is that an important question Carl?
Carl:	Because you ask someone else their opinion.
Sarah:	I think this because.
Teacher:	Why did you add 'because' to the end of that sentence?
Girl:	Because then they know why you made that remark.
Teacher:	Well done. Brilliant. You need to explain so that everybody understands what you think.

Comment

At the very start of this part of the lesson the teacher's questioning re-establishes the reasons for using a collaborative approach with the class. It is made clear through the children's responses that they are likely to be able to develop their ideas further and achieve more through thinking together than if they were to tackle the task alone. Thus, the culture of collaboration is constructed through the teacher's line of questioning. The class is encouraged to re-construct their list of rules through recall. This has more impact than simply displaying a list and referring to it. There is now a shared memory of previous joint experience to consider before they apply the rules to a new situation. The teacher is extremely positive in her responses to the contributions. The rules are thus given high status and are seen to be valued. The children are in no doubt that this set of rules is a vital element of the learning objectives for the lesson and are shown how their success in using these will be achieved; if the teacher hears certain words and phrases she will know that the groups are using the ground rules to think together about the maths activity.

Another important strategy employed by teachers who are successful in teaching children to collaborate effectively is that of modelling the kind of talk that is useful in discussion. In Transcript 2: *Choosing a Number* the teacher demonstrates this strategy as she introduces a maths activity to the whole class. The objectives for the session have already been explained and the ground rules have been revised together. The maths activity uses the software called 'Function Machine' in which the children are asked to consider what operation might have been done to one number in order to end up with another. As well as deciding on the operation, the groups have to come up with a strategy for discovering it and for testing their ideas about it.

Transcript 2: Choosing a Number

Teacher:	OK. I'm going to put a number in –
Louis:	One thousand.
Teacher:	OK Louis immediately said one thousand – is that a good number to put in?
Child:	No
Teacher:	You are shaking your head – why do you think it is not? Shall we come back to you? You've got an idea but you can't explain it? OK Louis had one thousand. Anybody think yes or no to that idea? David.
David:	Start off with an easier number.
Teacher:	Start off with an easier number. By an easier number what kind of number do you mean?
David:	Um. Something like -lower – five.

Teacher:	Fine. A smaller number – a lower number – yes. Louis can you see that point of view?
Louis:	Yes
Teacher:	If we put in a thousand we could end up with a huge number. If we put in five do you think it will be easier to work out what the machine has done?
Class:	Yes
Teacher:	Everyone agree?
Class:	Yes
Teacher:	OK I'm going to type in five...

Comment

The teacher is modelling the ground rules for talk in her demonstration of the activity. They are embedded in her own language as she speaks with the class. She is sharing relevant information with the group, in this case the whole class, about the number which is to be put into the input box of the function machine. She initiates discussion about the number by questioning the first suggestion of one thousand, followed by requests for reasons for opinions and assertions. The language she uses is full of indicator words, such as 'what', 'how', 'if' and 'why' as she leads them through a line of reasoning. She accepts and discusses the challenges made by David and the un-named child to Louis' suggestion, whilst respecting his contribution in initiating the discussion. She demonstrates how to consider the validity of alternative suggestions, at the same time as seeking clarification. She invites others to speak so that as many people as possible feel able to join in the discussion. This element is hard to model as part of a whole class introduction, but at other times she employs a strategy to address this by inviting the children to share their ideas with the person they are sitting next to so that everyone has a chance to say what they think. Finally she ensures that an agreement is sought and reached. In this way, through careful modelling of the ground rules for talk, the teacher is demonstrating to the children effective collaboration as an integral element of her introduction. The children are engaged in the discussion, motivated to participate and are real partners in the learning. By witnessing the usefulness of this modelling of the ground rules they are prepared to employ the same approach when they continue the activity in small group discussion.

TEACHER STRATEGIES 2: GROUP WORK

By the time the children begin to talk together in their groups, effective means of collaboration have been made explicit to them as well as having been demonstrated implicitly in the teacher's own style of talking. During the group work section of the lesson children are specifically asked to *think together* about the task they have been given. Group work is not something that carries on independently of the teacher. Observing and listening to the quality of group interaction is a valuable formative assessment opportunity for the teacher, both in terms of determining the level of understanding of curriculum objectives and of making judgements about the effectiveness of talk within each group. Intervention in group talk allows the teacher to address speaking and listening or curriculum issues as they arise. In Transcript 3: *Which Dog?* the teacher intervenes after listening to the group talk for a short time. This citizenship activity involves deciding which dog from a dogs' home would suit a particular owner. The teacher has observed that one group member, Jane, has been finding it hard to express her ideas in a way that engages the others. She approaches the group and joins the discussion:

Transcript 3: Which Dog?

Teacher:	Who are you trying to find a dog for at the moment?
Robert:	Mrs Jenkins
Teacher:	Mrs Jenkins. Right. What do you know about Mrs Jenkins, Jane, so far? (Pause). You read it out to everybody?
Michael:	Yeah.
Teacher:	Right. What do you know about Mrs Jenkins so far? Who can tell me something?
Heidi:	She's got a small home and a tiny garden, so she can't have a big dog.
Teacher:	No, that wouldn't be sensible, would it?
Michael:	And she can't. And she can't walk very far.
Teacher:	Ah right.
Michael:	So it has to be a very lazy dog.
Teacher:	(laughs). Oh right! Good boy.
Robert:	Sits by the fire. Look! (Points to a dog card)
Teacher:	Have you got a lazy, small dog?
Jane:	We were thinking about Fifi. (Points to Fifi's card).
Heidi:	But this one – to be patted.
Robert:	I think this one – to be patted.
Teacher:	Why do you think that one? What's your reasons?
Robert:	Well to, it was like, laying down, so that the lady could reach it.
Teacher:	(Reading) Running and snow. It dislikes running and snow. It dislikes running, so yes, it would be quite a quiet dog. It likes to be patted by an old lady. That's quite a good reason. Why did you want Fifi, Jane? What were your reasons?
Jane:	(Silent)
	Another child contributes inaudibly.
Teacher:	(looking at Jane). Can you remember? What did you think about that one? Pick up Fifi and have a good look. Is there a reason that you chose that for Mrs Jenkins?
Jane:	Cos Mrs Jenkins has got a small garden and she needs a little dog.
Teacher:	And you think Fifi's a little dog?
Jane:	Yes.
Teacher:	Yes, she does look little, doesn't she? ...

Comment

The teacher is aware that Jane is finding it hard to express herself within the group. There are three other children in the group, two of whom are articulate and confident. Through her own engagement with the group, the teacher draws Jane into the discussion and demonstrates that she can make a valuable contribution. She addresses her first question, about Mrs

Jenkins, to Jane, who is either unable or reluctant to answer. At that point she encourages others to share the information about Mrs Jenkins, so that Jane is able to hear it again, in a non-threatening way. This reinforces the ground rule that all information should be shared. After the important criteria for the selection of the dog have been revisited, Jane begins to offer a suggestion, that Fifi might be a good choice. Heidi and Robert suggest another dog and explain their reasons. The teacher acknowledges their suggestions, but crucially redirects the discussion to Jane at this point, and supports her in her explanation of why Fifi might also be an appropriate choice. In this way she has modelled another essential ground rule, that all alternatives and the reasons for them are considered before moving towards a conclusion. She avoids direct questioning of whether the group has done this, but through her intervention she reminds them of this rule and models ways to implement it. Thus the children learn to consider a variety of perhaps conflicting options and are supported in developing their capacity to collaborate.

TEACHER STRATEGIES 3: THE WHOLE CLASS PLENARY

The concluding whole class plenary session is an opportunity to share with the class some of the issues that have been observed or dealt with during interventions in the group work, so that learning is evaluated and compared with the objectives. In this way learners receive feedback from the teacher about observations made of the groups' ability to use the ground rules whilst working collaboratively, using the success criteria as a measure. For example, (*Teacher addressing class in plenary session*)

'I heard a group where the talk was, 'It is this? No it isn't'. Does this meet the success criteria? How could it have been done better? Do we need to alter any of the ground rules following this activity?'

Another strategy is to invite feedback from each group using the ground rules to structure questioning and challenges by other groups. In this way some assessment of children's learning success is possible, both in terms of talk skills and the understanding of curriculum concepts.

Children's comments about their experience of learning to use the ground rules for talk show that they perceive benefits in learning to collaborate. Interview evidence suggests that the approach has helped children to see the importance of assessing various alternatives before reaching decisions:

'It has helped us if we are working in groups – now we've got the rules for it as well, it's made us think, 'Oh, if one person's talking we can't barge in and talk in front of them.'

'We normally take it in our turns and say 'What do you think?' instead of leaving someone out.'

'(I'm not) afraid to challenge someone with their answer – (I) don't just sit there and say 'Alright – pick that one. I don't care'.

'(It) makes us feel more confident if we're in a group'

'Before the project, ...If we'd been sitting in the group and got one answer we'd say like – 'Oh just say it's that'. But now we've been thinking 'Oh let's think of another answer it could be as well', not just...saying 'Oh it looks like that one'. Try *each*'

Children indicated that they felt more able to proceed by pooling their ideas than when working alone:

'It has helped us a lot doing this, being in groups with other people. At one point we had to say 'Is this food?' *(Food Sorting ICT activity)* When we were doing that one time I thought *this* was *that*, but then we discussed it and it helped us learn something else with it.'

'It's easier to work in a group than it is on your own because then you've got the time to talk to the person you are working with ... if you both get the same answer you know it's got to be right because two people have got more chance than just you working it out on your own. ... even if you do get it wrong you've got it wrong as a group and not just as a person.'

CONCLUSION

Group work is a way of organizing classroom activity that can support curriculum learning. The Thinking Together approach provides children with the capacity to engage in collaborative conversation and so enhance their work in groups. Successful collaborative conversation can develop an individual's ability to think and reason in a way that is helpful when subsequently working alone. Effective group discussion thus provides children with the essential language tools for raised individual achievement. Children's capacity to collaborate may be under-developed in ways that make it difficult for them to contribute to group work. However, direct teaching can help children to understand the importance of learning conversations with one another. It is possible to teach not just this awareness but also talk skills and strategies which enable children to engage in effective discussions. Children's emerging capacity to collaborate requires a classroom culture which supports Exploratory Talk.

Teaching children how and why to use Exploratory Talk, as defined in a set of ground rules for talk, encourages them to begin to engage with each other in an educationally effective way, freeing them from some of the problems created by personal relationships.

The classroom teacher has a crucial role in the process of developing children's capacity to collaborate. Teachers whose classes benefited from the Thinking Together approach exhibited a range of strategies directed towards this end. Most importantly, these effective teachers:

- stressed the collaborative element of the lesson as a central focus alongside other learning intentions;
- explained the criteria by which individuals would be judged to have succeeded in achieving the learning intentions;
- incorporated Exploratory Talk skills into their own use of language;
- modelled the kinds of conversations that the children were being asked to engage in during introductory work, group work, closing plenaries and 'internally' during individual work;
- encouraged children to reflect on and evaluate the quality of their discussion as well as their achievement in the curriculum content of the lesson. This involved identifying their own contribution to the group talk and noting good practice in their peers.

In these ways teachers can create a talk-focused classroom community where discussion supports all the learning that takes place, and where whole class and group sessions have a coherence of style which helps to build, reinforce and develop the child's capacity to collaborate.

The classroom context is critical if organizing group work is to be a dependable strategy for teaching and learning. We advocate intervention to establish a context where an understanding of the importance of speaking and listening in children's development is integrated into the design of teaching and learning activities. Such a context can be generated by the direct teaching of specific skills which support group talk. In addition ground rules which govern group interaction are clarified and made explicit. This input helps children to generate Exploratory Talk during their group work, an outcome with profound implications for their learning. Thinking Together is based on a belief that all children have a capacity to collaborate which can benefit from focused input and systematic fostering. We place the teacher at the heart of the classroom in managing and organizing intervention to develop this capacity on behalf of the child. In this way, speaking and listening to one another allows teachers and learners to generate an environment in which the cognitive outcomes of collaboration can be less uncertain, and even reliably positive.

REFERENCES

Barnes, D., & Todd, F. (1977). *Communication and learning in small groups.* London: Routledge & Kegan Paul.

Bennett, N., & Cass A. (1989). The effects of group composition on group interactive processes and pupil understanding. *British Educational Research Journal, 15*(1), 19–32.

Bullock Report (1975). *A language for life.* London: HMSO.

Clarke, S. (2001). *Unlocking formative assessment.* London: Hodder & Stoughton.

Dawes, L., Mercer, N., & Wegerif, R.. (2000). *Thinking Together.* Birmingham: Questions Publishing.

Ding, S. A. & Flynn, E. (2000). Collaborative learning: An underlying skills approach. In R. Joiner, K. Littleton, D. Faulkner, & D. Miell (Eds.), *Rethinking collaborative learning.* London: Free Association Books.

Fisher, E. (1993). Distinctive features of pupil-pupil classroom talk and their relationship to learning: How discursive exploration might be encouraged. *Language and Education, 7*(4), 239–257.

Grugeon, E. Hubbard, L. Smith, C., & Dawes, L. (2001). *Teaching speaking and listening in the primary school. London*: David Fulton Press.

Galton, M., & Williamson J. (1992). *Group work in the primary school.* London: Routledge.

Galton, M., Simon, B., & Croll, P. (1980). *Inside the primary classroom.* London: Routledge & Kegan Paul.

Johnson, D. W., & Johnson, F. (1997). *Joining together: Group theory and group skills* (6th Ed.). Boston: Allyn & Bacon.

Kutnick, P., & Rogers, C. (1994). *Groups in schools.* London: Cassell.

Light, P., & Littleton, K. (1994). Cognitive approaches to group work. In P. Kutnick & C. Rogers, *Groups in schools.* London: Cassell.

Maybin, J (1996). Everyday talk. In Maybin, J, & Mercer, N. (Eds.), *Using English: From conversation to canon*. London: Routledge.

Mercer, N. (1996). The quality of talk in children's collaborative activity in the classroom. *Learning and Instruction*, 6(4), 359–377.

Mercer N. (2000). *Words and minds*. London: Routledge.

Mercer, N., Wegerif, R., &. Dawes, L. (1999). Children's talk and the development of reasoning in the classroom. *British Educational Research Journal*, 25 1(1), 95 – 111.

Norman, K. (Ed.) (1992). *Thinking voices: The work of the National Oracy Project*. London: Hodder & Stoughton.

Kutnick, P., & Rogers, C. (Eds). (1994). *Groups in schools*. London: Cassell.

Raven, J., Raven, J. C. & Court, J. (1993). *Manual for Raven's Progressive Matrices and Vocabulary Scales*, Oxford: Oxford Psychologists Press.

Vygotsky, L. S. (1978). *Mind in Society: The development of higher psychological processes*. London: Harvard University Press.

Wegerif, R., & Dawes, L. (2002). Talking solutions: The role of oracy in the effective use of ICT. In Monteith, M. (Ed), *Teaching Primary literacy with ICT*. Buckingham: Open University Press.

Wertsch, J. (2002). *Voices of collective remembering*. Cambridge: Cambridge University Press.

Chapter 7

EXPLANATIONS AND MODES OF COLLABORATION IN TUTOR-TUTEE INTERACTIONS AT SCHOOL

Karin Bachmann and Michèle Grossen

INTRODUCTION

Peer-tutoring has a long history in the field of education. In France, the idea that students could teach peers goes back to mutual teaching, practised in the 16th century (see Barnier, 1994 for a review). In England, it goes back to the end of the 18th century when Bell (1797) and Lancaster (1803, cited in Goodlad, 1979) suggested that more advanced students could teach younger ones and assist teachers in their work. Despite its success, the method quickly disappeared and only reappeared in the United States two centuries later during the 1960s when it became part of various educational programmes (see Goodlad, 1979). Rather than providing assistance to teachers, peer-tutoring was then generally defined as systematic and sustained *help* provided by students for their peers under the supervision of a teacher. Research into peer-tutoring later showed, however, that taking on a teaching role, led tutors to improve their own learning and understanding (a result which is referred to as the 'tutor-effect', see Allen & Feldman, 1973; Barnier, 1989, 1994; Cloward, 1967; Cohen et al., 1982; Devin-Sheehan, 1976). This observation led to a further definition which put more emphasis on the interaction between tutor and tutee and defined peer-tutoring as an 'instructional system where the learners help each other and learn by teaching' (Goodlad, 1979, p. 16).

The fact that the method of peer-tutoring has led to students being considered as teaching resources and has tried to move teachers away from their central position, may explain why peer-tutoring continues to arouse enthusiasm among school specialists. It certainly explains why Swiss secondary schools (covering 11-15 year-olds) in which our study was carried out, introduced peer-tutoring to help students experiencing learning difficulties. On a practical level, a few basic guidelines were set up. One of them, which could be questioned in the light of previous research into the 'tutor-effect', specified that 'a good' student should act as a tutor in order to help another student (or sometimes two) having difficulties, under a teacher's supervision. The schools assumed that because the tutors were peers who had experienced the same school curriculum they would engage in a less asymmetric relationship with the tutees and align more easily with their perspective by delivering 'simple' explanations. In one of the schools, for example, an information leaflet announced that 'through peer-tutoring, the tutees might accede to direct contact and simple explanations'. Our general approach to the study of peer-tutoring, however, has been to question these assumptions through the detailed observation and analysis of tutor-tutee modes of collaboration.

Social Interaction, Discourse and Cognitive Development

In analysing the peer-tutoring situations that we observed we draw upon a vast body of research on peer collaboration carried out in the post-Piagetian and post-Vygotskian traditions. Many of these studies have paid particular attention to the relationship between children's modes of collaboration and learning (for recent work see for example, Cowie, van der Aalsvoort, & Mercer, 2000; Gilly, Roux, & Trognon, 1999; Joiner et al., 2000). In this context, researchers have shown a growing interest in examining discourse and talk-in-interaction. Also, on an empirical level, studies in experimental contexts have gradually given way to observations of situated practices (e.g., in school or in workplaces) (Golay Schilter et al., 1999; Joiner et al., 2000; Littleton & Light, 1999; Mercer, 2000). This body of research has shown that the type of dialogue that best accounts for learning in collaborative situations is based on certain forms of reciprocity and mutuality, together with divergences (critical questions, counter-arguments, for example). One example of this type of dialogue is the 'transactional discussion' described by Teasley (1997). Another example is 'exploratory talk', (Mercer, 2000; Wegerif & Mercer, 2000) which is characterized by the partners' critical and constructive involvement with the task in hand, and by their capacity to challenge each other's suggestions and offer alternative solutions. In exploratory talk, children are able to justify their own reasoning and are also able to take their partner's perspective into consideration when making their own contributions. In their latest studies, Mercer and Wegerif have set up experiments where children are taught how to engage in genuine exploratory talk rather than other less productive forms of discussion (see also Rojas-Drummond et al., 2003). These have shown that teaching modes of collaboration known to promote learning is not only possible, but also that it has positive outcomes for the children's learning. These studies have thus reversed the initial area of enquiry, 'collaborating to learn', and replaced it with enquiries on 'learning to collaborate'.

Our own contribution in this field had been concerned with adult-child or child-child interactions in test or learning situations (Grossen, Liengme Bessire, & Perret-Clermont, 1997; Grossen, 2000). We have proposed fine-grained analyses that attempt to account for the interactional dynamics through which participants negotiate the meaning of the situation and the task, and through which they also negotiate the nature of their relationship and identities. Adopting a dialogical perspective, we have shown that the processes involved in solving the problem, that is the mode of collaboration employed and the identities that the children display can be regarded as *interactional accomplishments*. Peer-tutoring can thus be seen to be a dynamic process which, within a restricted temporal scale, also amounts to 'learning to collaborate'.

Modes of Collaboration in Tutor-Tutee Interactions, and Didactic Contract

In our previous work (Grossen & Bachmann, 2000), we drew upon this general framework to analyse one tutor-tutee dyad over five German-language lessons. Focussing upon the way in which the tutor (a girl) and the tutee (a boy) learned the asymmetric and complementary relationship of their roles, we demonstrated that a central element of this learning process was that it offered the tutor the opportunity to diagnose the tutee's state of knowledge. In fact, since the tutor did not know exactly which subject matter the tutee had already learned, each time she asked a question the tutee could not answer, she had to decide whether it was due to his lack of understanding, to his forgetting, or to the fact that he had not yet studied this subject matter. However, the longer the lessons went on, the more the tutor attributed the errors to the tutee and the more she appeared to feel entitled to guide him and to give him advice (and even homework!). The negotiation and construction of the tutor's and tutee's roles was also observed in sequences where the tutor explained certain bodies of knowledge that had already been taught in class. In these sequences, the tutor mostly used indirect questioning in order to guide the tutee towards the expected answer. The tutee, however, also developed indirect strategies that enabled him to obtain the expected answer from the tutor. His apparent passivity thus provoked the tutor's activity. According to our interpretation the tutor's guidance strategies could not be solely attributed to her *individual communicative skills*, they were seen to result from situated interactional work and changed and developed over time.

An emphasis upon fine-grained analyses of the verbal interaction, however, should not lead us to neglect the context in which the interactions take place. Tutor-tutee interactions are part of a larger system of interactions. For example they are located within a school institution with its own rules, definitions of roles, categorisations and assumptions about teaching and learning. From this perspective, the notion of the *didactic contract* (Schubauer-Leoni & Grossen, 1993) is useful as it allows one to grasp the specificity of the peer-tutoring situation. This notion refers to the tripolar system of expectations (or *ground rules* in the terminology of Edwards & Mercer, 1987) that link the *teacher*, the *student* and the *object of knowledge* to be learned or taught. In the case of peer-tutoring, the didactic contract has at least two specific characteristics. Firstly, when the tutor and the tutee do not belong to the same class (which is usually the case), the peer-tutoring didactic contract is based upon *two pre-existing didactic contracts*, the one at work in the *tutor's class* and the one at work in *the tutee's class*. The second characteristic is that both tutor and tutee are supervised by a teacher. The contract can be conceptualized, therefore, as an interaction among *four*, and not three, *poles*, with the tutor remaining a student with respect to the teacher, and the tutee being subjected to both the tutor and to the teacher.

This analysis reveals that 'good' students who become tutors face two related problems: a) Although their school marks allow the school institution to legitimize them as tutors, they have never learned to be teachers. Their institutional role does not imply that they will be able to adopt the role of a teacher or that their peers will willingly take on the complementary position of students. In this respect, a tutor's ability to master the subject matter brought by a tutee might be a way of achieving his or her role; b) A second problem, however, is that the tutors' ability to master the subject matter cannot be taken for granted. In fact, when the tutor and the tutee happen to be in different school grades, there is a *temporal lag* between the stage of the school curriculum that each has reached. In other words, the tutors are questioned about subject matters that are topical for their tutees, but that are not necessarily part of their own school curriculum. Because of this temporal lag, the tutors run the risk of being unable to remember the required piece of knowledge or to explain it and thus they might experience difficulties or even make errors in attempting to teach it to others.

This analysis shows that the construction of the asymmetry and complementarity of the tutor's and the tutee's roles allow us to define the situation as a teaching-learning activity and can be considered as a condition for learning to occur.

Starting from this general framework, in this chapter we aim to investigate the way in which tutors and tutees construct the asymmetry and complementarity of their roles, and to analyse their modes of collaboration. We shall focus upon an activity that pervades any teacher-student interaction: *explanation*. Providing explanations is part of a teacher's rights and obligations and is integral to any teaching-learning situation, including tutor-tutee interactions (Baker, 1999; Brixhe, 1999; Crahay, 2001; Kaartinen & Kumpulainen, 2002).

As our starting point we have chosen to adopt a definition of *explanation* as '[...] a discursive verbal activity which aims at transforming, through various procedures and differing processes, a problematic state related to a field of knowledge of a subject (or of several subjects) into one that the subject claims to be unproblematic', (Bruxelles & de Gaulmyn, 2000, p. 50, our translation from French).

According to this definition, explanation is not only a linguistic device. It is also *a discursive device* that takes place within *a social activity* that involves the actors' roles and identities, and that has illocutory effects. From this perspective, *who* is entitled to give an explanation *to whom*, in *which context* and for *what purpose* are important features to consider. For example, in certain situations, giving an explanation may highlight the recipient's ignorance and thus threaten him or her with loss of face. In other words, the identity of the deliverer or recipient of an explanation may not only reveal the two partners' present role system, but may also transform it. Consequently, on a methodological level, an examination of *how* explanations are given and *who* gives them may help identify different modes of collaboration between tutors and tutees.

RESEARCH QUESTIONS

As we mentioned above, the assumptions of the teachers who introduced peer-tutoring into their schools were that the tutor-tutee relationship would be less asymmetric than the teacher-student relationship. While our data does not enable us to make a comparison between these two settings, it nevertheless gives us access to the peers' modes of collaboration and degree of asymmetry. A central assumption is that being a tutor or a tutee is an *interactional accomplishment* that results from the interactions between the tutor, the tutee and the subject matter on which they interact. In this chapter we shall account for this interactional accomplishment, firstly by taking 'explanation' as a general indicator of the asymmetry of the tutor-tutee interactions and secondly, by comparing the interactional dynamics of two dyads that demonstrate contrasting modes of collaboration. One dyad demonstrates rather a low level of asymmetry, the other rather a high level of asymmetry. How do these students enter into the roles of tutor versus tutee? How do they learn their roles and accomplish them during, and through, the interaction? How do different modes of collaboration relate to cognitive work and learning?

PROCEDURE

Corpus

The total corpus from which the data for this chapter is taken was composed of eight dyads. In the interests of unity and brevity, however, we will present an analysis of the quantitative data from four of the original dyads (2, 3, 5 and 6). We will then present a detailed qualitative analysis of two contrasting modes of collaboration of two of these dyads (3 and 6) as examples of the different ways in which the didactic contract can be negotiated. All peer tutoring dyads we observed were working on mathematical problems involving measure conversions (time, distance, volume, and liquid capacity), calculation of areas, fractions and decimal numbers. On a practical level, peer tutoring took the form of a six-lesson cycle between a tutor and a tutee. Once a week, the groups worked under the supervision of a teacher who was present to answer the students' questions

As shown in Table 1, the dyads were asymmetrical with respect to students' age, gender and school grades. The tutor was the same for groups 2 and 6. One session is missing for group 2, and group 6 withdrew after two sessions. In total, 19 sessions were videotaped and transcribed.

Table 1: Composition of the tutor-tutee dyads and number of recorded sessions

Dyads			Recorded Sessions
Number	Tutor	Tutee	N
2	Teo, boy, 14 years old	Evelyne, girl, 13 years old	5
3	Tania, girl, 15 years old	Emmanuel, boy, 12 years old	6
5	Thierry, boy, 15 years old	Edith, girl, 13 years old	6
6	Teo, boy, 14 years old	Eva, girl, 12 years old	2

Method of Analysis

The method consisted firstly of locating what we will call, *explanation moves*, (see also Gaulmyn 1991). An explanation move consists of three phases (see Excerpt 1):

1 An *opening phase* – the discursive, or behavioural event provoking the explanation;
2 A *core explanation* that consists of explicative strategies and procedures and that can begin with an evaluative statement;
3 A *closing phase* – the addressee's reaction to the explanation.

Excerpt 1 and following excerpts are translated from the original French. Interested readers can apply to the authors for the original transcriptions. The transcription conventions adopted are given in Appendix 1.

Excerpt 1 (51/move 7)

		Explanation move
92tutee	err zero point five, err	*Opening phase*
93Tutor	no wait, if you have a number above, err above the fraction bar	
94te	yeah	*Core explanation*
95Tr	it is larger than the one you have below, it will actually be divided by a smaller number, well it goes more than one time, this number, inside [inaudible] you have already a part or your answer there	
96te	one point five	*Closing*
97Tr	it's one point five (…)	

A coding scheme categorizing the opening and closing phases was then elaborated. For each phase, we also coded who was responsible for the action: the tutor, the tutee or both together. Tables 2 and 3 present the categories of opening and closing phases.

Table 2: Description of the categories of opening phases

Label of the Categories	Brief Description
Question	Typically, 'why' questions
Error or difficulty	One student makes a mistake or displays a behaviour (hesitation, silence) which is interpreted as a sign of difficulty by the partner.
Diagnostic	One student asks what difficulty was experienced, for example 'was it difficult for you to represent yourself three quarters of what ?'
Correct answer	One student gives a correct answer
Focus upon an element of the task	One student focuses the partner's attention upon an element of the task, for example the instruction.
Metadiscursive comment	One student comments the necessity of providing an explanation before continuing.
Self-refutation	One student claims that s/he is wrong
Summary of the current step of the work	One student summarizes the current step of their work
Other	

Table 3: Description of the categories of closing phases

Label of the Categories	Brief Description
Minimal participation	The addressee of the explanation reacts by a minimal feedback (yes, or a simple nod).
Elaboration or reformulation	The explanation is reformulated or elaborated by one student.
Mention of a solution	One student provides a solution, verbally or by carrying out the exercise.
Request for an answer	After his or her explanation, one student asks the partner to answer the problem ('how will you then do ?').
Check question	The student who gave an explanation checks the partner's understanding.
Failure statement	One student claims that something is wrong or that she or he does not understand, or that the partner did not understand.
Direct continuation	After the explanation, the student continues the same exercise or moves directly to another one.
Refutation	One student contests the partner's explanation.
Clarification request	The addressee's asks for more explanations.
Other	

ANALYSIS OF THE DATA

Explanations and Asymmetry in the Tutor-Tutee Interactions

Let us first note that 372 explanation moves were found and considered for analysis. Table 4 shows that of these 372 moves, the most frequent types of opening were: 'error or difficulty' (27%), 'question' (21%), 'focus' (19%), 'correct answer' (11%) and 'diagnostic' (8%). Tutors and tutees opened almost the same number of explanation moves. However, 'error or difficulty' and 'correct answer' were mostly provided by tutees (even though there are also a few errors given by tutors), while 'diagnostic', 'focus' and 'questions' were due to the tutors. In other words, the tutees' questions rarely opened an explanation moves (32 out of 372).

Table 4: Frequency of the types of opening phases contributed by tutors and tutees

Opening Phases	Tutors N	Tutees N	Total Number (column %)
Error/Difficulty	14	88	102 (27%)
Questions	47	32	79 (21%)
Focus on Element of Task	61	9	70 (19%)
Correct Answer	0	41	41 (11%)
Diagnostic	31	0	31 (8%)
Metadiscursive comment	17	0	17 (5%)
Self-refutation	11	5	16 (4%)
Summary	9	0	9 (2%)
Other	5	2	7 (2%)
Total (line %)	195 (52%)	177 (48%)	372 (100%)

Table 5 shows that 71% core explanations were provided by the tutors, 18% by the tutees and 11% were joint explanations. Table 5 also shows that when the 'errors or difficulties' were due to the tutors, the following core explanations were in 29% of the cases given by the tutees, while when the 'errors or difficulties' were due to the tutees, the tutors were mostly responsible for providing an explanation. As might be expected, 'questions' asked by the tutees were answered by a tutor's explanation, and vice versa. When the tutors focused upon an element of the task, in most cases they also gave an explanation. The reverse, however, is not true: when the tutees focused upon an element of the task, they provided themselves with an explanation only in half of the cases. 'Correct answers' (which were all given by the tutees) were mostly followed by the tutors' explanations. The tutors' 'diagnostic' questions were mostly followed by their own explanations.

Table 5: Percentage of core explanations generated by tutors, tutees or jointly depending on whether opening phase was Initially contributed by tutor or tutee (only for the five most frequent types of opening phases)

Opening Phase	Following core explanation given by		
	Tutor	Tutee	Jointly
Error or Difficulty by Tutor (n= 14)	57%	29%	14%
Error or Difficulty by Tutee (n= 88)	84%	5%	11%
Question by Tutor (n=47)	4%	85%	11%
Question by Tutee (n=32)	91%	0%	9%
Focus on a element of the task by Tutor (n=61)	90%	3%	7%
Focus on a element of the task by Tutee (n=9)	33%	56%	11%
Correct Answer by Tutor (n=0)	0%	0%	0%
Correct Answer by Tutee (n=41)	83%	12%	5%
Diagnostic question by Tutor (n= 31)	81%	3%	16%
Diagnostic question by Tutee (n= 0)	0%	0%	0%
N	71%	18%	11%

Other results not presented in Table 5 show that the tutees' 'errors or difficulties' were responsible for the largest part of the tutors' explanations (74 out of 264), while the tutors' 'questions' were responsible for the largest part of the tutee's explanations (40 out of 68).

As concerns the closing phases, Table 6 shows that the most frequent types of closing phase were 'requests for an answer' (22%), 'minimal participation' (13%), 'elaboration or reformulation' (13%), 'statement of a solution' (12%), 'check question' (11%). The tutors closed more moves than the tutees. Except for three types of closing phase ('minimal participation', 'statement of a solution' and 'clarification request'), all types of closing phase were carried out by the tutors.

Table 6: Frequency of the types of closing phases contributed by tutors and tutees

Closing phases	Tutors N	Tutees N	Total Number (column %)
Request for an answer	80	0	80 (22%)
Minimal participation	18	30	48 (13%)
Elaboration or reformulation	47	2	49 (13%)
Statement of a solution	8	36	44 (12%)
Check question	39	1	40 (11%)
Failure statement	18	7	25 (7%)
Direct continuation	20	4	24 (6%)
Refutation	20	3	23 (6%)
Other	20	1	21 (6%)
Clarification request	4	14	18 (5%)
Total (line %)	274 (74%)	97 (26%)	372 (100%)

Table 7 shows that the 'requests for an answer' (which were all made by the tutors) mostly followed a tutor's explanation. The same pattern is observed for the 'check questions' and for the 'statement of a solution'.

As regards 'elaborations or reformulations' and 'minimal participation', the pattern is different. The former (mostly carried out by the tutors) followed a tutor's or tutee's explanations in the same proportion (42%), while the latter (which was more frequent among the tutees) was, unsurprisingly, given by the tutees after the tutors' explanations, and vice versa.

Table 7: Percentage of core explanations generated by tutors, tutees or jointly depending on whether the explanation move was closed by tutor or tutee (only for the five most frequent types of closing phases)

Closing phase	Preceding core explanation given by		
	Tutor	Tutee	Jointly
Request for an answer by Tutor (n=80)	89%	5%	6%
Request for an answer by Tutee (n=0)	0%	0%	0%
Minimal participation by Tutor (n=18)	0%	94%	6%
Minimal participation by Tutee (n=30)	90%	0%	10%
Elaboration or reformulation by Tutor (n=47)	42%	42%	16%
Elaboration or reformulation by Tutee (n=2)	100%	0%	0%
Statement of a solution by Tutor (n=8)	87%	0%	13%
Statement of a solution by Tutee (n=36)	72%	0%	28%
Check question by Tutor (n=39)	92%	3%	5%
Check question by Tutee (n=1)	100%	0%	0%

Discussion

The results showed that tutors more often provided explanations than did tutees. This asymmetry was associated with a difference in the way in which tutors' and tutees' explanations were introduced. The tutees' explanations were mostly elicited by the tutors' questions. By contrast, the tutors' explanations were rarely elicited by the tutees' questions but rather by the tutees' errors or difficulties, or by the tutors' initiative ('focus' or 'diagnostic question') even when the tutees did not make an error or encounter a difficulty.

An intriguing result is that the tutors also delivered explanations after the tutees' correct answer. Different, but not incompatible interpretations may be offered. Firstly, it might be that, according to the tutors' conception of teaching and learning, a correct answer does not constitute a reliable sign of the tutee's state of understanding. Secondly, for the tutors, being a teacher may amount to knowing more than the learner, so that they showed what they knew. Explanation would thus be used as a relational device aimed at asserting and legitimating the tutors' competence. Thirdly, the tutors, especially if they had not fully mastered the subject matter, may use explanation as a metacognitive device aimed at guiding their own thinking and improving their own understanding. Fine-grained analyses should provide evidence regarding which of these interpretations is likely to be correct.

As regards the closing phases, the results also showed an asymmetry between the tutors and the tutees. This asymmetry was both quantitative and qualitative. The tutors closed more explanation moves than the tutees. Furthermore, they closed them either with activities that testified their reflective stance (like 'reformulations' or 'elaborations'), or with activities that showed that they enacted a guidance role and took on a leader role in the management of the relationship (like 'requests for an answer', or 'check questions').

So far, the analysis carried out gave us a general view of the construction of asymmetry. But it does not account for the interactional dynamics specific to each group. We examine this aspect in the next section.

Becoming a Tutor and a Tutee:
Modes of Collaboration in Two Contrasting Dyads

We shall now analyse two groups (groups 3 and 6) which, in the first session, showed contrasting modes of managing the explanation activity. In group 3, the tutor opened 5 moves (out of 12), gave 7 core explanations and closed 10 moves. There were also 2 joint explanations. Because of the tutor's low control over the explanation activity, we shall call this group the *'low asymmetry'* group. By contrast, in group 6, called the *'high asymmetry'* group, the tutor opened 16 moves (out of 28), gave all the core explanations and closed 27 moves.

The Interactional Accomplishment of the Tutor and
Tutee Roles in the 'Low Asymmetry' Group

Excerpt 2 presents the beginning of the first session between Tania, the tutor (Tr), and Emmanuel, the tutee (te) in group 3. They decided to work on time conversions.

Excerpt 2 (31)

1te	x there were things that weren't ok, that was with time conversions
2Tr	yeah
3te	in hours, minutes, seconds
4Tr	time conversions
5te	yeah
6Tr	have you- have you got your folder [and]'
7te	[yeah yeah] I have everything *((looks for his math folder))*
8Tr	in which class are are you' 2M *((label of the class))* hmm'
9te	yeah *((flips the pages in his folder))*
10P	xxx *((the observer arrives with a chair for the tutor))*
11Tr	thank you very much *((to the observer))*
12te	ah ok here are some- here there are some x- which- this is ok but it's for example, we have to change 20'000 seconds into hours, minutes, seconds, that's 5 hours 33 minutes 19 seconds *((correct solution))* . this is what I can't do *((20'000 s. =.... h... min. and... s.))*
13Tr	ooh (laughs) and besides this you don't have any problem at all'
14te	it's the pro- no time conversions, it's only with time conversions that I have problems
15Tr	for time conversions
16te	yeah
17Tr	well how am I going to explain this to you, I've always had a hard time myself (laughs). but you have- you have to tell yourself. if you want you can. you have to imagine a- a watch well

The tutee (1te, 2te) begins straight away by mentioning the subject matter that he finds difficult and by illustrating his difficulties with a school exercise. By so doing, he gives a first definition of the situation and the participants' roles. He positions himself in the role of an applicant for help and places the tutor in the role of an expert. However, despite this first framing, the tutor ignores the tutee's indirect request and checks whether some conditions for work (having his folder) are fulfilled. Her question concerning the tutee's school grade (6Tr-8Tr) can be seen as her way of orienting herself towards the body of knowledge which will be taught in this context. By the same token, she clearly positions herself as the one who will control the unfolding of the lesson and guide the dialogue. Still, by disclosing her own difficulties with time conversions (17Tr), she also positions herself as a student. Ten turns later, the first explanation move appears (Excerpt 3):

Excerpt 3 (31/move 1)

Between turns 18 and 26, the tutor suggested that one way of solving the problem is to imagine a watch (implicitly a watch with a dial and hands) and suggested they transform 14'000 seconds into hours, minutes and seconds.

27Tr	[in] hours . minutes. and in seconds hmm' ... so err . how xx do I explain it to you (laughs) (6 sec)	*Opening phase* *Diagnostic*
	I first try to- to tell myself me 60 . err seconds .. no hold on 60 ... 60 err . seconds, how much is that in hours'	
28te	mmm	
29Tr	it makes'	
30te	err .. 0 point 1 hour . < point err>	*Core explanation*
31Tr	hold on . 0 point.. 60 seconds. myself I really have . I really have to- I almost- I don't know. you must. the hour, the watch, you really have to- in any case for myself it helps me a lot, you must imagine it, err the watch .. and err .. hour hmm' .. in minutes, how many seconds . are there in one minute'	
32te	well there are 60	
33Tr	well yeah 60 seconds in one minute . hence 60, then how many minutes in one hour' 60, so you do 60 times 60 that is hours . is it correct' .. hold on. it's always (laughs) it's always x that I had a hard time (laughs)	
34te	there's a little problem here	*Closing phase* *Failure statement*

The whole explanation move is pervaded by the tutor's difficulty. The tutee's reaction (30te) to her first question (27Tr: *60 seconds, how much does it make in hours?*) reveals the irrelevance of her question and leads her to reformulate it (31Tr: *how many seconds are there in one minute?*) and eventually to reconstruct the hour-minute-second inclusion. The movement between the use of the pronouns *I* and *you* in turn 31Tr can be interpreted as an indication that the tutor is involved not only in giving an explanation to the tutee, but also that she is involved in a thinking-aloud activity. This is aimed at reconstructing her reasoning and the strategies she formerly used to solve this type of problem. However, the computation she proposes (33Tr: *so you do 60 times 60 that is in hours*) leads to an implausible result as emphasized by the tutee's failure statement (34te: *there is a little problem here*) and opens the way to the next explanation move (Excerpt 4).

Excerpt 4 (31/move 2)

35Tr	mmm . I can't remember anymore how the teacher explained it to you	*Opening phase* *Error or difficulty*
36te	well he he does it err . on the calculator for example he puts	
37Tr	he does it with the calculator [xx]	
38te	[xx] with the calculator then	
39Tr	yeah	
40te	14'000 in .. <seconds> 14'000	
41Tr	yeah	
42te	after we do it . divided by 60. it gives us in	
43Tr	<one> <in> second, it gives us [in]	*Core explanation*
44te	[in] [[minutes]]	
45Tr	[[minutes]] yeah	
46te	so there are 233 of them *((14'000:60=233.33))*	
47Tr	yeah	
48te	if we don't need the 233 anymore xx	
49Tr	233 point 3 yeah	
50te	so we subtract the two hundred- minus 233 *((14'000-*	
51Tr	*233=13'767))*	
52te	yeah	
53Tr	divided once more by 60 *((13'767:60=229.45))* yeah	
54te	we get 229 seconds, so it's not very logical his system	*Closing phase* *Failure statement*

The tutor's reformulation *I can't remember anymore how the teacher explained it to you* (35Tr) shows that, even though absent, the tutee's teacher is part of the tutor-tutee didactic contract. It also illustrates one of the main difficulties in being a tutor: being able to remember subject matter that is outside the tutor's current curriculum. The tutee interprets this reformulation as an indirect request for him to describe the teacher's procedure. His explanation, (which is tightly monitored by the tutor and reverses the teacher-student asymmetry), retains the main principle of the tutor's prescribed procedure: transforming seconds into minutes, and minutes into hours, by dividing by 60 each time, and by rounding off the decimal numbers. However, he makes a mistake which he amusingly attributes to the teacher's procedure (54te: *so it's not very logical his system*). Nevertheless, as Excerpt 5 shows, the tutee's incorrect reconstruction enables the tutor to elaborate a correct explanation and to regain control of the situation.

After having opened the explanation move by pointing out the tutee's mistake, the tutor (55Tr) provides an explanation showing that she is now able to articulate the hour-minute-second inclusion with the mathematical computation to be done at each step (See Excerpt 5). The whole move restores the asymmetry of the tutor and tutee's roles. However, the correct solution (3 hours, 53 minutes and 20 seconds) is still not found and two further explanation moves showing a close collaboration between the tutor and the tutee were needed to solve the problem. Afterwards, the tutor and the tutee engage in an exercise that expands the conversion to a broader time unit, the day (Excerpt 6).

Excerpt 5 (31/move 3)

		Opening sequence
55Tr	but why by' . no here *((229))* it's seconds- you get hours	*Error or difficulty*
56te	yes hours . 229	
57Tr	well yes because you must first, well because we said that 60 seconds . there was one minute- no . there were 60 seconds in [one minute]	
58te	[one minute]	
59Tr	there were 60 minutes in one hour . so for the seconds to get hours you first divide by 60 to get the minutes	*Core explanation*
60te	.mm	
61Tr	and one more time to get the hours	
62te	yeah	
63Tr	did you understand this'	*Closing sequence*
64te	yeah	*Check question*

Excerpt 6 (31/moves 6 and 7)

The tutor asks the tutee to convert 3600 minutes into days.

95Tr	3600 minutes – well what I would first do is . you convert this in.. into hours first . in order to have hours what do you do now'	*Core explanation*
96te	well you divide by 60	
97Tr	you divide *((3600 minutes))* by 60 . minutes into hours yeah.. which gives well 60 .. 60 hours . then one hour .. there is- no 24 hours is a day, right'	
98te	x	
99Te	hence one day .. if you have the- hold on, if you have the hours… in order to get days you must . actually I do a drawing \<and> what I've done to go from here to there . then I do the same to go from here to there but in doing a conversion err,	
	so I'd do .. 60 divided by 24 . 2 point 5 . 60.. hold on, by 2 point 5 [150] (multiplies 60 times 2.5)	*Closing phase* *Mention of a*
100te	[150]	*solution*
101Tr	no it's wrong . what I'm telling you here is wrong	*Opening phase* *Self refutation*
102te	yeah	
103Tr	hold on . from hours to days .. here I .. I divide . 60 divided per 24	
104te	2 point 5	
105Tr	2 point 5 days . because 60 here we said that 24 hours it makes one day	*Core* *explanation*
105te	yeah	
107Tr	so you divide by 24 . so here if you have hours, you also divide by 24 . I always ask myself what is the most logical, the- 60 minutes what's that in in seconds . what you can see on the watch or what you know because with- with such numbers err – so I just-	
	did you understand what I have done here'	*Closing phase*
108te	yeah	*Check question*

The tutor's explanation (95Tr) guides the tutee's procedure towards the two steps of the procedure: converting minutes into hours and hours into days. She suggests using a 'drawing' (e.g., a sort of diagram) to guide the procedure. With the help of her drawing but with some hesitations and mistakes (99Tr, 101 Tr), she succeeds in providing both the computation (60 divided by 24) and the corresponding result. Finally when the tutee (104te) gives the answer (*2 point 5*) without indicating units, she is able to say that there are 2.5 *days*.

In these explanation moves, the tutor obviously had some difficulties. Her difficulties led her to express her reasoning out loud several times in a way that seems to be aimed both at eliciting the tutee's understanding (as shown by the fact that she regularly asks for the tutee's reaction) and at reconstructing her own understanding. Similarly, her drawing seemed to be a device, which she, as well as the tutee, could use as a scaffold for the procedure.

The interactional accomplishment of the tutor and tutee roles in the 'high asymmetry' group

During the whole session, the tutor, Teo and the tutee, Eva, work on a schoolbook exercise containing eleven items (*items a-k*) relating to the notion of integers (namely numbers from the sequence ..., -2, -1, 0, 1, 2, ... Positive members of this sequence are often called *counting* or *natural numbers*. Sometimes, but not in this school context, the word *integer* denotes the natural numbers). Excerpt 7 is the very beginning of session 1.

Excerpt 7 (61)

Off record, the tutee just indicated the number of the 'theme' in the schoolbook that was causing her difficulties.

1Tr	ok' then... theme 8... err it doesn't ring a bell for me well
2te	I don't understand this (*shows exercise 14 of her notebook and the instruction: 'Find the integers which may complete these lines'*)
3Tr	well a natural number, do you know what it is' ... (...)

Contrary to what was observed in the 'low asymmetry' group, the tutee does not give any precise information about her difficulty. After having mentioned the number of the 'theme', she points to an exercise she found difficult. This is sufficient to elicit the tutor's first explanation (Excerpt 8) and to enable the partners to assume complementary roles.

The tutor's explanation is threefold. First the tutor (2Tr) asks for a definition of the notion of 'natural number'. He hesitantly defines integers as positive numbers and makes a distinction between 'natural numbers' *(numbers that do not have a point)*, 'integers' *(positive numbers)*, and 'negative numbers' *(numbers below zero)*. Secondly, in 6Tr, he reformulates this definition with the aid of a concrete device: the drawing of a line with zero in the middle, positive numbers on the right, *(integers according to his definition)*, and negative numbers on the left. He uses this diagram during the whole session to support and illustrate his explanations. Finally, in turn 8Tr, he reformulates his first definition: integers are numbers without a point that are above zero.

Excerpt 8 (61/move 1)

		Opening phase
2Tr	well a natural number, do you know what it is'	*Diagnostic*
	it's a number that doesn't have a point	
3te	yeah	
4Tr	x three- three is a natural number . 3 point 4 is a number with a point err . . an integer' (4 sec) so if I am not mistaken an integer is a number which is positive, you see' this is a negative number (points to a number on the page) . because it's below zero	
5te	(nods)	*Core explanation*
6Tr	you see often one can dr- one can draw for example err a straight line where you have the ze- a mark where the zero is . you have 1, 2, 3, 4, 5, you have minus 1, minus 2, minus 3, minus 4, minus 5	
7te	(nods)	
8Tr	etcetera . so so these are the negative numbers, the positive numbers are the numbers which are above zero . they are called integers. ok'	
	.. so err thus the numbers . thus the numbers without a point which are above zero (2 sec) (...)	*Closing phase* *Direct* *continuation*

The tutor's wrong definition is not challenged by the tutee and in the first item of the exercise, the tutor initiates the second explanation move (Excerpt 9).

After having reformulated the problem corresponding to *item a* with some hesitations and self-corrections, the tutor (8Tr) focuses upon the instruction (working with relative integers) and by referring to his previous definition of the notion, deduces that the solution cannot be a negative number. Finally, he simplifies the task by drawing the tutee's attention to the different answers allowed by his definition (*between zero and plus 3*). Since the solution of the problem allows a positive number, the tutor's definition of the notion of 'integer' is not challenged. As a consequence, neither he nor the tutee has a chance of noticing the error. The solutions of *items b* and *c* also allow a positive number so that, again, the tutor's definition, which is repeated several times over the next third explanation moves, has no chance to be challenged. During that time, the tutee's participation is minimal and the tutor's guidance efficiently leads her to produce a correct solution.

Excerpt 9 (61/move 2)

8Tr	[item a: (-4) < ... < (+3)] so here what possibilities could we have'	*Opening phase* *Focus*
	. you see . here it's larger.. xx you have the sign xx larger than minus 4. rather minus 4 is smaller than the number you have to find . but the number you have to find is smaller than minus 3 . err than- than than plus 3 . so . since they say that it's- that it must be an integer . it means that it could not be for example minus 3 . you see'	*Core explanation*
9te	(nods)	
10Tr	so it will be between zero and plus 3 .. since it must- you see' between zero and plus 3	
11te	(nods)	
12Tr	so what could it be' (5 sec) between zero and 3 there is'	*Closing phase*
13te	2'	*Answer request*
14Tr	ok' so here there could be 2 (...)	

However, things dramatically change in relation to *items d* and *e* where the solutions can only be a negative number:

Excerpt 10 (61)

30Tr (...) ((*reads item d: [(-20) < ... < (-8)]*)) there is a problem here however ... mm ((*reads item e: [(-11) < (+4) + ... < (-2)]*)). well we take the f ((*item f*)) because with these two there is a problem ((*continues with item f*))

After some signs of puzzlement (30Tr), the tutor skips these items and goes to *items f, g, h* and *i* which allow a positive number. Things go smoothly again with the tutor taking charge of the explanations and the tutee participating minimally. However, the problem bursts out in the very last item (*item k*) where the solution has to be a negative number (Excerpt 11).

Excerpt 11 (61/move 27)

	Item k: (-7) ≤ (+18) + ... ≤ (+8)	
106Tr	(...) this number here (shows the dots) is smaller than 18 or equal .	*Core explanation (part)*
	so what' ... hmm' . x it's not possible (10 sec) . (he stands up) I'll be back because . there is an error . it makes no sense . I'll be back in two small seconds (goes to the teacher and comes back after 2 minutes) I think I've done a stupid thing (5 sec) so (7 sec) well err I have a question (suggests to complete [10 + ... = 5]; 2 minutes later the session is over)	*Closing phase* *Failure statement*

Now, the tutor notices that his previous definition is contradicted by the data and decides to ask the teacher. When he comes back, he does not comment on his wrong definition and just decides to leave the exercise. Without being questioned by the tutee, he invents another exercise, namely additions and subtractions that involve negative numbers.

Discussion

In the previous section, we examined the progressive construction of the roles of tutor and tutee in two contrasting groups in which the activity of explanation was differently managed. In the 'low asymmetry' group (group 3), we observed how, starting from a subject matter (time conversions) that was not part of her current school curriculum, the tutor gradually managed to reconstruct her understanding and, eventually, to guide the tutee's actions. Even though the tutee's explanation was incorrect, it enabled her to reconstruct the procedure and the underlying reasoning. Taking advantage of the tutee's incorrect explanation, she could position herself as an expert, set up the asymmetry and the complementarity pertaining to a teacher-student relationship, and demonstrate her legitimacy as a tutor. The tutee played a central role in this reconstruction. Firstly, he was partly able to report the procedure that he had learned in class with his teacher. Secondly, his errors gave the tutor the opportunity to go over her reasoning many times whilst demonstrating the procedure with the help of a semiotic tool (a watch with a dial). So, on the one hand, the tutor guided the tutee's actions, but on the other, the tutee's reaction and active participation elicited the tutor's activity, the specifics of which was directed at both the tutee as well as at herself, and thus giving it a metacognitive dimension.

On a relational level, the interactional dynamics of the whole session showed that this progressive mastery of the subject matter then served as an interactional resource that the tutor used to legitimate her role and expertise. The tutee's participation here was essential both for the construction of the solution and for the construction of the tutor's and tutee's roles.

In the 'high asymmetry' group, the situation was quite different. Here the tutor gave an incorrect definition of the mathematical notion of 'integers'. His error remained unnoticed, partly because many items of the exercise required a solution that did not challenge the tutor's incorrect definition, and partly also because the tutee let the tutor take a strong control over the interaction and the management of the explanation moves. Even when at the very end of the session, the tutor noticed his error, he did not tell the tutee and avoided discussing his error. Here again, the tutee's mode of participation was essential to the construction of the tutor's and tutee's roles. By her minimal participation, the tutee did not only position herself as an applicant for help, but she also put the tutor in the position of carrying out the task and of reducing it to its procedural dimensions.

CONCLUSION

In this chapter, we have described the specific nature of the peer-tutoring educational setting that we observed in terms of a didactic contract. A first description of the complexity of this contract led us to question the assumption that tutor-tutee interactions would have a low level of asymmetry. Taking the management of explanation as an indicator of the tutor-tutee level of asymmetry, we showed that the tutors clearly took the role of providing explanations and deciding when explanations were needed. In a complementary mode, the tutees positioned themselves as recipients of the explanations and let the tutors decide more often than not when an explanation was required.

By considering explanations as a situated activity, we have shown that explanation is (according to our first definition) a discursive device used to transform the tutees' problematic state of knowledge into an unproblematic state (Bruxelles & de Gaulmyn, 2000). However, it is also an *interactional resource* through which the asymmetry and complementarity of the tutor-tutee relationship is accomplished and through which the tutors construct their legitimacy. Finally, it is also a *semiotic tool* that tutors use to self-regulate their cognitive activity and thus has a metacognitive function (which, by the same token, may account for the classical 'tutor-effect' evidenced by research on peer tutoring).

Indirectly, these results also provide some insight into the students' implicit assumptions about the activities of teaching and learning. Tutors provided more explanations than the tutees and used explanations to correct or even hinder the tutees' errors. This suggests that, for these students, teaching is more a process of inculcating ready-made forms of knowledge in their peers, rather than one of 'drawing out' the competencies that would allow them to find the solution or the explanation by themselves. Following the etymological pun by Edwards and Mercer (1987), it is more a way of '*in*-ducating' bodies of knowledge into their peers, than of '*e*-ducating' them. In this sense, tutor-tutee interactions do not seem to differ radically from the classical teacher-student interactions described in the scientific literature.

Finally, our analysis also raised an unexpected issue concerning the role played by the tutors' errors or difficulties. We observed two contrasting modes of management of the tutor's errors or difficulties. In the 'low asymmetry' group, the tutor's difficulties or hesitations, far from hindering the development of the tutee's activity, brought about the tutee's participation and collaboration in the construction of the solution. In a way, the tutor's errors and difficulties slowed down the pace of the didactic interaction and gave time for reflection and discussion. Thus, the tutor's difficulties were transformed into a cognitive and interactional resource and led to a type of discourse which shared many characteristics with the exploratory type of dialogue described by Mercer and his colleagues (Wegerif & Mercer, 1997). By contrast, in the 'high asymmetry' group, the error was treated as critical event liable to challenge the tutor's legitimacy and thus did not provide an opportunity to engage in cognitive work.

So, a question that remains for further research, is to investigate whether the tutors' errors or difficulties, instead of being unwanted by-products (as the institutional role distribution suggests), might instead create a space for reflection. Do these errors, as might be expected from previous research, result in (socio) cognitive conflicts liable to stimulate students' understanding of the body of knowledge to be learned?

AUTHOR NOTE

Correspondence concerning this chapter should be addressed to Michèle Grossen, Department of Psychology, University of Lausanne, BFSH 2, 1018 Lausanne, CH. Electronic mail may be sent to michele.grossen@ip.unil.ch

REFERENCES

Allen, V. L., & Feldman, R. S. (1973). Learning through tutoring: Low achieving children as tutors. *Journal of Experimental Education, 42,* 1-5.

Baker, M. J. (1999). Argumentation and constructive interaction. In P. Coirier & J. Andriessen (Eds.), *Foundations of argumentative text processing*: Vol. 5 (pp. 179-202). Amsterdam: University of Amsterdam Press.

Barnier, G. (1989). L'effet tuteur dans des situations mettant en jeu des rapports spaciaux chez des enfants de 7-8 ans en interaction dyadique avec des pairs de 6-7 ans [The tutor-effect in situations involving spatial relationships in 7-8 year old children in dyadic interactions with 6-7 year-old peers]. *European Journal of Psychology of Education,* 4(3), 385-399.

Barnier, G. (1994). *L'effet-tuteur dans une tâche spatiale chez des enfants d'âge scolaire [The tutor-effect in a spatial task in school children].* Unpublished doctoral dissertation, University of Provence, Aix-en-Provence, France.

Brixhe, D. (1999). Construction d'un savoir dans l'interaction tutorielle: Vers le concept de nombre négatif [Construction of a body of knowledge in tutorial interaction: Towards the concept of negative numbers]. In M. Gilly, J.-P. Roux, & A. Trognon (Eds.), *Apprendre dans l'interaction [Learning in interaction]* (pp. 201-218). Nancy: Presses Universitaires de Nancy and Publications de l'Université de Provence.

Bruxelles, S., & de Gaulmyn, M.-M. (2000). Explication en interaction: Facteurs déterminants et degré d'efficacité [Explanation in interaction: Determinant factors and level of efficiency]. *Psychologie de l'Interaction, 9-10,* 47-76.

Cloward, R. D. (1967). Studies in tutoring. *Journal of Experimental Education, 36,* 14-25.

Cohen, P. A., Kulik, J. A., & Kulik, C. L. (1982). Educational outcomes of tutoring: A meta-analysis of findings. *American Educational Research Journal, 19,* 237-248.

Crahay, M., Hindryckx, G., & Lebe, M. (2001). *Analyse des interactions entre enfants en situation de tutorat [Analysis of intercations between children in a tutoring situation].* Paper presented at the biennial conference of the European Association for Research on Learning and Instruction (EARLI), Fribourg, Switzerland.

Devin-Sheenan, L., Feldman, R. S., & Allen, V. L. (1976). Research on children tutoring children: A critical review. *Review of Educational Research, 46*(3), 355-385.

Edwards, D., & Mercer, N. (1987). *Common knowledge: The development of understanding in the classroom.* London: Methuen.

Gilly, M., Roux, J.-P. & Trognon, A. (Eds.) (1999). *Apprendre dans l'interaction [Learning in interaction].* Paris: Presses Universitaires de France.

Golay Schilter, D., Perret, J.-F., Perret-Clermont, A.-N., & De Guglielmo, F. (1999). Sociocognitive interactions in a computerized industrial task. In K. Littleton & P. Light (Eds.), *Learning with computers* (pp. 118-143). London, New York: Routledge.

Goodlad, S. (1979). *Learning by teaching: An introduction to tutoring.* London: Community Service Volunteers.

Grossen, M. (2000). Institutional framings in thinking, learning and teaching. In H. Cowie, G. van der Aalsvort, & N. Mercer (Eds.), *Social interaction in learning and instruction: The meaning of discourse for the construction of knowledge* (pp. 21-34). Oxford: Permagon Press.

Grossen, M., & Bachmann, K. (2000). Learning to collaborate in a peer-tutoring situation: Who learns? What is learned? *European Journal of Psychology of Education, 15*(4), 491-508.

Grossen, M., Liengme Bessire, M.J., & Perret-Clermont, A.-N. (1997). Construction de l'interaction et dynamique socio-cognitives. [Construction of the interaction and socio-cognitive dynamics.] In M. Grossen & B. Py (Eds.), *Pratiques sociales et médiations symboliques* (pp. 221- 247). [Social practices and symbolic mediation.] Bern: Peter Lang.

Joiner, R., Littleton, K., Faulkner, D., & Miell, D. (Eds.). (2000). *Rethinking collaborative learning.* London: Free Association Books.

Kaartinen, S., & Kumpulainen, K. (2002). Collaborative inquiry and the construction of explanations in the learning of sciences. *Learning and Instruction, 12,* 189-212.

Littleton, K., & Light, P. (1999). *Learning with computers.* London, New York: Routledge.

Mercer, N. (2000). *Words & minds. How to use language to think together.* London, New York: Routledge.

Rojas-Drummond, S., Pérez, V., Vélez, M., Gómez, L., & Medoza, A. (2003). Talking for reasoning among Mexican primary school children. *Learning and Instruction, 13*(6), 653-670.

Schubauer-Leoni, M. L., & Grossen, M. (1993). Negotiating the meaning of questions in didactic and experimental contracts. *European Journal of Psychology of Education, 8*(4), 451-471.

Teasley, S. D. (1997). Talking about reasoning: How important is the peer in peer collaboration? In C. B. Resnick, R. Säljö, C. Pontecorvo, & B. Burge (Eds.), *Discourse, tools, and reasoning. Essays on situated cognition.* (pp. 361-384). Heidelberg: Springer Verlag.

Wegerif, R. (2000). Applying a dialogical model of reason in the classroom. In R. Joiner, K. Littleton, D. Faulkner, & D. Miell (Eds.), *Rethinking collaborative learning* (pp. 119-136). London, New York: Free Association Books.

Wegerif, R., & Mercer, N. (2000). Language for thinking. In H. Cowie, G. van der Aalsvoort, & N. Mercer (Eds.), *New perspectives in collaborative learning.* Oxford: Elsevier.

APPENDIX 1: TRANSCRIPTION CONVENTIONS

Overlaps   [ ]
     [ ]
and   [[..........]]
     [[ ]] when two overlaps or more are next one to the other
Intonation markers
     ': rising intonation (not necessarily a question)
     , : falling intonation
Pauses
     a dot = 1 sec   two dots = 2 sec
Unintelligible syllables
     x: one syllable unintelligible
     xx: approximately two syllables unintelligible
Latches between two turns
     end of turn 1: =
     beginning of turn 2: =
Interruption by the speaker him/herself or by the hearer: -
Comments by the transcriber: (( ))

Chapter 8

MUSICAL COLLABORATIONS

Raymond MacDonald and Dorothy Miell

INTRODUCTION

In this chapter we want to suggest that since engaging with music is an essentially social activity it can be a useful site within which to examine collaboration, since it extends our understanding of joint working into a creative and personally significant area of life. Perhaps surprisingly there has been little research until recently on such creative collaborations.

Music holds great personal significance for most people – we are motivated to engage with music throughout our everyday lives and to collaborate and identify with others through engagement with musical activities – and it has this personal significance for a number of reasons. Trevarthen (2002) for example suggests that the earliest communications between a parent and a child are essentially musical and as a result claims that to respond emotionally to music is a defining feature of our humanity. Furthermore, as Cook (1998) puts it:

'In today's world, deciding what music to listen to is a significant part of deciding and announcing to people not just who you 'want to be'…but who you are. 'Music' is a very small word to encompass something that takes as many forms as there are cultural or sub-cultural identities' (p.5).

Exploring how people engage with music is therefore potentially a particularly fruitful domain for researchers in the field of collaborative learning to study, since we can see how being involved with others in both listening to and making music can afford opportunities for identity development and creativity.

Music as a Social Activity

Composing and Playing Music

The old stereotype of a musician locked away in a dingy garret working alone on a composition, not caring about critics' or audiences' responses but driven only by some personal, internal inspiration is being altered by a significant body of research highlighting the indisputably social nature of our musicality (Hargreaves & North 1997; MacDonald, Miell & Hargreaves, 2002; Sawyer, 2001). Although there was an early recognition of the social nature of music (and other arts) in the work of the philosopher Collingwood (1938), this has not prevented the continuing folklore of the solitary artist:

> 'The work of artistic creation is not a work performed in any exclusive or complete fashion in the mind of the person whom we call the artist. That idea is a delusion bred of individualistic psychology....This activity is a corporate activity belonging not to any one human being but to a community. It is performed not only by the man whom we individualistically call the artist, but partly by all the other artists of whom we speak as 'influencing' him, where we really mean collaborating with him. It is performed not only by this corporate body of artists, but (in the case of the arts of performance) by executants.... and...there must be an audience, whose function is therefore not a merely receptive one, but collaborative too. The artist stands thus in collaborative relations with an entire community.' (cited in Sawyer, 2001, p103)

This view opens up our thinking to consider the otherwise 'hidden' social and cultural milieu within which an individual composer works - the traditional repertory or canon which he or she is developing, the musicians who will later interpret and play the piece and the audience who will hear and react to it. But if we can recognize this hidden social milieu how much easier is it to see the social nature of other aspects of the musical world? Consider improvisations, where a group of musicians develop a novel piece of music together as they play. These are characterized, as Monson's (1996) interviews with jazz musicians reveal, by intense intersubjectivity and highly developed communication between members of a band. The musicians liken a good improvised set to a good conversation, where the quality of the interaction is the key to success. As one musician she interviewed put it:

> 'That happens a lot in jazz, that it's like a conversation and one guy will ...create a melodic motif or a rhythmic motif and the band picks it up. It's like sayin' that you all are talking about the same thing.' (Richard Davis, cited in Monson, 1996, p32)

Even where the musicians are not creating the music as they perform within improvisations (such as in performances of classical music), there are subtle yet important social features to be observed as the musicians communicate with each other, for example in order to adapt to mistakes in the performance or to remind each other of discussions of timing or emotional tone that they had during rehearsal, as well as the various processes involved in communicating with their audience (Goodman, 2002; Moran, 2002). In a recent study we conducted where the members of a rock band kept a video diary of their rehearsals over several weeks, they emphasized the importance of communication and close, empathetic understanding of each other's intentions in their joint playing. In the extract below we hear two members of the band talking between playing about why they seem to work well together:

John: I would say that it's also got to do with the fact that me and Mark and Max have been playing for three years together.

Harry: When you look at you guys playing, usually if you're playing something that's quite new, you can definitely tell there's a chemistry between you and Mark.

John: The eye thing

Harry: yeah you'll just sort of give a glance and Mark will know exactly what to do. It doesn't really happen with Louise generally.

John: Yeah Louise is in a world of her own.
            [...]

John: I think what you're saying about the Mark thing is very true. A lot of eye signals go on and I'll tell sometimes what I kind of want or just by nodding and things like that and he'll pick up on it.

This level of mutual understanding and effective communication is what we already know to be characteristic of good collaborations in other domains (Rogoff, 1990; Hartup, 1996) and it is interesting to see the importance of these same social strategies when collaborating on music.

Listening to Music

Beyond the realms of performance, we can also consider the social meanings involved in *listening* to music – the music that individuals choose to listen to carries immense cultural significance and, as we saw in the quote from Cook which opened this chapter, consequent personal significance. A growing body of literature within the psychology and, particularly, the sociology of music have highlighted the importance of social and cultural factors upon developing musical identities through listening patterns, however there is still much to learn about the impact these factors have (Hodges & Haack, 1996; MacDonald & Miell, 2000). Popular culture - through television, radio and related magazines - plays a central part in all our lives, and this 'informal learning environment' is one within which many young people are developing musical identities that are as a result intrinsically linked with social and cultural factors. As Willis (1978) and Frith (1978; 1981) have demonstrated in their studies of 'bikeboys' and of rock culture, individuals see music as a resource 'through which [their] agency, identity and peer culture are produced' (deNora, 2001, p166).

This chapter will be examining the social and collaborative aspects of both playing *and* listening to music, drawing on illustrative examples from previous studies we have conducted which involved interviews with young people about their musical tastes and activities, and observations of Gamelan workshops for people with learning difficulties.

THE PERSONAL AND SOCIAL IMPORTANCE OF MUSIC

Modern technological advances mean that now, more than at any other time in history, music is pervasive and functions not only as a pleasurable art form, but surrounds many activities of daily life, including (perhaps especially) our most mundane and routine activities such as exercising, dressing, housework, travelling and shopping (deNora, 1999; Sloboda, O'Neill & Ivaldi, 2001). The recognition of the ubiquitous presence of music has been one of the factors motivating significant research interest in the effects that music listening might have on a range of psychological and even physiological variables (Overy, 1999). These include the effects of listening to music on cognitive skills (Rauscher, 2000), on heart rate and blood pressure (Aldridge, 1996), on emotional responses (Juslin & Sloboda, 2001) and on consumer behaviour (Hargreaves & North, 1997). While these studies highlight the effects of listening, and are not focused on musical collaboration, they do signal the ubiquitous nature of musical stimuli and the wide ranging effects of listening - not only does music provide a soundtrack to our lives but it can also affect the listener in quite profound ways.

Young People's Music Listening

It has been suggested (Larson *et al.*, 1989; Sloboda *et al.,* 2001) that music plays a particularly important role in the lives of young people, not only because they have more 'free' time to engage in leisure activities such as listening to music and watching TV, but also because music does not seem to be something that they listen to 'passively' in the way that some adults do who are more likely to use music as a background to their everyday routines (Sloboda *et al.,* 2001). Instead, adolescents are reported to see music as their most preferred leisure activity (Fitzgerald *et al.,* 1995; Zillman & Gan, 1997) and their music collection as one of their most special, important or treasured possessions (Kamptner, 1995). In interviews we conducted with young people aged 13-16 (Miell, Littleton & MacDonald, 2002), the importance of music to them was clear – as one young man said, 'Music is my life'.

The reason for this greater importance to young people is likely to be the role that music plays as a resource for them in their construction and presentation of self. This activity is an almost all-consuming preoccupation throughout the teen years when young people are exploring, trying out and rejecting a range of different possible identities. In studies by North and Hargreaves and colleagues (North, Hargreaves & O'Neill, 2000; Tarrant, North & Hargreaves, 2000), adolescents were asked to say the extent to which possible reasons for listening to music applied to them. These researchers found that in both UK and US populations the factor that explained most of the variance in responses was one labelled 'impression management', which included agreement with statements such as 'I listen to music in order to create a particular self-image', 'I listen to be trendy/cool' and 'I listen in order to please others (e.g. peers)'. The young people are achieving a great deal through their engagement with music, notably in managing their self-presentation and sense of identity in relation to their peer group.

The importance of music may manifest itself in a variety of diverse yet related ways, and it has a fundamental relevance for young people's lives which is being studied by a growing number of psychology of music researchers. A recent study we have carried out contributes to this literature (Littleton, Miell & MacDonald, 2002; Miell, Littleton & MacDonald, 2002). The study involved in-depth interviews with 13-16 year olds about their experiences of music both within school and in more informal settings such as community centres, youth clubs and at home. We asked about their tastes and preferences and also, if they took part in informal music making (such as in their own bands), their experiences of writing and performing

music. From the thematic analysis of these interviews it is apparent that the young people .
were using music to negotiate specific identities, identities which derived from their
exploration of particular musical genres, and that these identities were 'relational', being
based on comparisons with others in their immediate circle of peers as well as with young
people more generally through representations within popular culture. They were actively
using their reports about choosing music to buy and to listen to in order to construct particular
identities and communicate these identities to others, rather than simply as a passive
reflection of personal preferences.

This notion of consumption as identity construction can be seen if we consider Ossie's
exploration of Hip-hop. Ossie's growing into 'very underground Hip-hop' necessitated
deliberate efforts on his part to cultivate an appreciation of 'quite obscure, hard to listen to
things' by 'very clever musicians':

Ossie: I was sort of growing into Hip-hop, very underground Hip-hop, which, so
               quite obscure, hard to listen to things, like people like James Ravell and
               people like that who are actually very clever musicians to be able to make
               the tunes that they do and drum and bass I know a lot of people don't like it
               but I think it's good

It is also echoed in John's comment about his taste in music being deliberately acquired:

John: in a sense I almost made myself like industrial - coz I didn't really like it at
               the beginning but I really wanted to like it because for me it was like the last
               kind of type of music which was kind of just pristine from this, kind of
               marketing trend thing – it was the only one that was kind of untouched

In taking on the identity of 'listener to industrial music' he was deliberately distancing
himself from what he saw as the typical market/fashion led taste in music that was detested by
all the young people in our study. It was certainly more important for the young people in our
sample to stake claims for individual, often idiosyncratic musical tastes than to be seen as
'following the crowd' in the way that they saw others doing. They preferred to display their
individuality by claiming tastes that they did not associate with 'the masses'. However, the
young people we interviewed were keen to associate with the tastes of others when those
others were friends or members of a group that they were happy to be identified with:

Craig: most musicians tend to like the same sort of thing, for example everyone at
               the Academy who I know likes Jamiroqui but a lot of people who don't play
               instruments don't – it's probably because of some of the musical aspects of
               their music – it's got quite a lot of depth to it - a lot of the chords might
               sound a little weird to people…a lot of their music is really complicated'.

Young People's Music Making

The young people's accounts above reveal the complexity and subtlety of the 'identity
work' involved in the construction of specific musical identities within and in relation to

particular musical genres. This identity work is even more apparent when we hear young people talking about *making music*. Many of those we interviewed were involved in composing and performing music in informal settings such as their own rock or folk bands and were if anything even more passionate about this than about listening to music (although such enthusiasm was not at all evident when they discussed their experiences of school music. We will not be dealing with this issue here, but further details are in Littleton *et al.* (2002). Their accounts revealed their commitment to the process of making music – which, for almost all of them, was a collaborative venture which entailed extended discussion, rehearsal and negotiation about all aspects of the process - the make up of the band, the changing membership and individual members' contributions, potential gigs and, not least, the developing music itself. The important role that music played in their lives meant that they were very motivated to ensure that their collaborations were productive, and so examining what they said about these interactions can tell us something interesting about the nature of this form of collaboration (i.e. informal and open-ended), which is not a form which is studied very often in the collaborative learning literature. Since most of that literature involves studies of tasks such as science and maths tasks with pre-existing 'correct answers', we can extend our understanding of collaboration by studying how people collaborate when working on open-ended tasks such as music composition and this will add to the gradually increasing body of literature on such collaborative creativity (e.g. Barrett, 2004; Sawyer, 2004). As we saw in the earlier quote taken from the rehearsal conversations between John and Harry, many of the same underlying processes seem to be as important for creative collaborations as for those in other domains, in terms of the need for intersubjectivity and effective communication.

Ollie was typical in his emphasis on the need for everyone involved to be both individually skilled and attentive to the others in the group:

Interviewer: Do you improvise a lot together or does it depend on what you're playing?

Ollie: um when we are using the jazz stuff we improvise a bit but I improvise a lot on my own [...] yes it's hard it's hard you have to have a group of really good players each one has to be individually very good

Interviewer: yes and also very um in tune, intuitive and..

Ollie: yeah you have to listen to what's going on and be aware of how things are going [...]

However it was recognized that in a supportive group of friends, even someone without much musical skill could achieve well:

Kelly: I think, I mean certainly, certainly last year some people who had very little musical ability could do really good compositions [at school]

Interviewer: mmm

Kelly: in a group together.

Interviewer: Really, yeah?

Kelly: They were with their friends

This view is consistent with the findings of the observational study we conducted of young people's collaborative compositions at school (Miell & MacDonald, 2000). In that study, 11-12 year old children without any formal musical training who were working with a friend were able to develop better quality compositions (as judged by an independent music teacher) than those who were working with a non-friend, even if these non-friends had previous musical training. The better quality of the communication between friends and their stock of shared experiences and mutual understanding was particularly helpful in enabling them to succeed in this creative collaborative task.

As Vass (2003) has shown in her studies of young people collaborating on creative writing projects, in such domains some other factors which are less typically associated with productive collaborative working practices become particularly important – such as this closeness of the personal relationships between partners ('the chemistry' that Harry noted above between John and Mark) which means they can draw on their shared history of experiences for inspiration and can communicate in a form of shorthand (e.g. 'the eye thing' as John said above). Vass' research also stressed the importance in creative collaborations of cycles of 'brainstorming', where partners build cumulatively and uncritically on each other's ideas to generate new ones, rather than the carefully reasoned-out and explicit discussion more often associated with successful collaborations on science and maths tasks where there is a 'correct' answer. Whilst our interviews here only provide accounts of these processes rather than observations of them taking place, there was evidence of this form of brainstorming being fundamental to the process of collaborative composition. As Ollie put it when asked how his band worked together: 'We just sort of spark off each other'. Rachel gives a more detailed account of the creative process and emphasizes the cumulative, brainstorming approach and the importance of keeping everyone involved:

Rachel: Then we sort of say, 'allright, we'll make a song', and then somebody arranges, strung a few chords that we all like, but we've all got to like them, you know, otherwise it's not really any point, and then, um, and maybe someone will come up with a phrase, and then.. and then ...and then it just comes together, or somebody will know they've got to make some words

Interviewer: Yeah

Rachel: OK so it starts off, maybe Carol going away and writing the words, and we'll think 'Oh they are really nice words', and then she does some record, and 'Oh, you could do this sort of tune', and 'this sort of tune', and gradually it changes with people's opinion and you've got some tune and some words, and we don't really like, and then Ros will go away and do her violin bit, 'cos we think 'Oh well, the violin makes it sound a bit sort of less teenagery',

Interviewer: Yes, yes I know what you mean.

Rachel: And, um, then Kate can't sing very well anyway, but we just sort of have a good time with them. They sort of add their ideas, cos like, me and Ros have our sort of type of music, Carol has her sort of Corr-ish, loving sort of music, and they have the more modern music influence and they sort of maybe add little bits here and there, but usually it's Carol, me and Ros, really, cos Kirsty and Kate just tag along really (laugh)

Many of the young people stressed the importance of all being fully involved and committed to the process of working together as a group. The personal importance that the music held for them meant that they felt they were 'laying themselves on the line' and potentially exposing themselves emotionally in group sessions, so it was vital that there was a sense of trust between them and commitment from all. When this failed it could lead to the breakdown of the band, as Ros explains when she described the destructive behaviour of two members of her band:

Ros: They don't really seem to be enjoying themselves in band practices
Interviewer: mm
Ros: I mean they're always dissing everything we do but they're never, never putting their own views forward.
Interviewer: mm
Ros: I mean, I mean like ideas forward. We're the ones that have done the hard work but they, you know, but they never like call it quits
Interviewer: mm
Ros: You know. I mean, we sort it, we sort it out amongst us three and suddenly there's a problem when, when Kirsty can't do something or, I mean. I mean, one, one time all Kirsty had to do was play her violin and she refused and
Interviewer: Yes
Ros: I thought, you know if you really want to be in this band I think you would be willing to do practically anything to make the sound, sound okay

One of the consequences of the deep association between music and identity development - described in the previous section - seems to be that in these musical collaborations the young people are concerned to retain ownership of at least some of their own contributions to the final composition. They also show respect for others' contributions, recognizing their personal significance, and are careful in how they suggest changes to such sections. In other forms of joint working it is often seen as a sign of 'true' collaboration that the partners lose sight of who made individual contributions (Vass, 2003), but we can see from the extracts below from Dan, Rachel and Trevor that these young people felt their music was too personally significant to lose ownership of:

Interviewer: Is there ever conflict about what goes into the song?
Dan: Well no not really I mean if someone has written a song I sort of respect what they've written […] it also depends what we're playing because if it's like um a rocky piece um and someone has written some words I wouldn't say no these are rubbish just change it because they're going to feel I mean […]
Dan: you can be more what's the word hurt I suppose if you've written a song and people have a go at it. You've got to be more careful…

Trevor: Well, em (.) I don't know. Well, what (.) basically one of us will (.) write the song, or whatever, and then, the other person will say, well maybe you could put this here or this would work, or you could reverse this. We just all like we just collaborate ideas.
Interviewer: Yeah. So it's still, it's sort of basically your song
Trevor: Yeah but

Interviewer: with bits from someone else.
Trevor: Yeah.
Interviewer: and (.) it might be either of you
Trevor: Yeah
Interviewer: that's written it (.) but kind of always know who's song it is
Trevor: yeah

Rachel: They [another band in a workshop] were working on one of our songs, but
               we didn't want them to work on it, and we couldn't exactly say No, because
               it's just one of those things you just don't do.
Interviewer: Um yes,
Rachel: And they were just making up all these little bits that we didn't like and we
               thought well, it's our song, we didn't like that, leave it out, you know. But
               we couldn't say anything.
Interviewer: It's difficult, because if you start all together from scratch it's different, but
               if you've already made a song as a group of people.
Rachel: And then they began to think about it as theirs – like it's just not on.

This section has shown the close inter-relationship for young people between the personal and social in music. The extracts discussed have provided indications of which features are common to processes of collaboration across domains and those which are distinctive to working on music. We suggest that further detailed observational work would be valuable to explore these and other aspects of creative collaborations further.

Collaborative Music Making in Special Needs Group

As we have seen in our studies with young people in bands, when working together on musical activities participants need to develop and use skills of empathy, communication, listening and respect. These are in many cases skills that not only make for good joint music making, but in any case are the skills required to collaborate well on any task. Therefore learning to participate in musical activities can be a good place for learning to collaborate generally. We can see this in other populations and contexts too. For example, a series of studies were conducted by MacDonald *et al.* (1999) that have highlighted the importance of these communicative and social factors in music education environments. These studies demonstrated how structured music workshops for individuals with special needs could facilitate general development in musical and communication skills. The practical activities involved in all these studies were music workshops focused on the playing of a Javanese Gamelan, undertaken within a group context where participants were working towards a shared goal, and "success" on the task required all participants to work together collaboratively.

Gamelan is a generic name for a set of percussion instruments consisting of tuned gongs, metallophones, cymbals and drums. These can be found throughout Malaysia and Indonesia and range in size from four to forty instruments (Lindsay, 1989). In Gamelan music there is no conductor present. Instead all coordination is accomplished musically by one drum player playing with and leading all the other musicians. Effort is required by all members to follow the variations in tempo that occur and therefore in training the emphasis is placed on developing and fostering good group communication. Effective communication is achieved by a sensitive and detailed understanding of the social and musical conventions involved in playing the Gamelan, and all musicians must be collaborating effectively in order to successfully complete any piece of Gamelan music. Its relative obscurity within Western cultures makes it an ideal instrument for use with special needs populations as individuals can approach the Gamelan, as both listeners and performers, without any preconceived cultural stereotypes. Another important feature of the Gamelan for use with a special needs population is its accessibility. Complicated digital dexterity is not required to commence playing the instrument. In this and other ways the Gamelan caters for all levels of ability and is therefore an ideal instrument to use for both educational and therapeutic applications of music.

In the MacDonald et al. (1999) studies, one group (N=19) participated in a ten week music workshop programme, and were compared on a number of measures with two control groups, one who took part in no activities for the same length of time (N=16), and a second who took part in cooking or art activities for the ten weeks (N=24). Results indicated significant improvements in both musical ability and self-perception of musical ability for participants in the workshop group in comparison with the other two groups. This finding is not surprising given the nature of the activities engaged in by the different groups, but a significant improvement in more general communication skill measures was observed *only* in the music workshop group. None of the participants in the other groups made gains on any of the measures taken. A longitudinal investigation indicated that both the musical and communication gains made by the music workshop group remained six months after the end of the workshops. The musical activities seemed to provide an environment that facilitated lasting developments for individuals with learning difficulties in not only their musical skills but also in both self confidence (related to their musical ability) and in general communication skills.

MacDonald and Miell (2002) argue that one of the main reasons for these developments occurring in the music workshops was the focus on fostering skills of attending to and synchronizing with others, which involved not only carefully watching and listening to others' actions and musical contributions but also observing others' reactions to their own musical suggestions. Various methods were employed by the workshop facilitators to enable such effective collaboration between the participants, but all involved communicating through music rather than verbally, since many of the participants' special needs made verbal communication difficult. (In these circumstances, it is interesting to note the way in which music can communicate so effectively and enable learning and development non-verbally (Ansdell & Pavlicevic, in press; Magee, 2002)). All Gamelan workshops began with a warm-up session that involved participants standing in a circle and participating in a series of rhythmic games. This period was vital to the success of a workshop as during this period the workshop facilitators managed to set up – entirely through music - a strong sense of the group as a cohesive whole, of the value of attending to each other's contributions, and the idea of following each others' musical suggestions. The games (as well as the later experiences within the workshops themselves) focussed on encouraging the development of what might be seen as transactive musical communication – where participants attended to and built on previous musical suggestions made by others in offering their own musical contributions, rather than only following their own ideas or experimenting with the sounds their instrument could make. As Miell and MacDonald (2000) established in studies of children's collaborative compositions, the use of musical (and verbal) transactive communication was significantly positively correlated with successful outcomes for the task (as judged by a music teacher assessing the final compositions), and Kruger (1993) has suggested that this form of communication is generally found to be a component of successful collaborations.

The musicians at the workshops had to be enabled to integrate their own playing with the overall group in such a way that the individual elements came together to form a convincing whole. This process involved not only intense listening skills but attending to subtle features of the interaction such as non-verbal communication. Sustained effort was required by everyone to follow the variations in tempo that occurred. Initially participants were asked to repeat a rhythmic pattern being played on one of the Sarons (one of the instruments in the Gamelan orchestra). More complex patterns were played as the workshop progressed and there was opportunity for improvisation within the context of any piece of music. The participants also had the opportunity to select a particular part of the Gamelan to play. The emphasis was on group involvement and rhythmic awareness through musical participation while at the same time attempting to cater for the individual needs of participants. Both improvisational and compositional activities were utilized during these workshops. Thus, there was a sensitive interplay between the facilitators and the participants and this interaction between everybody taking part was a crucial feature of the collaborative dynamic.

In conclusion, musical activity (both listening and playing) can be seen as intrinsically social in nature. Not only do social processes crucially influence musical identities but music also has a relevance and importance for individuals that make it a particularly good site to further develop our knowledge of collaboration and learning. The chapter illustrates these points with reference to two empirical studies. Our transcripts from interviews with young musicians highlighted some of the key issues for young people doing identity work through their listening to and collaborative playing of music. Collaborative musical activity as a vehicle for developments in communication, music, and wider social awareness is also illustrated in our discussion of Gamelan music workshops for individuals with learning difficulties. The notion that we are all musical is not a vague utopian ideal, but rather the conclusion drawn by an increasing number of researchers interested in researching the foundations of musical behaviour (MacDonald, Hargreaves & Miell, 2002). Research into collaborative learning may find there are significant insights to be gained by studying the processes involved within the musical environment that young people find so important.

REFERENCES

Aldridge, D. (1996). *Music therapy research and practice in medicine: From out of the silence*. London: Jessica Kingsley.

Ansdell, G., & Pavlicevic, M. (in press). Musical companionship, musical community: Music therapy and the process and values of musical communication. In D. Miell, R.A.R. MacDonald, & D.J. Hargreaves (Eds.), *Musical communication*. Oxford: Oxford University Press.

Barrett, M. (2004). *Creative collaboration: Exploring the teaching-learning relationship in music composition*. Paper presented at the Society for Education, Music and Psychology Research International Conference, Milton Keynes, UK, April.

Cook, N. (1998). *Music: A very short introduction*. Oxford: Oxford University Press.

Collingwood, R. G. (1938). *The principles of art*. New York: Oxford University Press.

deNora, T. (1999). Music as a technology of the self. *Poetics: Journal of Empirical Research on Literature, the Media and the Arts, 26*, 1-26.

deNora, T. (2001). Aesthetic agency and musical practice: new directions in the sociology of music and emotion (pp.161-180). In P. Juslin & J. Sloboda (Eds.), *Music and emotion*. Oxford: Oxford University Press.

Fitzgerald, M., Joseph, A.P., Hayes, M., & O'Regan, M. (1995) Leisure activities of adolescent schoolchildren. *Journal of Adolescence, 18*, 349-358.

Frith, S. (1978). *The sociology of rock*. London: Constable.

Frith, S. (1981). *Sound effects: Youth, leisure, and the politics of rock 'n' roll*. New York: Pantheon.

Goodman, E. (2002). Ensemble performance. In J. Rink (Ed.), *Musical Performance: A guide to understanding* (pp.152-167). Cambridge: Cambridge University Press.

Hargreaves, D. J., & North A. C. (1997). *The social psychology of music*. Oxford: Oxford University Press.

Hartup, W. W. (1996) Cooperation, close relationships, and cognitive development. In W. M. Bukowski, A. F. Newcomb, & W. W. Hartup, (Eds.), *The company they keep - Friendship in childhood and adolescence* (pp.213-37). Cambridge: Cambridge University Press.

Hodges D.A., & Haack P.A., (1996). The influence of music on human behaviour. In D. A. Hodges (Ed.), Handbook of music psychology (pp.467–557). Texas: IMR.

Juslin, P., & Sloboda, J. (2001). *Music and emotion*, Oxford: Oxford University Press.

Kamptner, N. L. (1995). Treasured possessions and their meanings in adolescent males and females. *Adolescence, 30*, 301-318

Kruger, A. C. (1993). Peer collaboration: conflict, co-operation or both?. *Social Development, 2* (3), 165-182.

Larson, R., Kubey, R., & Colletti, J. (1989). Changing channels: early adolescent media choices and shifting investments in family and friends. *Journal of Youth and Adolescence, 18*, 583-599.

Lindsay, J. (1989). *Javanese Gamelan: Traditional orchestra of Indonesia*. Oxford: Oxford University Press.

Littleton, K., Miell, D., & MacDonald, R. (2002 September). *Music in the lives of young people*. British Educational Research Association Annual Conference. Exeter.

MacDonald R. A. R., & Miell, D. (2000). Creativity and music education: The impact of social variables. *International Journal of Music Education, 36*, 58-68.

MacDonald, R. A. R., & Miell, D. (2002). Music for individuals with special needs: A catalyst for developments in identity, communication and musical ability. (pp.163-178). In R.A.R. MacDonald, D.J. Hargreaves, & D. Miell (Eds.), *Musical Identities*. Oxford: Oxford University Press.

MacDonald, R. A. R., Hargreaves, D. J., & Miell, D. (2002). *Musical identities*. Oxford: Oxford University Press.

MacDonald, R. A. R., O'Donnell, P. J, & Davies, J. B. (1999). Structured music workshops for individuals with learning difficulty: an empirical investigation. *Journal of Applied Research in Intellectual Disabilities, 12*(3), 225 - 241.

Magee, W. (2002) Disability and identity in music therapy (pp.179-198). In R.A.R. MacDonald, D.J. Hargreaves, & D. Miell (Eds.), *Musical identities*. Oxford: Oxford University Press.

Miell, D., & MacDonald, R. (2000). Children's creative collaborations: The importance of friendship when working together on a musical composition. *Social Development, 36,* 348-369.

Miell, D., Littleton, K., & MacDonald, R. (2002 September). *Musical collaboration as identity work*. Paper presented at the BPS Developmental Section Annual Conference, Sussex.

Monson, I. (1996). *Saying something: Jazz improvisation and interaction*. Chicago: University of Chicago Press.

Moran, N. (2002). *Interaction in and as North Indian music*. Unpublished MPhil thesis, Queens' College, Cambridge.

North, A. C., Hargreaves, D. J., & O'Neill, S. (2000) The importance of music to adolescents. *British Journal of Educational Psychology, 70,* 255-272.

Overy, K. (1999). Can music really improve the mind? *Psychology of Music, 26,* 97–103.

Rauscher, F. (2000) *Musical influences on spatial reasoning: Experimental evidence of the Mozart effect*. Paper presented at the biannual conference of Society for Research in Psychology of Music and Music Education. Leicester, UK.

Rogoff, B. (1990). *Apprenticeship in thinking: Cognitive development in social context*. Oxford: Oxford University Press.

Sawyer, R. K. (2001). *Creating conversations: Improvisation in everyday discourse*. Cresskill, NJ: Hampton Press.

Sawyer, R. K. (2004 April). *Musical collaboration*. Paper presented at the Society for Education, Music and Psychology Research International Conference, Milton Keynes, UK.

Sloboda, J., O'Neill, S., & Tvaldi, A. (2001). Functions of Music in Everyday Life: An Exploratory Study Using The Experience Sampling Method. *Musicae Scientiae, 5,* 9-32.

Tarrant, M., North, A. C., & Hargreaves, D. J. (2000). English and American adolescents' reasons for listening to music. *Psychology of Music, 28,* 166-173.

Trevarthen, C. (2002). Origins of musical identity: Evidence from infancy for musical social awareness. In R.A.R. MacDonald, D.J. Hargreaves, & D. Miell (Eds.), *Musical identities*. Oxford: Oxford University Press.

Vass, E. (2003). *Understanding Collaborative Creativity: An observational study of the effects of the social and educational context on the processes of young children's joint creative writing*. Unpublished PhD thesis, The Open University

Willis, P. (1978). *Profane culture*. London: Routledge.

Zillmann, D. & Gan, S. (1997). Musical taste in adolescence. In D. J. Hargreaves & A. C. North (Eds.), *The Social Psychology of Music* (pp. 161-187). Oxford: Oxford University Press.

Chapter 9

CONFLICT AS A CHALLENGE TO PRODUCTIVE LEARNING DURING LONG-TERM COLLABORATION

Jaana Lahti, Anneli Eteläpelto and Sanni Siitari

INTRODUCTION

Conflict as a challenge to learning has been addressed in theories of learning and development in a number of ways. The Piagetian theory of intellectual development has suggested that cognitive conflict represents a fundamental condition for learning and intellectual development (Doise & Mugny, 1984).) Psycho-dynamic theories (Luft, 1970) of the individual's emotional and personal development have located conflict between different levels of awareness, with involvement of the affective and emotional aspects of the self (Agazarian, 1999). In addition to these individual-level conceptualisations of conflict, the topic has been addressed within theories of social psychology dealing with small-group interaction. In such theories, conflict has been analysed in terms of the social roles and power relations between participants.

Theories describing the social dynamics of group-processes have perceived conflict as an important aspect of the phase of 'storming', which is typically thought to emerge after the initial phase of group formation (Agazarian, 1999; Kieffer, 2001; Tuckman, 1965). The phase of storming, which can contain many affective conflicts between group members, is seen as useful for the development of a functional group, i.e. a group which would have enough cohesion and enough awareness of each participant's set of resources for effective task management. Indeed, the phase of storming has been suggested as necessary in all groups that utilize group processes. It has been thought that a successful resolution of the conflicts arising during the storming phase makes the group more productive. It is believed that the processes at work during and after conflict lead to productive interaction, with increased awareness of participants' roles, motives, interests and capacities. Thus, conflict has been perceived in some theories of group dynamics (Yalom, 1995) as so important that it has been the task of the group leader to promote conflict, through active confrontation with the group and its members.

In recent research on collaborative learning, group processes have been analysed mainly from the cognitive perspective, and from the perspective of knowledge building. Based on analyses of group discussion, questions have been asked about the contextual conditions necessary for shared knowledge building and high-level dialogue (Littleton & Light, 1999; Mercer, 2000). So far, it has been found that the necessary conditions for high-level knowledge construction include the participants having at least a shared knowledge base, with common ground for mutual understanding and perspective taking (Baker *et al.*, 1999). In addition, it has been found that any group task must be a genuine group task, and that it must include enough space for negotiation and argumentation in order to serve as a starting point for high-level learning (Arvaja et al., 2000; Schwartz, 1995; Dillenbourg, 1999). A further necessary condition for productive group work seems to be the participants' involvement and motivation to work towards completion of the task (Littleton & Light, 1999). Instructional programs and specific courses have also been implemented with a view to teaching social interaction skills and competencies for collaboration (Dawes et al., 2001; Pohjonen & Lindblom-Ylänne, 2002).

The main aim of such intervention has been the promotion of collaborative knowledge construction. However, with a few notable exception (e.g. Crook, 2000; Murphy, 2000), the social and emotional aspects of collaboration have in fact been neglected, and they are relatively under-theorized. Despite this, they have great importance in academic and professional domains such as in teaching and education, where social, emotional, and interaction competencies are of crucial importance. Moreover, wherever learning means constructing personal skills and corresponding professional identities, social and emotional aspects will also be important objects of learning. Teachers need to develop qualities such as a reflective orientation to their personal qualities and their interaction skills, and they need to become aware of the emotional aspects of interaction (Calderhead, 1996; Hargreaves, 1998; Oosterheet & Vermunt, 2001). Not much attention has been given to how teacher students might develop such competencies within an intensive small-group-based learning environment, or to how they might become more aware of these aspects of personal identity and socio-emotional competency.

In this study, we shall address the learning processes and outcomes of an intensive small-group-based learning environment. We shall present some results from a small-group-based pre-service teacher education program in which interactive and collaborative processes are utilized to promote learning. Our starting point in this is that the social and emotional aspects of collaboration and interaction are themselves important objects of learning. Based on an analysis of student interviews and observations of group functioning, we shall show how the social conflicts emerging in the first year of studies have been a central challenge – yet a challenge that can advance student teachers' professional competencies. We shall demonstrate how conflict is manifested in group work, and point out ways in which it can become a resource for learning.

The article is case-based, but we shall also point out certain theoretical aspects. In order to utilize intensive small-group-based learning environments for developing teacher students' professional identities, it is important to understand the group-level conditions and processes through which the learning takes place. Through this understanding we can gain a better grasp of how the resolution of conflicts can promote productive learning. In the study reported here, we inquire into the processes and situational conditions which cause emotional and social group processes to become manifested as social conflicts, with the aim of discovering how these can be used to promote the learning of personal, emotional and social competencies required for teachers. We also try to discover the solutions and understandings of conflict situations which seem most favourable to students' learning, and to examine the kinds of conflict situations that are less fruitful for learning.

We shall deal first of all with the kinds of conflicts that are most common in intensive group-based learning among teacher students. After that we shall examine certain necessary conditions of group-based learning which in our group seemed to be connected to the successful resolution of conflicts.

METHOD

Participants

In our analysis of group processes we focussed on a trainee teacher group of ten students, consisting of eight females and two males. The students were aged 20–40, and at the time of data collection they were starting their second year of university study. The students were enrolled on an experimental programme of teacher education at the University of Helsinki, Finland. Five students in the group had studied previously at the university, most of these on the traditional programme of teacher education which is taught in the same department.

A Small-group Based Learning Environment in Teacher Education

The experimental program, founded in 1998, was from its inception based on constructivistic ideas of learning and studying (Rauste-von Wright, 1999). An intensive small-group based method was used to promote the qualities needed in teachers, with an emphasis on developing skills in social interaction and group-based planning (Wirtanen et al., 2003). Intensive small-group-based work was initiated right from the start of the students' first year. In the experimental programme, students took educational psychology as the main subject of their Master's Degree studies in teacher education for primary school level. These studies would last five years altogether, with the group-based studies planned for the first three years.

The work in the small group was based on a process curriculum; which is based on the ideas of the teacher as a social agent and the concept of the teacher as a team worker whose main competencies will include the promotion of collaborative learning processes. Within the curriculum, the evaluation and assessment of learning processes and outcomes was seen as a continuous group-based process. It was envisaged that in this process students would work towards a specification of the goals and aims of learning on which their later learning would be based. Thus, the groups have considerable autonomy in defining such matters as the methods and ways of learning. The groups also have to reconcile individual and group-level goals while making plans for their studies.

The student group is scheduled to work together for three years in all. During the first year of their studies, the students have the task of constructing a group-based plan for their studies. The main content-specific themes for the first year include issues of social interaction and learning. During this first year, students also make short visits to schools, and analyse the schools from the perspective of whether they truly function as learning organizations.

At the beginning of the first year there is one main tutor and one assistant tutor. These individuals guide and tutor the group. During the first two months, the tutors are usually present at all group meetings. However, as the group gradually starts to take more responsibility and to rely more on its own ability to solve problems, the tutors move more into the background. The goal is that the group should become the agency referred to, so that the tutor becomes more like a consultant who is available when needed.

DATA GATHERING AND ANALYSIS

From the inception of the group, we collected a good deal of empirical data including videotapes of group sessions, evaluations and assessments of the group atmosphere and its communication culture, individual and group-level study plans and portfolios, electronic platforms for the group's e-mail messages, and learning diaries written by group members.

All of this material gives some necessary background information concerning the general conditions within the group. However, for this chapter we will focus on the data from the individual interviews conducted at the beginning of the students' second year of study. This interview material has been transcribed, and analysed using qualitative content analysis methods, the unit of analysis being the semantically meaningful unit (Chi, 1997). The authors read and re-read the transcribed interviews, and discussed the interpretations of the interviews together and also with the tutors who were in charge of the group during the first year of studies. The students from the group also read and gave comments on how the interviews were used, and the kinds of interpretations that could be derived from them (the students' comments are not reported in this chapter).

The study as a whole can be seen as an example of the kind of endeavour known as a design-based research study (Brown, 1992), i.e. a design experiment or teaching experiment (Cobb et al., 2003; Shavelson et al., 2003) which attempts to engineer innovative educational environments in authentic contexts. Our general theoretical underpinnings adhere to socioconstructivistic and sociocultural approaches to learning (Vygotsky, 1986) with the emphasis on subjective identity development (Edwards, 2002; Eteläpelto, 2003; Eteläpelto & Collin, 2004; Murphy, 2000; Phillips, 2002).

The interviews used for the study were conducted at the beginning of the second year of studies, after the summer holiday. Both the interviewers were unknown to the students, in the sense that they had not worked with them as either tutors or researchers during the first year of the studies (i.e. the period mainly discussed in the interviews).

In the following sections we shall use direct quotations from the students' own evaluations, as presented in the interviews. These are used to shed light on the students' conceptions of group processes, and to illustrate their conceptualizations of the learning processes they went through during their first year of studies.

CONFLICT AS A PART OF THE GROUP PROCESS

Conflict situations of various kinds were among the most challenging situations encountered by the students in this small-group environment. This was clear from our observations as monitors and tutors of the group, and also from students' own evaluations of their first year studies. In their evaluations, most of the students indicated that social conflicts were very clearly present, and that they had demanded a lot of energy from the group. The conflicts seemed to have a good deal of personal significance for individual students; they also had an important influence on group atmosphere and coherence, and on the extent to which the group could work together effectively.

In the interviews, our students brought out the multi-layered aspects of conflicts. They perceived conflicts as a challenge for the continued functioning of group work. They also mentioned that the conflicts had affected them personally.

Although the conflict often manifested itself as individual irritations and emotional contradictions between two persons, there are very complex interaction between the individual's emotional regulation, dyadic relationships and group level interaction and atmosphere. Erik demonstrates the awareness of the different levels where conflict emerged and was manifested and emerged in the group as follows:

Extract 1

"... if I say to the person in question who's been annoying me in some way; for example, that he or she annoyed me; well is that sufficient, or is that a matter for the whole group, and pretty much the kinds of things we've actually had in our group, that there is some kind of schism between two people, then it affects the activities of the whole group, because there aren't ten separate persons forming a group and a group formed from them, as separate individuals, but those ten people making up the group, and if there is a clique somewhere in there, then it becomes something visible in the group as well."

Although conflicts mostly manifested themselves as aspects of social interaction, personified and taking place between group members as interpersonal issues, conflicts also manifested themselves in terms of content-specific argumentation between different views and conceptions. In our group, disputes arose from opinions representing different ideological notions, concerning ethical issues or questions of tolerance towards ideological differences.

In addition to these conceptual conflicts, the shared planning of the group curriculum caused many conflict situations. Later in the year, the division of responsibilities and tasks among group members was addressed on several occasions. And in addition to these more inherent conflicts, there were conflicts that emerged between the group and its external context.

Conflicts Concerning Responsibilities and the Division of Tasks

Research on cooperative and collaborative learning has demonstrated that the division of tasks and the management of responsibilities have often been among the most difficult problems for groups working together (Littleton & Häkkinen, 1999). In addition, a problem frequently mentioned has been that of taking other group-members' perspectives into account. In our group (long-term, intensive), this was indeed a factor which became a source of irritation and conflict. After the first year of the group-based studies, Helen described difficulties of this kind in a very illuminating way:

Extract 2

"... [the fact is that] we're together... and that has proved to be the most difficult factor... for the whole... – you know – activity when not everyone takes equal responsibility for that being together... I have always felt that our biggest obstacle is ... that people aren't always able to understand each other and that people have a certain preconception about each other... so that perhaps it in a way – you know – in a particular way that slows down that collaboration and through that the learning together was so, in a way, difficult, that you had to give everything you could so that something could go forward at all."

In this statement, Helen demonstrates the awareness of the twofold task of the group, which includes working on cohesion and continuity in order to stay together at all, as well as the effective completion of learning tasks. Questions of task division and responsibilities were much discussed right from the initial formation of group, as were questions of commitment. A large number of important rules, norms and useful practices, such as writing diaries after every meeting, were developed as solutions for these conflicts. The group also sought to develop rules on how participants could compensate for any absence from group meetings.

Conflict Concerning Different Conceptions and Ideologies

In the interviews, our students described one of the most significant conflicts as emerging between opposing ideologies. These manifested themselves in terms of differing religious beliefs, and attitudes towards sexual orientations. The differences obliged group members to specify and elaborate their world views. In this sense the group served as a platform in which the students could further specify their conceptions of what it was to be a professional teacher, and from this examine various facets of themselves: their prior knowledge, their beliefs concerning learning, their epistemic conceptions, their image of humanity, and diverse ethical issues in teaching and education. From such a specification, a degree of tolerance of different conceptions became more or less a necessity. In our case, ethical and ideological differences were discussed right from the first year of study. This differs from the more typical situation in which ethical and ideological issues become objects of professional learning only in the later stages of pre-service education, once the students' professionalism is more developed (Ropo, 2004).

Although there were many serious disagreements and arguments between people holding different conceptions and views, the students seemed to understand that they needed to have tolerance for the conceptions of others. Indeed, the value of individual ways of thinking was highly valued in the group. Nelda describes this in the following way:

Extract 3

"... if the group ends up... with some kind of really grand consensus, general agreement on things, I think that too is rather alarming."

In developing a professional identity as a teacher, Nelda demonstrates an awareness of the responsibility of all group members to make their own voice heard in the group. If conflict is going to promote professional learning for teachers, it needs to be manifested through all members of a group voicing their views – however different – rather than aiming for consensus.

CONFLICTS AS A RESOURCE FOR LEARNING

Conflict as a resource for learning can be described from both individual and group viewpoints. Our students faced conflicts right from the beginning of the first year of their studies, perceiving the conflicts mainly as individual affective states or as disagreements between some of the group members. In our tutoring of the group we took it as our goal to increase students' awareness about how these personal issues were connected to group level issues. From the beginning of the group's activities, our aim was to offer students tools to handle the conflict situations, through raising their awareness of group level issues. This involved providing assessment tools concerning group atmosphere and communication styles. The group was taught to face the problems manifested as conflicts, and from this to develop as a group. To achieve the learning goals, the group was encouraged to take into account affective and emotional needs on the one hand, and the needs of efficiency in task completion on the other (Bion, 1961).

Research on collaborative learning has suggested that a significant advantage of collaborative - as compared to individual – learning emerges through processes in which individuals have to articulate and explicate their own thoughts (Roschelle & Teasley, 1995; Schwartz, 1995). This is believed to increase individuals' metacognitive awareness of their own thinking, and to give them a better grasp of each other's perspectives. In our group, the conflict situations seemed to promote similar challenges: the students were obliged to articulate and make visible their own position and relationship to the group. Conflict situations also seemed to have the benefit of challenging the most silent members of the group to explicate their opinions regarding the conflict.

It has to be emphasized that although the conflict situations had particular significance in terms of getting students to articulate their opinions, non-conflict situations too had a strong motivating effect in getting students to clarify and present their individual views. The very existence of the group itself, perceived as a carefully listening audience, seemed to promote this aspect. Helen describes below the effect of the group in her case:

Extract 4

".. I'm basically quite a shy person and almost all my life have been picked on at school and been a bit isolated, so when I suddenly got into a situation where someone really seriously, or like it's, there are nine people who listen to you and you can talk and join the group and you can just be there, I don't know, it was tremendously nice... it was a really good feeling.."

The main sources and processes of learning which were taking place during the first year of the group emerged from their shared planning of the group curriculum and from the need for individuals to explicate their own views and positions in the group. These will be discussed below.

Learning from Shared Planning of the Group Curriculum

In constructing the group curriculum, the group had to specify the goals and objects of learning and to choose appropriate methods for studying. In this process, the students also had to reconcile their individual and group level interests, and these might be in conflict. The group had to negotiate intensively if it was to succeed in achieving such a reconciliation.

When students evaluated their learning experiences they perceived the reconciling of group-level and individual interests as important learning experiences during their first year of study. Peter described the first year learning experience as follows:

Extract 5

"... everyone has their own personal interests to look after, so the question is how to get them fitted in with the other interests in the group. That must have been absolutely the number one learning thing we've gone through in the group."

The group was encouraged to do everything possible to negotiate a group-level plan. It was suggested that this would help students to utilize their background knowledge and also increase the commitment of individuals to the group plan. The emotional aspects bound up with commitment are thought to be of a great value in promoting the cohesiveness of a group. These aspects are also connected with becoming an agent, and with become a subject of one's own teachership. If these aspects are not promoted by group collaboration, important aspects of professional learning for teachership will be neglected. If, on the other hand, the group is used to advance identity development as teachers, through the identity negotiation that occurs during the process of giving feedback on the subjects' interaction skills and on their other distinctive qualities, it will be useful for professional learning.

In the shared planning of the group curriculum, students had to face differences in each others' previous knowledge. This might have caused emotional confusion arising from the comparison of this with that of other members of the group. Ella describes such comparison as follows:

Extract 6

"... when I've had a certain idea about myself, feeling now I know a bit more about things than the others and so on, it's really good when you've noticed that, that, well okay the others know a bit about these things too; so after that I've faced a kind of little personal crisis, on the other hand..."

In the long run, students' awareness of other group members' knowledge and intellectual resources is important. Such awareness is needed if the group is developing to utilize these resources while constructing an authentic learning community.

Learning Arising from the Need to Explicate
One's Conceptions and Positions in the Group

In this study, we have not addressed the possible changes taking place in individuals' conceptual understanding (Limon, 2001). Rather, we have addressed emotional processes and social skills that may promote such changes in small-group based learning. In the interviews in which the students spoke about their learning experiences in the group, they often referred to various kinds of social interaction skills. In the learning of such skills, students perceived the intensive small-group experience as crucial: Nelda describes her experience in the following way:

Extract 7

"to latch onto some people's... well... ways of interacting, so that you see that someone... somebody handles things in a totally different way; and for some people that kind of forceful way, for example like shouting or something is immediately a bad thing, whereas for me on the other hand it's terribly natural..., it's characteristic of me to, you know, speak quickly or speak loudly or express myself strongly; so they've been real, you know, learning experiences when I've just... well... had to get the message that I can't do that in the group because this is a group, and here one has had to, you know, take everybody's styles into consideration."

The extract above shows how the student was able to reflect on her communication skills and on their development in context of a small group. The student-teachers seemed to understand that social skills – which include listening carefully to others and also being alert to non-verbal cues – are important skills for future teachers. Student Nelda demonstrates this understanding:

Extract 8

"... for a teacher one important skill in thinking is the ability to put oneself in somebody else's position, some kind of identification and sensitivity, the sensitivity to notice many kinds of – you know – wordless messages too, because... not everything is said and you really need to..., for example, if you want to carry through some kind of learning that would somehow originate from the learners themselves, you need to be quite a sensitive person to see what they're actually interested in and the topic that really matters to them at that moment."

The conflict situation can be hypothesized to promote the emergence of individual subjectivities. This will take place through the process in which group members are challenged to explicate their conception and position in relation to the conflict. In our group, the rule regarding expressing one's opinion was perceived as an indication of tolerance in which no limitations were set on the individual's freedom of expression. However, the rule was not made explicit until after the first year and it came more or less as a surprise to the group that such a rule had existed. The avoidance of explicitness was deliberate: during the first year, such direct rules would themselves have been perceived as a kind of regulation governing people's freedom of expression. It was in fact this freedom that was perceived as the most important value in the group.

THE COLLABORATIVE CONDITIONS ALLOWING PARTICIPANTS TO LEARN FROM CONFLICTS

The Time Dimension

Prior studies on collaboration have emphasized the importance of the history of the group. Mercer (2000) suggests that a shared group history is a necessary condition for a learning community to emerge. Short-term groups do not have the kind of shared history which would give participants an understanding of the different stages of group development and the shared experiences included in them. Shared experiences can be used in the future as objects of reference, for example in planning the future goals and activities of the group.

The critical aspects in promoting productive learning are thus connected with the time dimension. Our students regarded long-term working together as important both for emotional support and for task completion. Student Erik describes this as follows:

Extract 9

"... the further the studies have progressed of course the better It [studying in the group] works because the group is more welded together, and there's that certain degree of support, so that even if I myself stumble at a given point, in my own way of thinking, then there's someone who reaches out his hand to me and lifts me up."

Deep-level growth and transformation in one's professional identity can occur in the course of long-term collaboration. But it takes time for such real collaboration to develop. Our students thought it vitally important that the group process should last for more than just one year. If a group is aware of having sufficient time available, it seems that the group itself can regulate the level of the conflict and the depth at which it is to be handled. (Öystilä, 2001)

In the interviews, our students were relieved that the group was going to meet again after the first year and after the summer vacation. They made a connection between the first year that had just passed and their studies to come, wishing that they could have even more time to work on the conflict during the following year. This indicates the desire of the group to include learning about the group process within the overall time available for study. One student, Ella, made clear the importance of having opportunities to work out conflicts in the year to follow, and her awareness of time as a factor:

Extract 10

"..yes, it [group process] remained a little bit open, I mean that the situation is OK and it stayed that way, for it had got like that before the summer vacation, but definitely there is still some underlying thing, and undercurrents, so many things that I'm really awaiting with interest this coming autumn."

Emotional Security within the Group

Studies on therapy groups have emphasized the importance of feeling emotionally safe within the group. Although our intensive long-term groups are not therapy groups, an emotionally secure atmosphere appeared to be an important condition for addressing personally meaningful issues in the group. The element of trust and the ability to listen to others were often mentioned in interviews as being important for students' learning. The point is made by Nelda, below:

Extract 11

"...those kinds of... tensions that are present come up in a subordinate clause and one sees ... that they're there – so they really make it more difficult to be in the group, and because of that also to learn. And then one thing too ... if you don't feel safe in the group, if you don't... feel that you're becoming fully accepted and if you get the feeling that there's somebody checking how you do things, what you say and how you behave, it makes things much more difficult too."

Emotional aspects were not only expressed by words but were also communicated through non-verbal acts such as tears, blushing, sweating, movements of eyebrows, gestures and other bodily movements. These aspects of non-verbal communication were discussed a good deal during the group meetings.

SOME PITFALLS CONCERNING LEARNING FROM CONFLICTS

If the conflict is neglected or if the group simply falls apart when it encounters conflict, the process of learning to collaborate is aborted. In addition, an inability to reflect on group-level phenomena may lead merely to a search for a scapegoat in identifying a 'guilty party' (i.e. the person who had the role of triggering the conflict). Such an inability to reflect is destructive to any sense of security within the group and can prevent any movement towards working out conflicts.

Rogoff et al. (1996) have noted that in productive collaboration the participants' varying roles are determined according to their understanding of the particular task in question, and that differing responsibilities serve as resources for task completion. From the socio-emotional point of view, long-term collaboration can fail if participants get stuck in their roles, or if they express only the emotions that the group regards as appropriate.

Azmitia (2000) has raised the question of whether group members who have collaborative relationships are better able to regulate each other's negative affects and frustrations because they can read each other's emotional cues. But on the basis of our interviews, one could hypothesize that close relationships between group members might actually postpone the appearance of conflict and hence constructive solutions.

The discussion culture of the group was noted by the tutors as one drawback in the process, in the sense that the mentality within the group seemed on occasion to become too self-centred. The demand that everyone should be allowed to express immediately his or her feelings of irritation without considering the feelings of others received adverse comments. In addition, stress was caused by the collision of individual differences – the 'chemistry' – and the ways in which individuals tried to or were unable to regulate it as heard from Helen:

Extract 12

"it's so dependent on that chemistry between people... when it's not only that we do research and do work but it's that we are together... and that has proved to be the most difficult thing for... the whole, you know, activity... and when not everyone takes an equal amount of responsibility for that being together then I... felt terrible stress."

Negative emotions connected to the conflict situation do not necessarily mean negative feelings between collaborators. If the various aspects can be separated out, there may be the option of using positive relationships between collaborators to prevent frustration in difficult tasks. However, the opposite outcome is also possible. Azmitia (2000) has described both positive and negative implications, referring to cases where frustration at a difficult task has resulted in a breakdown between two friends. Yet sometimes working with others generates positive emotions and reduces negative affect in such a way as to prevent irreparable breakdowns caused by frustrations. And sometimes these conflict-based frustrations that have caused breakdowns can be productive, if the partners can use them to work out an idea. More often than not, working with others generates positive emotions and can reduce negative actions (Azmitia, 2000). In any case, focusing on this positive aspect can help to promote positive solutions when conflicts arise.

CONCLUSIONS AND DISCUSSION

This study aimed to discover how the conflicts emerging in an intensive small-group based learning environment helped student teachers to develop the emotional and social competencies they will need as teachers. We wanted to know what was learned through the solution of conflicts, and to determine the conditions promoting successful learning in such situations.

Our analysis showed that the various kinds of conflict situations during the first year of the group's operation did indeed have implications for participants' learning. The conflict situations functioned as real challenges for group members, obliging them to make visible and specify their beliefs, their prior conceptions, and their relationship to the group. Without the conflicts and their resolutions, the need for students to articulate positions in relation to these issues might have remained unspoken.

Another important learning outcome emerging from the conflicts and their solution is increased awareness of the difficulties of collaboration, and especially the difficulties involved in dividing up tasks and responsibilities, and awareness of the task of turning the group into an effective learning community. The solutions to problems of task division and responsibilities emerged as group-level outcomes that led to novel working practices: for example, group sessions were tape-recorded, and the absent member was obliged to write a report on group decisions as compensation for his/her absence. What, then, are the necessary conditions for conflict to become useful for productive learning? On the basis of our experience, a number of conditions seem to apply.

First of all, the nature of the group task seems to be important, in the sense that the task should be sufficiently open and require genuine participation from all members if it is to be completed. In our study, the planning of the group curriculum seemed to function well as a task, since it demanded that all participants should look after their own personal interests and make use of their prior knowledge. An open planning task also seemed to offer enough space for negotiation – something which is necessary in order to involve everyone and to ensure real commitment to the task.

In creating individual and group plans, students learned to negotiate between individual- and group-level interests. Such negotiations are needed in all kinds of group-based learning and working environments. At its best, negotiation between individual and shared goals can promote students' awareness of their professional identities and the contextual aspects related to it. The relational identity (Murphy, 2000) of a student in a learning group can thus become manifest: the identity actually takes its form as a consequence of such negotiations. For our part, we hope that this will also offer tools for continuous identity work in those future communities in which our students will eventually work as teachers.

Mercer (2000) defines an ideal learning community as a place where individuals have access to each other's intellectual resources. If we widen this definition to include also emotional and social aspects, we could posit an ideal learning community as a place in which individuals have access to each other's emotional and social resources – these resources being what in fact causes the group to continue as a unified group. We would further suppose that it is the actual articulation by individuals of their perceived relationship to each other that will help them to become aware of each other's social and emotional resources, including for example the commitments and responsibilities that people are willing to take on.

In our situation – a small group existing over an extended period – the students used the group as a stage on which preconceptions and misunderstandings could be brought into view. At the same time, the group functioned as an environment for learning social skills and for developing a reflective orientation towards one's personal ways of communicating. Furthermore, the negotiations on the group curriculum created a basis for reciprocal commitment and responsibility. This is a necessary precondition for the building of a community (Wenger, 1998).

Based on our analysis, we suggest that conflict is a phenomenon which can decrease or increase identification with the group, make prevailing standards visible and reveal the emotional and social factors at work behind factual statements. Thus, conflicts involving the relationship between an individual and the group may actually have the function of making explicit and thereby defining the relationship between the individual and the group. At the same time, conflict may promote the identification of common ground through which the personal goals, interests, and motives of others may be perceived. In this way, conflict contains the potential for increased mutual understanding.

From another perspective, that of problem-solving, a conflict can be seen as itself providing an authentic problem for solution. In order to complete the learning projects, the group has to confront the conflict and develop a solution of some kind. In our case, the awareness of group atmosphere and the culture of communication during meetings became in themselves tools for dealing with conflict. These were not the only tools, however, since conceptual tools were offered also through the books and articles on group processes that students were advised to read.

On the basis of the interviews and our own observations, it seemed that conflict situations were particularly empowering to those individuals who had previously been most withdrawn in the group. In this sense, one could say that the conflict either forced or encouraged silent participants to voice their opinions and to define their position relative to the group.

Our own students made their ideas clear regarding the contextual conditions which make social conflict productive for promoting competencies. The conditions involve the existence of a long-term group with enough time for reflection and emotional security as part of the group atmosphere. The long term existence obliged the group to attend to two issues: (i) effective completion of immediate tasks in hand, and (ii) taking care of the emotional and social issues impacting on group cohesion. In short-term groups, where cohesion is not such a pressing problem, the need to become aware of the group's emotional and social dynamics is not so much emphasized. A long-term group offers a remarkable opportunity to learn about emotional and social dynamics – those aspects which truly represent the submerged part of the iceberg that is group functioning. Hence, a long-term collaborative group offers a unique chance to elaborate one's own 'ideal self' as it appears under the scrutiny of one's peers.

On the basis of our experience, we would argue that in a long-term, small-group-based learning environment, social and emotional aspects are of crucial importance in creating, maintaining and promoting the community as a lasting entity. Conversely, it appears that long-term communities by their nature offer an advantageous environment for becoming aware of and learning to manage the social and emotional aspects of collaboration.

From the perspective of professional learning, we would suggest that an intensive long-term small group, in which participants have to face different kinds of conflicts, does indeed offer a productive environment for developing the professional subjectivities of future teachers. A collaborative learning community can benefit from the growth of its members' individual subjectivities, and the interplay of the voices of individual learners (Eteläpelto, 2003; Phillips, 2002; Walkerdine, 1997). This has been our experience also with the group in the present study. By becoming attuned towards the viewpoints of others in the group, group members can give support to each individual's process of becoming a subject of his or her own learning and taking on the professional identity of teacher.

AUTHORS' NOTE

This chapter is, to a large extent, the product of our interactions with students, colleagues, and fellow researchers. We are deeply indebted to all the students we interviewed, who shared their opinion with us and gave us the opportunity to explore our ideas with them. Our interactions with colleagues in seminars and in the Research Centre of Educational Psychology stimulated our thinking. We owe a great intellectual debt to Karen Littleton, who made a substantial scientific contribution – helping us identify key analytic themes. We would also like to thank Mr Donald Adamson for help with the translation.

REFERENCES

Agazarian, Y. M. (1999). Phases of development in the systems-centered ™ psychotherapy group. *Small Group Research, 30,* 1, 82–107.

Azmitia, M. (2000). Taking time out from collaboration: Opportunities for synthesis and emotion regulation. In R. Joiner, K. Littleton, D. Faulkner, & D. Miell (Eds.), *Rethinking Collaborative Learning.* Great Britain: Free Association Books.

Arvaja, M., Häkkinen, P., Eteläpelto, A., & Rasku-Puttonen, H. (2000). Collaborative processes during report writing in a science learning project: The nature of discourse as a function of task requirements. *European Journal of Psychology of Education, 15,* 455–466.

Baker, M., Hansen, T., Joiner, R., & Traum, D. (1999). The role of grounding in collaborative learning tasks. In P. Dillenburg (Ed.), *Collaborative learning: Cognitive and computational approaches* (pp.31–63). Oxford: Elsevier Pergamon.

Bion, W. R. (1961). *Experiences in groups.* London: Tavistock Publications.

Brown, A. L. (1992). Design experiments: Theoretical and methodological challenges in creating complex interventions in classroom settings. *Journal of the Learning Sciences, 2,* 141–178.

Calderhead, J. (1996). Teachers: beliefs and knowledge. In D. C. Berliner & R. C. Calfee (Eds.), *Handbook of educational psychology.* (pp.709–725). New York: MacMillan Library Reference.

Chi, M. (1997). Quantifying qualitative analyses of verbal data: A practical guide. *The Journal of the Learning Sciences, 6* (3), 271 –313.

Cobb, P., Confrey, J., diSessa, A., Lehrer, R., & Schauble, L. (2003). Designing experiments in educational research. *Educational Researcher, 32*, 9–13.

Crook, C. (2000). Motivation and the ecology of collaborative learning. In R. Joiner, K. Littleton, D. Faulkner, & D. Miell (Eds.), *Rethinking Collaborative Learning.* Great Britain: Free Association Books.

Dillenbourg, P. (Ed.) (1999). *Collaborative learning: Cognitive and computational approaches.* Amsterdam: Pergamon, Elsevier Science.

Dawes, L., Mercer, N., & Wegerif, R. (2001). *Thinking together: Classroom activities for key Stage 2.* Birmingham: Questions Publishing Company.

Doise, W., & Mugny, G. (1984). *The social development of the intellect.* Oxford: Pergamon Press.

Edwards, A. (2002). *Contriving the formation of professional minds; Conflicting cultures in the preparation of beginning teachers.* Paper presented at the symposium of American Educational Research Association (AERA), New Orleans, USA.

Eteläpelto, A. (2003). Commentary on Roger Säljö's presentation 'Technologies, knowing and the transformation of work practices: what do we need to learn?' In J. Kirjonen (Ed.), *Knowledge work and occupational competence,* (pp. 23–29). Jyväskylä, Finland: University Printing House.

Eteläpelto, A., & Collin, K. (2004). From individual cognition to communities of practice; theoretical underpinnings in analysing professional learning and expertise. In E. Boshuizen, H. Gruber, & R. Bromme (Eds.), *Professional learning: Gaps and transitions on the way from novice to expert.* Kluwer Academic Publishers.

Hargreaves, A. (1998). The emotional practice of teaching. *Teaching and Teacher Education, 14*, 835–854.

Kieffer, C. C. (2001). Phases of group development: A view from self psychology. *Group, 25* (1/2), 91–105.

Limon, M. (2001). On the cognitive conflict as an instructional strategy for conceptual change: A critical appraisal. *Learning and Instruction, 11*, 357–380.

Littleton, K., & Häkkinen, P. (1999). Learning together: Understanding the processes of computer-based collaborative learning. In P. Dillenbourg (Ed.), *Collaborative learning: cognitive and computational approaches* (pp.20–31). Oxford: Elsevier Pergamon.

Littleton, K., & Light, P. (Eds.) (1999). *Learning with computers: Analysing productive interactions.* London: Routledge.

Luft, J. (1970). *Group processes; an introduction to group dynamics.* Palo Alto, CA: National Press Books.

Mercer, N. (2000). *Words and minds: How we use language to think together.* London: Routledge.

Murphy, P. (2000). Gender identities and the process of negotiation in social interaction. In R. Joiner, K. Littleton, D. Faulkner, & D. Miell (Eds.), *Rethinking collaborative learning* (pp.139–160). London, New York: Free Association Books.

Oosterheert, I. E., & Vermunt, J. D. (2001). Individual differences in learning to teach: relating cognition, regulation and affect. *Learning and Instruction, 11*, 133–156.

Phillips, D. K. (2002). Female preservice teachers' talk: Illustrations of subjectivity, visions of nomadic space. *Teachers and Teaching: Theory and Practice, 8*(1), 9–27.

Pohjonen, S., & Lindblom-Ylänne, S. (2002). Challenges for teaching interaction skills for law students. *The Law Teacher, 36*(3), 294–306.

Rauste–von Wright, M.-L. (1999 August). *A learning based teacher training project. The first two years*. Paper presented at the conference of European Association for Research on Learning and Instruction (EARLI), Göteborg, Sweden.

Rogoff, B., Matusov, E., & White, C. (1996). Models of teaching and learning: Participation in a community of learners. In D. Olson, & N. Torrance (Eds.), *The handbook of education and human development: New models of learning, teaching, and schooling* (pp.388–415). Cambridge, England: Blackwell.

Ropo, E. (2004). Teaching expertise: Empirical findings on expert teachers and teacher development. In E. Boshuizen & H. Gruber, & R. Bromme (Eds), *Professional learning: Gaps and transitions on the way from novice to expert*. Kluwer Academic Publishers.

Roschelle, J., & Teasley, S. (1995). The construction of shared knowledge in collaborative problem solving. In C. O'Malley (Ed.), *Computer supported collaborative learning* (pp.69–97). Berlin: Springer-Verlag.

Schwartz, D. L. (1995). The emergence of abstract representations in dyad problem solving. *The Journal of the Learning Sciences, 4*(3), 321–354.

Shavelson, R. J., Phillips, D. C., Towne, L., & Feuer, M. J. (2003). On the science of education research studies. *Educational Researcher, 32,* 25–28.

Tuckman, B. (1965). Developmental sequences in small groups. *Psychological Bulletin, 63*(6), 384–399.

Vygotsky, L. S. (1986). *Thought and language*. Cambridge: MIT Press.

Walkerdine, V. (1997). Redefining the subject in situated cognition theory. In D. Kirschner & J. A. Whitson (Eds.), *Situated cognition: Social, semiotic, and psychological perspectives* (pp.57–70). Mahwah, NJ: Lawrence Erlbaum Associates, Inc.

Wenger, E. (1998). *Communities of practice: Learning, meaning and identity*. Cambridge University Press.

Wirtanen., S., Eteläpelto., A., & Lahti, J. (2003). Ryhmäprosessien hyödyntäminen luokanopettajakoulutuksessa – mahdollisuudet ja haasteet [Utilization of group processes in class teacher education – possibilities and challenges]. In H. Sinevaara-Niskanen, & R. Rajala (Eds.), *Kasvatuksen yhteisöt – uupumusta, häirintää vai yhteisöllistä kasvua?* Lapin yliopiston kasvatustieteellisiä julkaisuja 3, Rovaniemi, Finland: Finnish Educational Research Association. (http://ktk.urova.fi/kasvatuspaivat/opettajat_koulutuksessa_ja_tyossa.htm)

Yalom, I. D. (1995). *Theory and practice of group psychotherapy*. New York: Basic Books.

Öystilä, S. (2001). Ryhmäprosessin hyödyntäminen yliopisto-opetuksen haasteena [The utilization of group processes as a challenge for higher education]. In E. Poikela, & S. Öystilä, S. (Eds.), *Oppiminen on tutkimista ja tutkiminen oppimista [Learning is studying and studying is learning]* (pp. 30–50). Tampere, Finland: Tampere University Press.

Chapter 10

PREREQUISITES FOR CSCL: RESEARCH APPROACHES, METHODOLOGICAL CHALLENGES AND PEDAGOGICAL DEVELOPMENT

Päivi Häkkinen, Maarit Arvaja and Kati Mäkitalo

INTRODUCTION

One of the essential requirements in a rapidly changing society is to prepare learners for participation in socially organized activities and in building socially shared expertise. An earlier focus on purely individual cognition has shifted to an emphasis on the social construction of knowledge (Greeno, 1998), and new learning environments are often based on collaborating and sharing expertise (Dillenbourg, 1999). Collaborative learning is nowadays a fashionable phenomenon, but collaboration among students in various learning settings (e.g. in classrooms) is a much more complex phenomenon than has often been thought. Let's just think about the following typical cases of collaborative learning in small-group working described by Salomon (1992):

- "Free-rider effect": one team member just leaves it to the others to complete the task.
- "Sucker effect": a more active or capable member of a team discovers that (s)he is taken for a free ride by other team members.
- "Status sensitivity": active or capable members take charge and have an increasing impact on the team's activity and products.
- "Ganging up on the task": team members collaborate with each other to get the whole task over with as easily and as quickly as possible.

This makes one ask why true collaboration does not happen more often? What makes it so difficult? And yet why is it, on the other hand, so tempting as a spontaneous phenomenon among small children? This article will first discuss the central concepts and recent research trends in the area of collaborative learning. Further, the sometimes contradictory findings of research on Computer-Supported Collaborative Learning (CSCL) are presented. And finally, methodological, as well as pedagogical and contextual prerequisites and constraints are considered.

FROM INDIVIDUAL MINDS TO COLLABORATIVE KNOWLEDGE CONSTRUCTION

In the history of research on collaborative learning, several researchers have anchored their research on two main traditions: namely Vygotsky's (1978) sociocultural approach and neo-Piagetian ideas of socio-cognitive conflict (e.g., Doise 1985). Later notions of social aspects of learning vary from perspectives focusing on individuals that participate in group activities (Anderson, Reder & Simon, 1997) to perspectives focusing on groups that are made up of individuals (Greeno, 1998). In addition to individual, cognitive perspectives on learning and expertise (Anderson et al., 1997), the focus of recent learning research has moved more to examining how experts typically function in social contexts such as in teams and communities of practice. Theories referred to as situated cognition describe training as the process of entering a community of practice through peripheral legitimate participation (Lave & Wenger, 1991). It is assumed that learning becomes more effective when an individual participates more centrally in a community of practice. In other words, learning is not viewed as the mere acquisition of concepts or skills but as the appropriation of the culture specific to the target community.

Anderson *et al.* (1997) and Greeno (1998) have framed conflicts between cognitive and situated learning theories. The main difference between cognitive and situated perspectives can be seen in their interpretations of social processes. Lave and Wenger (1991) have argued that participation in social practices does not only influence otherwise autonomous psychological processes, but that learning is synonymous with changes in the ways that an individual participates in social practices. In the situated approach, participation into social practice or context is not restricted to face-to-face interaction with others. Instead, all individual actions are viewed as elements of a broader system of social practices. Therefore, individuals can be seen as participating in social practices even when they act in physical isolation from others (Cobb & Bowers, 1999; Forman, 1996). Furthermore, theories of distributed cognition emphasize a process in which cognitive resources are socially shared in order to extend individual cognitive resources or to accomplish something more than what individuals could achieve alone. In this approach, cognitive processes can be distributed, not only between social actors, but also between social actors and physical artefacts of learning environments (Hutchins, 1995; Salomon, 1993). However, while emphasizing knowledge as an aspect of practice, discourse and activity, what is often overlooked is the question of how much or how well organized is the knowledge that individual students acquire. Besides the description of activities and discourse processes, we should also consider the knowledge acquisition of individual students in collaborative learning environments (Lehtinen, Hakkarainen, Lipponen, Rahikainen & Muukkonen, 1999).

While emphasizing the meaning of social context in learning, researchers also often struggle with issues related to the unit of analysis. Cobb and Yackel (1996) have claimed that the choice in any particular case is pragmatic and depends on the purpose at hand. In sociocultural theories, the unit of analysis is groups of individuals participating in broad systems of practices (Lave & Wenger, 1991). Socio-constructivist theories, on the other hand, focus on individual students' seeking after meaning and understanding while simultaneously viewing reasoning as an act of participation in evolving communal practices (Palincsar, 1998).

While some studies concentrate on understanding how individuals become members of a large community as they do in apprenticeship studies (Rogoff, 1990), other studies focus more on how members of cognitive communities can construct shared understanding in the first place (Roschelle & Teasley, 1995). For instructional design of powerful learning environments, it is also important to recognize the qualitatively distinct ways in which individual students participate in particular practices (Cobb & Bowers, 1999). In addition, students must have a way to participate in the practices of the classroom community. If they cannot participate, they are not members of the community any more. Therefore, what is needed now is to better understand how individuals' mental and developmental processes relate to social and situational factors that influence collaborative learning and performance.

It has become clear that the line between individual and social processes of learning is blurring, and the main message of many researchers is that we should see individual minds in interaction with group understandings (Stahl, 2002). In research on collaborative learning, we should also call for approaches that bring together different streams of research. One example of such convergence is presented by Baker, Hansen, Joiner and Traum (1999). In order to understand the role of grounding in collaborative learning tasks, they combined sociocultural approaches and cultural-historical activity theory (Cole & Engeström, 1993) with cognitive studies of collaborative problem solving which focus on the mechanisms by which partners maintain a shared and mutual understanding of the task at hand (Roschelle & Teasley, 1995; Schwartz, 1995). Further, to understand how two partners maintain some mutual understanding (grounding process), they referred to linguistic studies (mainly in pragmatics). According to their perspective, culture is the language that subjects have to develop to interact efficiently about the task at hand. Furthermore, conversational and other interactional conventions of communities are well-coordinated patterns of participation in social practices. It can also be hypothesized that systematic development in the ability to participate in practice (e.g. turn-taking and other means of using language) occurs over a long period of time.

DEFINING THE CONCEPT OF COLLABORATIVE LEARNING

There is a consensus among researchers that collaboration involves the construction of meaning through interaction with others and can be characterized by a joint commitment to a shared goal (Littleton & Häkkinen, 1999). Furthermore, collaborative learning is often defined in a way that necessitates participants to be engaged in a co-ordinated effort to solve a problem or perform a task together. This coordinated, synchronous activity is the result of a continued attempt to construct and maintain a shared conception of a problem (Roschelle & Teasley, 1995).

One of the emerging themes in research that is focusing on collaboration as a co-ordinated activity is research on grounding processes and social negotiations. In the grounding phase of co-ordinated problem solving, the participators negotiate common goals, which means that they do not only develop shared goals but they also become mutually aware of their shared goals. Common goals form the basis for joint work, and negotiation of common goals is part of the interactive process of grounding. The grounding process has been described in the settings that consider communication as a form of collaborative action (Brennan, 1998; Clark & Brennan, 1991; Clark & Schaefer, 1989). During the grounding process, individuals build and maintain common ground by sharing mutual understanding, knowledge, beliefs, assumptions and pre-suppositions (Brennan, 1998; Clark & Schaefer, 1989). Participants exchange evidence of their understanding and of the fact that they are talking about the same thing until they have reach the common ground (Clark & Schaefer, 1989). If shared understanding is incomplete, the continued interaction might be threatened, because too much effort and time are needed for the re-construction of shared understanding.

There is empirical evidence demonstrating the positive effects of social interaction for individual learning in organized problem solving settings (Light, Littleton, Messer & Joiner, 1994; Roschelle & Teasley, 1995). Collaborative learning situations seem to provide a natural setting for self-explanation and explaining to others as well as other forms of knowledge articulation, which have been shown to demonstrate positive effects for learning (Ploetzner, Dillenbourg, Preier & Traum, 1999). Collaborative cognitions can also promote the use of abstract representations among collaborators more efficiently than individuals working alone on the same problem (Schwartz, 1995). An explanation for this is that the collaborative task places demands on partners to create a common representation that bridges the multiple perspectives they hold individually on the problem structure and situation. This representation tends to be at a more abstract level than the representations formed from any single viewpoint.

Focus on Process and Context of Collaboration

Recent research interests have shifted away from analysing the outcomes and products of collaborative work or from establishing whether collaborative learning is more effective than individual learning. Instead of treating collaborative learning as a single learning mechanism, the focus has been directed more towards analysing interactions as a means of gaining insight into the processes of collaborative learning. The aim of such analyses is to identify what constitutes productive collaborative activity (Littleton & Häkkinen, 1999). Recent research on collaborative learning has also called for more exact use of terminology related to the specific forms of collaboration (Dillenbourg, 1999). Collaborating participants will learn if they generate certain collaborative activities (argumentation, explanation, mutual regulation etc.), which in turn trigger learning mechanisms such as knowledge elicitation and reduced cognitive load. Baker (2002) has suggested that there is a need to move beyond simple demonstrations of the advantage of group conditions and focus on studies that seek to understand the processes of collaborative interaction itself and its contribution to learning.

In addition to the cognitive variables, recent research trends have also emphasized the importance of affective and motivational variables of collaborative learning (Crook, 2000; Joiner, Littleton, Faulkner & Miell, 2000; Stahl, 2003). For example Crook (2000) has pointed out that current conceptions of collaboration focusing on cognitive skills do not pay attention to collaboration as something that is motivated. It is relevant, for example, to ask what then makes students engage in collaborative activities and how the circumstances for potential collaborations are enhanced. Furthermore, does seeking after shared meaning require intentional activity or does it happen spontaneously? What makes playful and informal collaborations so appealing? Examining these kinds of questions presupposes a strong emphasis on situated and sociocultural theories of learning.

Crook (2000) has introduced the idea of the ecology of collaboration, which refers to certain forms of productive joint engagement in learning. He uses this term to focus on the settings in which collaborations are organized, in other words actual spaces within which collaborations are either constrained or resourced. This kind of ecological perspective helps us to understand which circumstances will lead people to work together well and which circumstances will lead them to prefer to work alone. He argues that the ecology is about the immediate environments within which collaborative learning is supported – the artefacts, the technologies, and the spaces for acting. Also Stahl (2003) has emphasized contextual features of collaborative learning by suggesting that the situation reflects previous social activities, and is transformed by current interactions and projections of the future. To sum up, while aiming to understand the diverse viewpoints on collaborative learning, we have to consider an extremely complex set of variables: cognitive, social, emotional, motivational and contextual variables interacting with each other in a systemic and dynamic manner.

COMPUTER-SUPPORTED COLLABORATIVE LEARNING (CSCL) AND COMPUTER-SUPPORTED CO-OPERATIVE WORK (CSCW)

Research on collaborative learning and the use of Information and Communication Technologies (ICT) has been integrated in the emerging research area called Computer-Supported Collaborative Learning (CSCL), which aims to create powerful learning environments with the aid of groupware and communication technologies (Koschmann, 1996). Two traditions that have strongly contributed to the development of CSCL tradition are research on co-operative (e.g. Forman & Cazden, 1985) and collaborative (e.g. Dillenbourg, 1999) learning as well as research on Computer-Supported Cooperative Work (CSCW) (Dourish, 1998). Although there is no unified theory of CSCL, the common feature shared by the diverse standpoints is a focus on how collaborative learning supported by technology can enhance peer interaction and work in groups, and how collaboration and technology facilitate the sharing and distributing of knowledge and expertise among community members. CSCW, on the other hand, focuses on the collaborative nature of work supported by groupware. The latter tradition has excluded the issues of learning, but has provided the basis for developing groupware tools for learning purposes.

Guribye, Andressen and Wasson (2003) have outlined the organisation of interaction in distributed collaborative learning. They have particularly contrasted the field of CSCL to the field of CSCW. In Computer-Supported Cooperative Work, the focus of attention is put on cooperative practices, and cooperative work is mainly seen as an activity in which workers are interdependent of each other (Schmidt & Bannon, 1992). Schmidt (2001) has also claimed that compared to Computer-Supported Collaborative Learning, discordant interests and motives among workers in CSCW are often relegated to the background. Furthermore, in a typical cooperative work setting, the workers perform the same tasks everyday and work is a routine activity exploiting domain-specific skills. In contrast to learning situations, making sense is also viewed as effortless, and outcomes and actions of others are seen as predictable (e.g. Heath & Luff, 1996). CSCW systems support sharing and archiving of knowledge that is an aggregate of the contributions of cooperative individuals (Guribye et al., 2003).

The field of CSCL, on the other hand, focuses on the functioning of collaborative groups when they are building knowledge that is the shared creation and property of the group (Stahl, 2002). Compared to workers, students form a more diverse population with unstable membership and no shared objective. In CSCL communities, the process of collaboratively constructing the shared knowledge and arriving at instructions of what actions to perform is important (Stahl, 2002). It is also worth noting that making sense of each other's actions is a constant struggle, and the issues of interests and motives are important ones to attend to (Guribye et al., 2003).

CSCL tools usually offer a fairly open collaboration space where learners are in the centre of the communication process (Bourguin & Derycke, 2001). An important feature of open spaces for collaboration is the need to negotiate the flow of actions, which emphasizes the importance of coordination and awareness of each other's support needs in distributed collaborative learning more than in distributed collaborative working. When participants negotiate a shared objective, they need to understand the conditions for collaboration and rules for coordinating the collaborative effort at the same time as solving the learning tasks (Guribye et al., 2003). The situation becomes even more complex when people meet in distributed learning groups who are previously unknown to each other. It is hard to reproduce the creation of mutual understanding or shared values and goals in a distributed learning environment because of the absence of visual information and non-verbal cues (Järvelä & Häkkinen, 2002). At the beginning of an interaction there will be some degree of common ground between individuals once they establish that they share some aspects of the same cultural background, but nevertheless participants with a shared culture still need to build and maintain common ground during the interaction itself in order to explore new aspects of their mutual knowledge (Baker et al., 1999).

Benefits and Constraints of CSCL

Positive results have been received in CSCL experiments, and many advanced technical infrastructures (such as CSILE and Knowledge Forum, created by Scardamalia and Bereiter, 1994) for fostering higher-level processes of inquiry-based interaction have been developed (e.g. Scardamalia & Bereiter, 1994). For example, shared workspaces and communication tools can provide a natural setting for explanation, knowledge articulation, argumentation and other demanding cognitive activities (Häkkinen, 2001; 2002). They can also enable sharing and distributing of the cognitive load and bring thinking out into open (Miyake, 1986). In other words they can function as a collective memory for a learning community, helping the storage of the history of the knowledge construction process for revisions and future use. Recent studies have revealed that in connection with corresponding pedagogical practices, CSCL environments can facilitate higher-level cognitive achievements such as critical reasoning, explaining, generating one's own research questions, setting up and improving one's own intuitive theories, and searching for scientific information (Scardamalia & Bereiter, 1994; Hakkarainen, Lipponen & Järvelä, 2002).

There is also research demonstrating the possibilities that technology can provide to support, structure and re-organize shared problem solving in small groups around the same computers. Many researchers have argued that this way computer can offer a mediating artefact that fosters optimal conditions for reciprocal interaction (Järvelä, Bonk, Lehtinen & Lehti, 1999).

Results of studies of computer support for collaborative learning have, however, been contradictory, and several studies have indicated collaborative learning to be a complex phenomenon and difficult to realize in our institutionalized schooling (Baker, 2002; Häkkinen, 2001). Collaborative processes are often over-generalized and simplified by treating collaborative learning either as a single psychological process or as a pedagogical method. It is worth remembering that interacting in small groups around computers in face-to-face situations for one or two hours differs in many respects from the situation where hundreds of people participate in distributed on-line courses during one year. Furthermore, any tools for communication and correspondence are called 'collaboration tools' (Roschelle & Pea, 1999). The problem is that if almost any interaction situation is called collaborative, it is difficult to judge whether and when people learn from collaborative situations (Dillenbourg, 1999; Littleton & Häkkinen, 1999).

According to Kreijns, Kirschner and Jochems (2001), social interaction is taken for granted in CSCL environments. There is the assumption that interaction will automatically happen in CSCL environments, nevertheless many studies report that discussion threads are short and participation rates are low. Furthermore, it is typical for collaborative interaction in CSCL environments to deal with descriptive and surface-level knowledge instead of finding deeper explanations for the phenomena under study (Järvelä & Häkkinen, 2002; Arvaja, Rasku-Puttonen, Häkkinen & Eteläpelto, 2003). One of the problems seems to be in participants' engagement with web-based work (Oliver & Shaw, 2003). A crucial problem also related to the process of collaboration is the difficulty of making inquiry questions that would evoke elaborated explanations. Further on, particular challenges are related to reaching reciprocal understanding, shared values and goals in networked environments (Järvelä & Häkkinen, 2002).

To reach and maintain an adequate level of common ground, which is essential in collaborative activities (Dillenbourg, 1999), the participants need to be aware of 1) the presence of others, 2) the process of diagnosis; participants have to think what they are saying and also how they are saying it, and 3) feedback; participants need to show their understanding in some form of feedback (Baker et al., 1999; Brennan, 1998). Participants also have to maintain common ground during the interactive processes to be able to deal with emerging new aspects of the common situation or task (Baker et al., 1999). For maintaining common ground, individuals need to be willing and able to continue the interaction, observe a message in the web-based environment, understand the message, and react and respond to it. All these elements – contact, perception, understanding and attitudinal reaction – are linked together; an attitudinal reaction between persons cannot take place unless the message is first understood (or at least interpreted), which requires perception and contact (Baker et al., 1999; Clark & Schaefer, 1989).

According to Brennan (1998), even if the feedback consists of a simple acknowledgement that the message has been noticed and read, it is necessary for avoiding undue doubts of some participants that others are not reading the messages they post, and also for reaching mutual understanding. In the study of Mäkitalo, Häkkinen, Järvelä and Leinonen (2002), the results reveal that in deeper level discussions, supporting feedback was more frequent. The results suggest that positive feedback encourages people to participate in discussion and thereby engage in the group actively contributing to the web-based learning environment (see Hara, Bonk & Angeli, 2000). Furthermore, McMillan (1996) proposes, that the members of the community need support and to be able to offer support to others in times of need. According to Wegerif (1998), creating a sympathetic sense of community is a necessary first step for collaborative learning.

Also Kreijns *et al.* (2002) suggest that the social dimension of social interaction is not considered enough, instead there has been an emphasis on the role of the cognitive dimension. For example, Wegerif (1998) noted that for truly collaborative learning it is necessary that people feel that they can reveal their own feelings, assumptions and knowledge without being treated badly by their fellow participants in the web-based environment. Also Oliver and Shaw (2003) suggest that the enthusiasm and expertise of the tutor might foster engagement even more than e-moderating skills in the web-based conferences. It seems that also the enthusiasm of the fellow students might foster engagement, especially in small group contexts, which is an important ingredient in ensuring that interaction continues successfully (Mäkitalo, Pöysä, Järvelä & Häkkinen, 2004). Altogether it can be concluded that at best, CSCL environments can support cognitive, social, motivational and affective processes of learning, but also that constraints can be related to any of these viewpoints.

Methodological Challenges for Studying CSCL

In research on computer supported collaborative learning, typical research methods have been content analysis of networked discussions, different types of discourse analysis or quantitative summaries of computer-generated databases. Some researchers have also used social network analysis methods to visualize students' participation and roles in computer-supported collaborative learning. They report that a social network analysis is an appropriate method for studying structures of interaction and relationships in a technology based learning environment (Nurmela, Palonen, Lehtinen & Hakkarainen, 2003). These methods offer insight into the content and quantity of students' networked discussions as well as interaction structures at a general level. However, these methods are not capable of revealing the *quality* of collaborative processes in the network, or the ways in which collaborators shape each other's reasoning processes, neither do they reveal individuals' personal experiences or interpretations.

There is growing evidence that learning in collaborative learning environments cannot be explained as only the result of specific abilities but appears as the product of complex and dynamic interactions between cognitive, social, affective and motivational variables (Pintrich, Marx & Boyle, 1993). What is needed now is to better understand how individuals' mental processes relate to social and situational factors that influence cognitive performance and learning. Consequently, new methods are needed to capture the process of collaborative interaction and its contribution to learning. Furthermore, these methods should be able to understand the process of computer-supported collaboration as part of the wider social context of the participants.

While seeking methodological accounts for capturing e.g. the processes of collaborative learning or community-building, we should bear in mind that the analysis of collaborative interaction cannot be isolated from the context in which it is embedded (Crook, 1999). To find out more about the nature of collaborative learning processes and what promotes collaborative knowledge building, different features affecting learning must be studied in the context of the joint activity, i.e. in relation to and in the form they occur in different learning environments. Also Salomon (1997) has stated that it is the whole culture of learning environments with several intertwined variables that influence learning in a fundamental way. Thus, the analysis of CSCL settings should go beyond networked interaction by including the activities in face-to-face settings as well as taking into account the previous history of the students participating in the learning activity (Crook, 2000). The unit of analysis should be the whole activity system of tasks, artefacts, interactions, symbols, social practices, roles and community of practice, which absorbs the shared knowledge of the group (Stahl, 2003).

Pedagogical and Contextual Prerequisites for CSCL

The most optimistic views suggest that global networks and the use of computers for intellectual communication will further enhance and expand the ways in which humans connect, communicate, and create a sense of community. However, more critical questions about the possibilities and qualities of virtual learning environments have been presented earlier in this chapter. The biggest challenge of researchers and practitioners is to develop innovative, multi-faceted pedagogical practices and models, utilizing ICT that can support students in their efforts for deeper-level learning and interaction.

However, on the basis of the research on collaborative learning and CSCL, several lessons can be learned concerning the pedagogical and contextual prerequisites for successful collaborative learning situations. Some of the most important processes in human communication, like the creation of mutual understanding, shared values and goals, are hard to reproduce in a Web-based environment (Järvelä & Häkkinen, 2002). The absence of visual information (e.g. missing facial expressions and non-verbal cues) increases the social distance between the participants (Järvelä & Häkkinen, 2002; Rovai, 2000). Therefore, it is important to consider how common ground could be created and maintained in virtual environments (Mäkitalo et al., 2002). According to Dillenbourg and Traum (1999), grounding can occur at the linguistic level as well as at the cognitive level. Furthermore, Veerman (2000) proposes that grounding can take place also at the level of understanding thematic information in relation to certain task and learning goals. The recent research suggests that it is essential to consider also the role of socio-emotional level of grounding in future collaboration situations (Mäkitalo et al., 2004).

One crucial determinant of successful collaboration is related to the nature of learning task (Arvaja et al., 2000). Unlike fact-seeking questions and unambiguous tasks, open-ended and discovery tasks (Cohen, 1994) have been seen to promote joint problem solving and reasoning. Too obvious, or unambiguous tasks do not leave space for disagreements, misunderstandings, questions, negotiations, explanations and arguments. Therefore, one of the biggest challenges in instructional design and support of CSCL is to provide real group tasks and contexts that enhance questioning, explaining and other forms of knowledge articulation. Also when considering the role of cognitive conflict in learning, it is important to bear in mind that it is not the conflict itself that is crucial and beneficial in terms of learning, but it is the process of *solving* the conflict.

It has also been suggested that in instructional design of collaborative learning tasks and scenarios, the possibilities of cognitive diversity and participants' positive interdependency on each other should be taken into account. By utilizing cognitive diversity, the kinds of learning environments can be designed where participants have different perspectives and overlapping areas of expertise, but they also share expertise from different areas (Brown & Campione, 1994).

Dillenbourg (2002) has recently called for approaches that help us to structure collaborative learning situations due to the fact that free collaboration does not systematically produce learning. Collaboration can be promoted by structuring the collaborative process beforehand in order to favour the emergence of productive interactions. One way to structure interactions is to design predefined collaboration scripts into CSCL environments. These scripts are sets of instructions prescribing how students should form groups, how they should interact and collaborate and how they should solve the problem (Dillenbourg, 2002; Hoppe & Ploetzner, 1999). Scripts can be seen as a way to influence collaboration that is complementary to tutors' or mentors' attempts to regulate interactions afterwards.

According to Dillenbourg (2002), the effectiveness of scripts is based on the idea of integrating usually separate activities: individual, cooperative, collaborative and collective activities. Furthermore, scripts enable the integration of co-present activities and computer-mediated activities. They also introduce a time frame in distance education where students often lack landmarks for their time management. The other side of the coin in designing well-defined scripts is the risk of over-scripting collaboration. Predefined scripts can disturb the richness of natural interaction and problem solving processes. Furthermore, this kind of 'educational engineering' approach can lead to reaching for effectiveness at the cost of the genuine notion of collaborative learning (Dillenbourg, 2002). The balance between the benefits and risks of structuring collaboration depends on the core mechanism that the script is based on, in other words how the designer aims to foster productive interactions and learning. For example, drawing on participants' cognitive diversity and knowledge interdependency fosters different mechanisms than purely vertical task division in collaborative groups.

CONCLUSIONS

In this chapter, we first examined the recent research on collaborative learning and Computer-Supported Collaborative Learning (CSCL). On the basis of this, several methodological and pedagogical challenges were raised. In addition to the need for pedagogical and contextual models, the point was made that the collaborative tools themselves should be designed to take into account more effectively the challenges of human communication and learning in networked environments. From the viewpoint of technology, networked environments used in different learning environments just need to provide a learner with a relevant platform for communicating and sharing knowledge. Instead, more advanced technological solutions to support many problematic issues in virtual interaction, such as the difficulties in reaching shared understanding, in coordinating different perspectives or in establishing the sense of co-presence especially in distributed teams, are still missing (Gutwin & Greenberg, 1999; Häkkinen, Järvelä & Dillenbourg, 2000; Munro, Höök & Benyon, 1999).

It can also be assumed that collaborative learning sets new demands on students and teachers by challenging the traditional practices and support structures of educational settings. For example, learning from doing complex, challenging and authentic projects collaboratively requires resourcefulness and planning by the student, new forms of knowledge representation in school, expanded mechanisms for collaboration and communication, and support for reflection and authentic assessment (Häkkinen, 2001). Computers can be seen as essential elements in re-structuring social interaction and knowledge building, and social construction of knowledge is also strongly associated with the creation of new kinds of learning culture (Hakkarainen et al., 2002; Scardamalia & Bereiter, 1994). Although this culture offers real opportunities from the point of view of learning, it is not realized immediately or without problems. It can be hypothesized that the traditions, structures and processes of institutionalized schooling do not support collaborative forms of learning. However, learning environments that are seen as beneficial from the viewpoint of learning require reasoning, evaluation, critical discussion and transparent learning processes. If CSCL environments inspire these activities, they can serve a crucial role in innovating new instructional practices that depend on more open sharing of ideas.

Although the scientific community has regarded the principles of CSCL as highly promising, they are extremely difficult to implement among teachers and other practitioners. In addition, one of the critical points in CSCL research is the scaling up of the models of intensive pilot experiments – it has proved to be extremely difficult to implement schemes more broadly (Sinko & Lehtinen, 1998). Although teachers and students have access to computers, technology is not intensively used, at least not in pedagogically advanced ways. Good practices usually emerge in pilot projects supported by researchers rather than modifying and revising these practices to be part of a new culture of schooling (Hakkarainen et al., 2002; Lipponen, 2001). New sustainable pedagogical practices require long-term commitment to develop them in close collaboration between researchers and practitioners, and gradually they can trigger changes in the learning culture.

AUTHORS' NOTE

The study is supported by grant from the Academy of Finland (project no. 50986).

REFERENCES

Anderson, J. R., Reder, L. M., & Simon, H. A. (1997). Situative vs. cognitive perspectives: From versus substance. *Educational Researcher, 26*(1), 18-21.

Arvaja, M., Häkkinen, P., Eteläpelto, A., & Rasku-Puttonen, H. (2000). Collaborative processes during report writing of a science learning project: The nature of discourse as a function of task requirements. *European Journal of Psychology of Education, 15*(4), 455-466.

Arvaja, M., Rasku-Puttonen, H., Häkkinen, P., & Eteläpelto, A. (2003). Constructing knowledge through a role-play in a web-based learning environment. *Journal of Educational Computing Research, 28*(4).

Baker, M. (2002). Forms of cooperation in dyadic problem-solving. In P. Salembier & H. Benchekroun (Eds.), *Cooperation and complexity in sociotechnical systems* (Vol. 16, pp. 587-620). Paris: Hermes.

Baker, M., Hansen, T., Joiner, R., & Traum, D. (1999). The role of grounding in collaborative learning tasks. In P. Dillenbourg (Ed.) *Collaborative learning: Cognitive and computational approaches* (pp. 31-63). Pergamon: Oxford.

Bourguin, G., & Derycke, A. (2001 March). *Integrating the CSCL activities into virtual campuses: Foundations of a new infrastructure for distributed collective activities.* Proceedings of ECSCL '01. Maastricht, the Netherlands.

Brennan, S. E. (1998). The grounding problem in conversations with and through computers. In S. R. Fussell & R. J. Kreuz (Eds.) *Social and cognitive approaches to interpersonal communication* (pp. 201-225). Mahwal, NJ: Erlbaum.

Brown, A., & Campione, J. (1994). Guided discovery in a community of learners. In K. McGilly (Ed.) *Classroom lessons: Integrating cognitive theory and classroom practice* (pp. 227-270). Cambridge, MA: MIT Press.

Clark, H. H., & Brennan, S. E. (1991). Grounding in communication. In L. B. Resnick, J. Levine, & S. D. Behrend (Eds.) *Perspectives on socially shared cognition* (pp. 127-149). Washington, DC: American Psychological Association.

Clark, H. H., & Schaefer, F. S. (1989). Contributing to discourse. *Cognitive Science*, 13, 259-294.

Cobb, P., & Bowers, J. (1999). Cognitive and situated learning perspectives in theory and practice. *Educational Researcher, 18*(2), 4-15.

Cobb, P., & Yackel, E. (1996). Constructivist, emergent, and sociocultural perspectives in the context of developmental research. *Educational Psychologist, 31*, 175-190.

Cohen, E. (1994). Restructuring the classroom: Conditions for productive small groups. *Review of Educational Research, 64*(1), 1-35.

Cole, M., & Engeström, Y. (1993). A cultural-historical approach to distributed cognition. In G. Salomon (Ed.) *Distributed Cognitions: Psychological and educational considerations.* (pp. 1-46). Cambridge, MA: Cambridge University Press.

Crook, C. (1999). Computers in the community of the classrooms. In K. Littleton & P. Light (Eds.) *Learning with computers.* Analysing productive interaction (pp. 102-117): London: Routledge.

Crook, C. (2000). Motivation and the ecology of collaborative learning. In R. Joiner, K. Littleton, D. Faulkner & D. Miell (Eds.) *Rethinking collaborative learning.* Free Association Books: London.

Dillenbourg, P. (1999). Introduction: What do you mean by "'collaborative learning'"? In P. Dillenbourg (Ed.) *Collaborative learning: Cognitive and computational approaches* (pp. 1-99). Pergamon: Oxford.

Dillenbourg, P. (2002). Over-scripting CSCL: The risks of blending collaborative learning with instructional design. In P. A. Kirschner (Ed.) *Three worlds of CSCL. Can we support CSCL* (pp. 61-91). Heerlen, Open Universiteit Nederland.

Dillenbourg, P., & Traum, D. (1999). Does a shared screen make a shared solution? In C. Hoadly & J. Roschelle (Eds.) *Proceedings of the third conference on computer supported collaborative learning* (pp. 127-135). California: Stanford University.

Doise, W. (1985). Social regulations in cognitive development. In R. Hinde, A-N. Perret-Clermont, & J. Stevenson-Hinde (Eds.) *Social relationships and cognitive development* (pp. 294-308). New York: Oxford University Press.

Dourish, P. (1998). Software architectures for CSCW. In Beaudouin-Lafon (Ed.) *Computer-supported cooperative work* (pp. 195-219). London: Wiley.

Forman, E. (1996). Forms of participation in classroom practice: Implications for learning mathematics. In L. Steffe, P. Nesher, P. Cobb, G. Goldin, & B. Greer (Eds) *Theories of mathematical learning* (pp. 115-130). Hillsdale, NJ: Erlbaum.

Forman, E.A., & Cazden, C.B. (1985). Exploring Vygotskian perspectives in education: The cognitive value of peer interaction. In J. Wertsch (Ed.) *Culture, communication, and cognition: Vygotskian perspectives* (pp. 323-347). Cambridge: Cambridge University Press.

Guribye, F., Andressen, E.F., & Wasson, B. (2003). The organisation of interaction in distributed collaborative learning. *Proceedings of CSCL 2003 conference. Kluwer Academic Publishers.*

Greeno, J. G. (1998). The situativity of knowing, learning and research. *American Psychologist, 53*(1), 5-26.

Gutwin, C., & Greenberg, S. (1999). The effects of workspace awareness support on the usability of real-time distributed groupware. *ACM Transactions on Computer-Human Interaction, 6*(3), 243-281.

Hakkarainen, K., Lipponen, L., & Järvelä, S. (2002). Epistemology of inquiry and computer-supported collaborative learning. In T. Koschmann, N. Miyake, & R. Hall (Eds.) CSCL2: *Carrying forward the conversation.* Mahwah, NJ: Erlbaum.

Hara, N., Bonk, C.J., & Angeli, C. (2000). Content analysis of online discussion in an applied educational psychology course. *Instructional Science, 28,* 115-152.

Heath, C., & Luff, P. (1996). Line control and passenger information on the London Underground. In Y. Engeström & D. Middleton (Eds.) *Cognition and communication at work* (pp. 96-129). Cambridge: Cambridge University Press.

Hoppe, U. H., & Ploetzner, R. (1999). Can analytic models support learning in groups. In P. Dillenbourg (Ed.) *Collaborative-learning: Cognitive and computational approaches* (pp. 147-168). Oxford: Elsevier.

Hutchins, E. (1995). *Cognition in the wild.* Cambridge, MA: The MIT Press.

Häkkinen, P. (2001). Collaborative learning in technology-supported environments – two cases of project-enhanced science learning. *International Journal of Continuing Engineering Education and Life-Long Learning,* 11(4/5/6), 375-390.

Häkkinen, P. (2002). Challenges for design of computer-based learning environments. *British Journal of Educational Technology,* 33(4), 465-474.

Häkkinen, P., Järvelä, S., & Dillenbourg, P. (2000). Group Reflection Tools for Virtual Expert Community – REFLEX Project. In B. Fishman & S. O'Connor-Divelbiss (Eds.) *Proceedings of the Fourth International Conference of the Learning Sciences.* Mahwah, NJ: Erlbaum, 203-204.

Joiner, R., Littleton, K., Faulkner, D., & Miell, D. (2000). (Eds.). *Rethinking collaborative learning.* Free Association Books: London.

Järvelä, S., Bonk, C. J., Lehtinen, E., & Lehti, S. (1999). A theoretical analysis of social interactions in computer-based learning environments: Evidence for reciprocal understandings. *Journal of Educational Computing Research, 21*(3), 359-384.

Järvelä, S., & Häkkinen, P. (2002). Web-based Cases in Teaching and Learning – the Quality of Discussions and a Stage of Perspective Taking in Asynchrounous Communication. *Interactive Learning Environments,* 10(1), 1-22.

Koschmann, T. (1996). Paradigm shifts and instructional technology: An introduction. In T. Koschmann (Ed.) *CSCL: Theory and practice of an emerging paradigm* (pp. 1-23). Mahwah, NJ: Lawrence Erlbaum Associates.

Kreijns, K., Kirschner, P., & Jochems, W. (2002). The Sociability of Computer-Supported Collaborative Learning Environments. *Educational Technology & Society*, 5(1), 7-22.

Lave, J., & Wenger, E. (1991). *Situated learning: Legitimate peripheral participation.* Cambridge: Cambridge University Press.

Lehtinen, E., Hakkarainen, K., Lipponen, L., Rahikainen, M., & Muukkonen, H. (1999). *Computer Supported Collaborative Learning: A Review.* CL-Net Project. TSER.

Light, P., Littleton, K., Messer, D., & Joiner, R. (1994). Social and communicative processes in computer-based problem solving. *European Journal of Psychology of Education,* 9(1), 93-109.

Lipponen, L. (2001). *Computer-supported collaborative learning: From promises to reality.* Doctoral dissertation, University of Turku, Series B, Humanoira, 245.

Littleton, K., & Häkkinen, P. (1999). Learning together: Understanding the processes of computer-based collaborative learning. In P. Dillenbourg (Ed.) *Collaborative learning: cognitive and computational approaches* (pp. 1-20). Pergamon: Oxford.

McMillan, D. W. (1996). Sense of community. *Journal of Community Psychology*, 24(4), 315-325.

Miyake, N. (1986) Constructive interaction and the iterative process of understanding. *Cognitive Science*, 10, 151-177.

Munro, A., Höök, K., & Benyon, D. (1999). *Social navigation of information space.* Berlin: Springer.

Mäkitalo, K., Häkkinen, P., Järvelä, S., & Leinonen, P. (2002). The mechanisms of common ground in the web-based interaction. *The Internet and Higher Education*, 5(3), 247-265.

Mäkitalo, K., Pöysä, J., Järvelä, S., & Häkkinen, P. (2004). *Socio-emotional level of grounding in a Web-based conference of small group context.* Submitted.

Nurmela, K., Palonen, T., Lehtinen, E., & Hakkarainen, K. (2003). Developing Tools for Analysing CSCL Process. *Proceedings of CSCL 2003 conference.* Kluwer Academic Publishers.

Oliver, M., & Shaw, G. P. (2003). Asynchronous discussion in support of medical education. *Journal of Asynchronous Learning Networks*, 7(1), 56 – 67.

Palincsar, A. S. (1998). Social constructivist perspectives on teaching and learning. *Annual Review of Psychology*, 49, 345-375.

Pintrich, P. R., Marx R. W., & Boyle R. A. (1993). Beyond cold conceptual change: The role of motivational beliefs and classroom contextual factors in the process of conceptual change. *Review of Educational Research*, 63, 167-199.

Ploetzner, R., Dillenbourg, P., Preier, M., & Traum, D. (1999). Learning by explaining to oneself and to others. In P. Dillenbourg (Ed.) *Collaborative learning: Cognitive and computational approaches* (pp. 103-121). Pergamon: Oxford.

Rogoff, B. (1990). Apprenticeship in thinking: Cognitive development in social context. Oxford: Oxford University Press.

Roschelle, J., & Pea, R. (1999). Trajectories from today's WWW to a powerful educational infrastructure. *Educational Researcher*, 28(5), 22-25.

Roschelle, J., & Teasley, S. (1995). The construction of shared knowledge in collaborative problem solving. In C. E. O'Malley (Ed.) *Computer supported collaborative learning.* Heidelberg: Springer- Verlag.

Rovai, A. P. (2000). Building and sustaining community in asynchronous learning networks. *The Internet and Higher Education* 3(4), 285-297.

Salomon, G. (1992). *What does the design of effective CSCL require and how do we study its effects?* ACM SIGCUE Outlook. (http:// www.cica.indiana.edu/ cscl95/outlook/ 62_Salomon.html).

Salomon, G. (Ed.) (1993). *Distributed cognitions. Psychological and educational considerations.* Cambridge, MA: Cambridge University Press.

Salomon, G. (1997 August). *Novel constructivist learning environments and novel technologies: Some issues to be concerned with.* Invited Keynote Address presented at the 7th European Conference for Research on Learning and Instruction, Athens.

Scardamalia, M., & Bereiter, C. (1994). Computer support for knowledge-building communities. *The Journal of the Learning Sciences, 3*, 265-283.

Schmidt, K. (2001 July). Computer-supported cooperative work — and learning. *Proceedings of Travail coopératif et NTIC en environnements ouverts de formation, FREREF workshop.* Universitat Oberta de Catalunya, Barcelona.

Schmidt, K., & Bannon, L. (1992). Taking CSCW seriously: Supporting articulation work. *Computer Supported Cooperative Work (CSCW): An International Journal, 1*(1), 7-40.

Schwartz, D. L. (1995). The emergence of abstract representations in dyad problem solving. *The Journal of the Learning Sciences,* 4(3), 321-354.

Sinko, M., & Lehtinen, E. (1998). *The challenges of ICT in finnish education.* Helsinki: Atena Kustannus.

Stahl, G. (2002). Contributions to a theoretical framework for CSCL. *Proceedings of Computer Supported Collaborative Learning* (CSCL 2002) Boulder, Colorado, USA.

Stahl, G. (2003). Building Collaborative Knowing: Elements of a Social Theory of Learning. In J. W. Strijbos, P. Kirschner, & R. Martens (Eds.) *What we know about CSCL in higher education.* Kluwer, in press.

Veerman, A. (2000). *Computer-supported collaborative learning through argumentation.* Utrecht: Interuniversity Center for Educational Research.

Vygotsky, L.S. (1978). *Mind in society.* Cambridge: Harvard University Press.

Wegerif, R. (1998). The Social dimension of asynchronous learning networks. *Journal of Asynchronous Learning Networks,* 2(1), 34-49.

Chapter 11

UNDERGRADUATE STUDENTS' USE OF COURSE RELATED WEB-CONFERENCES

Sarah Brown, Nigel Wilson and Clare Wood

THE NATURE OF LEARNING IN HIGHER EDUCATION

Kirschner (2001) notes that the purpose and nature of education has changed over time from being goal orientated (e.g. Gagné, 1985), to vocationalist (Harvey & Knight, 1996), then critical and reflexive (Barnett 1997), and finally constructivist, where learners are seen as actively seeking meaning from rich learning environments that reflect real world contexts. In line with these changing conceptions of education, there is a call for higher education to enable students to acquire 'competencies' rather than just specific, knowledge-based learning outcomes:

> "Competencies are a combination of complex cognitive and higher-order skills, highly integrated knowledge structures, interpersonal and social skills, and attitudes and values" ***(Kirschner, 2001, p2).***

Similarly, Morrison and Collins (1996) argue for the need for 'epistemic fluency':

> "the ability to identify and use different ways of knowing, to understand their different forms of expression and evaluation, and to take the perspective of others who are operating within a different epistemic framework" (p109).

These more recent conceptions of education suggest that learning needs to be embedded in some form of group activity or learning community. Moreover, the type of activity occurring within these communities should include the opportunity for dialogue between peers about what is being learned. The role of talk in effective learning and thinking is seen as significant by Mercer (1995, 2000) who identified three types of dialogue based on his analysis of talk in classroom contexts: disputational talk, cumulative talk and exploratory talk. *Disputational talk* is characterized by disagreement and assertions by individuals with no attempt to work collectively as a group. *Cumulative talk* is where speakers offer support to others' suggestions without being critical, often just confirming or establishing an idea that has been offered. *Exploratory talk* is illustrated by a critical but positive exchange of ideas, with justifications and suggestions offered at the same time as a critique of an existing suggestion. Mercer (1995) suggests that this type of talk 'foregrounds reasoning' (p105):

> "it is like the kind of talk which has been found to be most effective for solving problems through collaborative activity...it typifies language which embodies certain principles – of accountability, of clarity, of constructive criticism and receptiveness to well argued proposals ...people have to use language to interrogate the quality of the claims, hypotheses and proposals made by other people, to express clearly their own understandings, to reach consensual agreement and make joint decisions....exploratory talk represents qualities that are a vital, basic part of many educated discourses. Encouraging it may help learners develop intellectual habits that will serve them well across a range of different situations." (p105-107).

Although these ideas were developed from research with school age children, this type of talk can be seen to be consistent with the earlier statements concerning the development of competencies and 'epistemic fluency' in higher education.

The discussion so far suggests that learners need to be given the opportunity to engage in collaborative learning activities as part of their experience of higher education. However, true collaborative learning is rarely supported within organized activities in university settings (e.g. seminars, lecturers, individual dissertation work). Collaborative learning is about symmetrical learning relationships where responsibility for learning and for the conduct of the 'group' is shared. This contrasts with cooperative learning, which is "more directive than a collaborative system of governance and closely controlled by the teacher. While there are many mechanisms for group analysis and introspection the fundamental approach is teacher centred, whereas collaborative learning is more student centred". (Kirschner, 2001, p4). Within higher education the idea of the teacher as the monitor and authenticator of learning persists.

Computer Mediated Communication in Higher Education

Changes in the conception of learning and education have occurred in parallel with an increased use of computer mediated communication (CMC) in higher education. 'Conference areas' and email lists are increasingly used by tutors as a means of countering the pressures of increased class sizes and the resultant lack of close contact with students as individuals. While, in theory, such environments seem to offer a number of advantages to both students and teachers, in practice there is limited evidence that they deliver all that they promise. In fact, it seems that the successful use of such resources, especially discussion forums, is dependent on several factors. Soong, Chan, Chua and Loh (2001) suggest that all of the following conditions must be simultaneously present if online course resources are to be effectively used:

- Adequate time and effort invested in resources by tutors
- Tutors who constantly urge and motivate students to use the resources, especially at the beginning

- IT literate tutors and students who share constructivist notions of learning
- Courses designed to encourage high levels of collaboration
- Students & staff perceiving the resource to be easy to use and useful, with technical support present.

While helpful, it is of concern that the presence of so many factors are necessary for students to engage in online learning and collaboration, as few higher education institutions are in the privileged position of being able to guarantee the presence of them all. However, what such a list does indicate is the need for online learning to be integrated into part of a wider cultural change that embraces computers and their potential to mediate collaborative activity.

A CASE STUDY IN WEBCT USE

The Psychology Subject Group at Coventry University is an example of a University department that has attempted to implement such a culture change, by using WebCT (short for Web Course Tools) to support all undergraduate students' learning throughout their experience at the University. The University operates a modular framework, in which students are enrolled on a course of study, which consists of a specified number of modules. Satisfactory completion of the required modules typically leads to a named degree e.g. BSc Psychology. Students aiming for different qualifications may be enrolled on the same module. Coventry University has supported and promoted the use of WebCT and it is available for all courses and all modules; however, the level of use varies across the University.

Through WebCT, students have access to a 'Study Web' for each module that they study, and a 'Course Web'. The study webs are used to provide information that is module specific, while the course web provides information that is more general in nature but which is related to the course of study. All students registered on a module or course have access to the relevant WebCT webs, as do the staff who contribute to the module or course. The relevant module or course leader is responsible for the management of each web. Students and staff can access WebCT from university computers and also from any other computer that can access the internet. As a result, WebCT is a particularly useful resource for students who have limited physical access to the University campus.

Module and course leaders can add useful information to the 'contents' and 'resources' sections of WebCT webs. Students can also mail via 'module mail' any student or member of staff who has access to the web. In addition, a 'discussion forum' is available to staff and students within each web. Students are advised to check WebCT regularly for updated information, module mail and discussion forum postings.

Psychology students at Coventry University therefore offer a useful case study of *how* students use web-based conference areas to support their learning in an institutional setting that supports and encourages the use of such resources. There is little study of the nature of the educational dialogue that occurs in the context of Web-based discussion forums that are related to specific modules. Similarly, there is little consideration of the conditions that facilitate instances of collaborative activity in these environments.

A Comparison of Approaches

This chapter will compare psychology students' use of second and third level study-web conference areas. These two modules have been selected because they offer a number of interesting contrasts. In addition to the difference in academic level, they differ in the extent to which the topics covered by them are applied or theoretical, and the extent to which they build on existing knowledge or require the assimilation of new content. The analysis of the students' use of the online resource in general and the nature of the academic discussion that takes place within the conference areas will form the basis of a discussion regarding the potential of online conferences for fostering collaborative learning and exploratory discourse amongst students in higher education.

Module Descriptions

Second Year Module: 211PY – Physiological Psychology.

This is a Level 2 module that is a core module for all students taking a psychology degree. The majority of students take psychology as a single discipline, but some are joint degree students or are studying sports science. Students are expected to have a basic understanding of biological terminology, having previously studied a Level 1 biological psychology module. The module extends the themes covered in the Level 1 module but focuses more on the interrelationship between biology and behaviour. Eight key topics are covered: functional organisation of the brain and cerebral asymmetry, the physiology of memory, hunger and thirst as motivations, stress, sleep, sexual development and behaviour, perception and psychopharmacology.

Students have a one-hour lecture per week. In addition they have four, three-hour supporting tutor-led workshops that occur (one per week) over four consecutive weeks. WebCT is used to supplement both types of session. Students are encouraged to engage in discussion and ask questions using the discussion forum. They are also provided with copies of the lecture material and supplementary material to support a practical report based on workshop work. Students are provided with guidance re the nature and use of the forum in the module handbook. This guidance orientates the students to the discussion board as a place where students can 'raise questions' about the module and its content, as well as any other queries about topics related to physiological psychology. They are told that the module tutor will check the site regularly, but that contributions do not need to centre on the tutor if other students feel that they have something to contribute. However, the guidance clearly assumes that any queries will be directed to the tutor in the first instance.

The module tutor has a PhD in an area of biological psychology, and has taught biological psychology at degree level for 9 years. Although he did not teach biological psychology to this cohort of students in their first year, a subset of the students are familiar with the tutor, as he delivered workshops on research methods to them during their first year.

Third Year Module: 318PY – Psychology and Crime.

This is a Level 3 module that is an option for students taking psychology as a single discipline and psychology joint degrees, with the majority of students studying single honours psychology. In contrast to the level two module selected, this topic is almost entirely new to the students who have chosen to study it, although it builds upon the students' methodological and theoretical understandings from the first two levels of their courses. For example, some aspects, such as eyewitness testimony, have been covered in theoretical modules earlier in the course. The module is split into six topic areas: theories of crime, serial murder and offender profiling, rape, courtroom behaviour (eyewitness testimony and juries' decision making), dangerousness and psychopathy, sex offenders and sex offender treatment programmes.

Students have a weekly two-hour lecture. The format for this is usually a 50 minute / 1 hour lecture, followed by a short break and then the presentation of a related video. Some sessions are more interactive, e.g. eyewitness testimony exercises, or a mock jury exercise. There are no seminars or workshops in the module.

Students are encouraged to discuss aspects of the module via the WebCT discussion forum. The module handbook offers a lengthy introduction to the discussion forum, which is introduced as an area where the students can discuss issues raised in the lectures with other students and the tutors. The students are also encouraged to exchange information by addressing their entries to the forum rather than to specific individuals. The tutors also inform the students that they will check the site regularly, but note that they will 'participate as appropriate'.

WebCT is also used to provide additional 'useful information', such as crime statistics, coursework advice, other web links. Lecture overheads are also put on the site prior to each lecture. Students are encouraged to use these to save copying in lectures, but not to avoid lectures altogether. Students are also provided with six Multiple Choice Tests (MCTs), one for each topic area, and they are encouraged to use these and the feedback provided to assess their learning and understanding of each topic as the lectures for that topic are completed. The availability of MCTs is staggered, so that they become available for a short period after the completion of the lectures for each topic, and then they are all made available at the end of all the lectures for revision purposes.

Two tutors run this module. One is an experienced lecturer in higher education, who had been teaching students full time for 13 years at the time of this study, and has taught criminological or forensic psychology for 9 of those years. The other tutor is less experienced, although she has a PhD in an area of criminological psychology. She has been teaching forensic psychology at this level for the last 4 years.

Overall Patterns of WebCT Access & Use

The level of students' use of these two module webs and the discussion forum entries posted to these webs during the period September 2001 to July 2002 are analysed below. Table 1 shows the frequency of student 'hits' for each of the two module WebCT sites in general.

'Hits' indicates the number of times the homepage, tool pages or contents pages were accessed and broadly indexes usage of the resource as a whole. So, for example, the first line of Table 1 shows that five students from the second level module never accessed WebCT (3.2% of the total number of students on the course), whereas two students from the level three module never accessed WebCT (1.4%).

Table 1: Number of student 'hits' on the two WebCT sites

Module	211PY		318PY	
Number of Hits	Number of students	Percentage of students	Number of students	Percentage of students
0	5	3.2	2	1.4
1-9	1	0.6	3	2.2
10-24	7	4.5	4	2.9
25-49	12	7.7	21	15.2
50-74	17	10.9	10	7.2
75-99	20	12.8	21	15.2
100-149	36	23.1	30	21.7
150-199	30	19.2	29	21.0
200-249	17	10.9	10	7.2
250-299	7	4.5	3	2.2
300+	4	2.6	4	2.9
Total	156		138	

The table illustrates the fact that for both modules the amount of 'interest' in the two sites in broad terms was similar. For example, 156 students were registered to use the study web for the Level 2 physiological psychology module. Of these, five students never made use of the module web site, and three did not log on after the first term. A further three students stopped logging on before March 2002 (at the end of the second term; it should be noted that the academic year began at the end of September and ended in the following July, with timetabled lectures/workshops ending at the end of March). The remainder continued to log on through the April to July period. A similar pattern of access was observed for the Level 3 psychology and crime module. 138 students were registered for the module, two students failed to use WebCT at all, and three students did not log on after the first term. Five students had a final log in date in March, but the remainder of the students had last log on dates in April to July.

However, there are differences between the modules in the students' use of the study web discussion forums. Within this area of the WebCT environment we see a higher level of use in the Level 3 module, both in terms of 'silent' activity (reading postings – see Table 2) and active use (posting contributions – see Table 3). Twice as many students contributed to the discussions in this module compared to its level two counterpart (23.2% of students registered on the module compared to just 10.3% in 211PY), and there were over twice as many postings in the level three module. This contrast is especially interesting given that the percentage of threads (related sequences of postings) initiated by students was broadly similar in both modules (55.6% in 211PY compared to 52.6% in 318PY). So although there was more activity overall in the third level module, the relative distribution of that activity between staff and students was broadly similar.

Table 2: Number of Discussion Forum Posting Students Read

Module Number of Postings Read	211PY		318PY	
	Number of students	Percentage of students	Number of students	Percentage of students
0	28	18.0	16	11.6
1-10	21	13.5	20	14.5
11-20	18	11.5	16	11.6
21-30	14	9.0	5	3.6
31-40	16	10.3	9	6.5
41-50	12	7.7	13	9.4
51-60	20	12.8	7	5.1
61-70	27	17.3	5	3.6
71-80	NA	NA	10	7.2
81-90	NA	NA	7	5.1
91-100	NA	NA	4	2.9
101-110	NA	NA	3	2.2
111-120	NA	NA	5	3.6
120-	NA	NA	18	13.0

Table 3: Number of Discussion Forum Postings Students Made

Module Number of Postings	211PY		318PY	
	Number of students	Percentage of students	Number of students	Percentage of students
0	140	89.7	105	76.1
1	11	7.1	17	12.3
2	2	1.3	5	3.6
3	2	1.3	6	4.3
4	0	0	2	1.4
5	0	0	0	0
6	1	0.6	2	1.4
7	0	0	1	0.7
Total	156		138	

Nature of Conference Use

In order to characterize the nature of the activity within each discussion forum, each posting was assigned one or more codes intended to capture the nature of that contribution (see Table 4). This coding was designed and developed by the third author, who was independent of the University setting, and who had no prior knowledge of the students or how they used the website. Initially each posting was considered from the perspective of what its purpose was, and a broad descriptor capturing that purpose was then applied to it. Where a contribution was observed to have multiple purposes, codes were applied to each part of the posting as appropriate. These broad descriptors were collapsed and relabelled where there was felt to be overlap between codes. The codes were deliberately labelled in a way that was intended to be as transparent as possible. That is, they were primarily *descriptive* terms, rather than interpretative. These codes and their relative frequencies were subsequently viewed by the relevant module tutors, who verified that the application of the categories to the transcripts offered an accurate representation of the activity within the discussion areas. These data are presented in Table 4.

Table 4: Summary of conference use

	Tutor 211py	Students 211py	Tutor 318py	Students 318py
Orientation & Purpose of Conference	1	0	1	0
Notification of Resource	3	0	16	0
Resource Request	0	1	0	5
Question about Resource	0	0	0	1
Assessment Question	0	8	0	12
Assessment Answer	8	0	12	1
Assessment Notification	3	0	4	0
Technical Question	1	7	0	0
Technical Answer	9	0	1	0
Question to Conference	4	2	2	3
Response to Conference Question	1	5	2	3
Thanks	0	2	0	1
Warning	1	0	0	0
Response to Warning	1	1		
Reminder	3	0	0	0
Further Study Question	1	0	1	2
Further Study Response / Notification	1	0	5	0
Activity Suggestion	0	0	1	0
Discussion Issue Raised	0	0	1	10
Discussion Response with Elaboration	0	0	13	20
Discussion Response without Elaboration	0	0	0	2
Course Content Question	0	0	0	1
Course Content Answer	0	0	2	1

Firstly, it is worth dwelling on the similarities between the two conferences, as these may be seen to characterize 'typical' use of such discussion areas. For example, both tutors opened their conference areas with a posting that orientated students to the purpose of the forum and the way that they would like to see students use it (see Extracts 1a and 1b). Please note that all conference postings are reproduced exactly as they were typed by the contributors.

Extract 1a (from the 211PY forum)

Subject: Welcome

Welcome to the 211py discussion board. Please use this board to ask questions about the course content or to begin a general discussion on any topic within physiological psychology.

[module tutor]

Extract 1b (from the 318PY forum)

Subject: Welcome

Welcome to the Psychology and Crime Module!

This module is taught in two hour lecture slot sessions. Generally, although not always, this will involve an hour long lecture, followed by a short break and a video presentation. This means that there are no seminars for the module, however issues covered in the module can be discussed using this forum.

Please use the forum for this purpose. Remember there are generally no 'right' or 'wrong' answers with the complex and often controversial issues covered in the module. Rather there are a number of different views, which are supported by a wide range of often conflicting or equivocal research studies and/or theories, which are open to debate. This is your forum; so make the best use of it that you can. Remember though, that many of the issues covered in the topic are sentive and emotive, so please take care with your entries.

You can also use the forum to ask questions of us or your fellow students that are of a general rather than individual nature (e.g. a query concerning the coursework). We will endeavour to check the forum regularly and contribute to the discussions or answer questions.

You can also use the module mail facility to email the module tutors or other students studying the module. To ensure that you receive any module mail sent to you, for this and other modules, it is helpful to set your WebCT account up to forward your WebCT mail to the email address you use most frequently.

Finally you can contact us at the end of lectures, or during our office hours (signs detailing these hours are posted on the notice boards by our offices). Please stick to these office hours, or use the facilities described above to contact us. We are very busy and it is very frustrating to be constantly interrupted outside office hours. Remember, [less experienced module tutor's first name] is the module leader, but you may want to contact [more experienced module tutor's first name] if you have a specific query about her topic areas or coursework questions.

We hope you enjoy the module. We have made every effort to make sure that the WebCT site provides material that enhances your learning on this module, and that the material covered in the module is clear, challenging and interesting. Please let us know, however, if you experience any problems with the module or the WebCT site.

[Module tutors]

There are immediate differences between these two orientation postings. The 211PY tutor's posting is not only extremely brief, but he also presents the forum as incidental to the module and offers the students no guidance on the appropriate use of it. This contrasts sharply with the detailed and careful orientation message provided by the 318PY tutors, who present the forum activity as *part* of the module strategy. They present the area as a place for discussion and explicitly assign ownership of the site to the students ('This is your forum').

The students also used the discussion forums for both modules to ask questions about module assessment and to make general module queries (see Extract 2).

Extract 2 (from the 211PY conference)

Subject: Workshop attendance

Hi! I lost Monday's workshop. Can I attend another group's workshop? I think there is one on Thursdays, too. So, is it all right if i go on Thursday's session?

Thanks anyway, Z. [Student]

This extract is particularly interesting as it characterizes a feature of the student's use of the 211PY site: the fact that often the students used it to ask questions that, arguably, should have been sent directly to the tutor's private mailbox rather than to the forum. The tutor did not comment on the appropriateness of these messages and, as we shall see, this contributed to what became a problematic issue for the 211PY site: that the students quickly turned the site into a frequently asked questions site rather than a place for discussion and collaboration.

Occasionally students were observed to use the sites to support the module tutors' efforts in some way (see Extract 3).

Extract 3 (from the 211PY conference)

I just wanted to say how disgusted and embarrassed I was at the behaviour in lecture today (10/12). Not only was there several people talking continually throughout the lecture but [module tutor] had to contend with people throwing things on the floor, others arriving late and to top it all a mobile phone going off!...

Surely we should show our lecturers more respect than this? I am sure [module tutor] goes to a lot of trouble preparing lectures but after today's performance I wouldn't be surprised if he is totally appalled and is wondering why he bothers.

If you feel that you cannot sit for an hour without talking could I suggest that next time you stay away, then those of use that want to learn can do so without continual background noise.

[Student]

This posting, the fact that it was followed by supporting messages, and the fact that the forum for the other module also included messages that showed students encouraging their colleagues to engage with the module fully in some way, is interesting for a number of reasons. Firstly it shows the extent to which students see the forums as safe and appropriate environments to talk frankly, even though their contribution will identify them by name. Secondly, it suggests that the students do see these areas as primarily for their use, rather than areas where the tutors are foregrounded. This student's defence of the lecturer is endearing as it almost assumes that the tutor is not in a position to speak so firmly. To do so would somehow break one of the 'rules' of the conference: that tutors cannot contribute in a way that would threaten the 'safe environment' in which the students, their actions and their words are not judged by academic staff. Finally, it shows an important but neglected aspect of collaborative activity – self management of the group, both within the discussion and in their engagement with the module as a whole (Kirschner, 2001).

Given the academic context in which these discussions are made, another interesting similarity between the postings to the webs of these two modules was in the writing style adopted by both the students and the tutors. Postings were made in a colloquial manner rather than the more formal manner required for most other written communication in an academic setting. For example, when referred to directly by name, tutors first names were used, many messages were begun with an informal 'Hi', and formal rules of grammar were not always adhered to. Postings used a more conversational tone and punctuation was often used to illustrate conversational points more clearly. This again may reflect the students' perception of the forums as safe places to 'converse' informally. A friendly, supportive tone was noted in the contributions of the tutors and students, and the students were generally happy to address questions to both staff and peers (see Extract 4).

Extract 4 (from318PY forum)

Subject: Quizzes

Is it possible to have all the quizzes available over the reading week for those of us who may wish to use them for revision purposes?

[Student]

Subject: re: Quizzes

Revision! Blimey ;-)

Ok – 'tis done – well except for the Courtroom behaviour one but you won't have any lectures on that until after reading week, so there doesn't seem to be much point in making that one available yet.

Have fun!

[Module tutor].

Subject: re: Quizzes

thanx, much appreciated!!! – now for all the students out there try not to let [module tutor's] and [module tutor's] hard work go to waste. Try out the quizzes and you may even find that they help with you revision of the different topic areas.

N [Student]

There are several points worthy of comment in Extract 4. One is the use by the tutor of an emoticon: the 'winking' smiley. This was used by the tutor to indicate that her initial comment is intended as a humorous statement, rather than sarcasm. The use of these kinds of paralinguistic cues is noted as being an important element of relationship building in computer mediated settings (Joinson & Littleton, 2002). The tutors of both sites typically made attempts to establish friendly and informal relationships with the students using the forums through the use of humour. Another aspect of Extract 4 is the student's response, in which she took the opportunity to encourage her fellow students to engage with the new resources. This type of 'rally call' was observed several times (in fact Extract 3 is a type of rally call) and appears to be a form of contribution peculiar to forum settings. It is difficult to conceive of a face-to-face equivalent of this, such as a student turning to the rest of the group after a tutor has issued a reading list, and beginning to exhort her fellow students to exploit the valuable resource provided by the tutor. Yet, the forum settings seem to elicit or make acceptable these types of statement.

Although tutors are often seen as being 'expert', there is a sense that the forums were owned by all engaged in the module and that they could be used to benefit both the tutors and students. Although the students are the more obvious beneficiaries of the forum, Extracts 3 and 4 above provide examples of where the students used the forum to benefit themselves *and* the tutor. Other postings by tutors and students requesting information, or postings providing useful information reflect the full range of support that was provided to all in the module group.

As Table 4 illustrates, there were important differences in the way the students and the tutors of the two modules used the forum. The contributions of the 211PY tutor can be characterized as predominantly *passive*. This passivity is indicated by the limited number of questions posed to the forum, notification of resources and suggestion of student activities compared to the number of times the tutor responded to questions raised by the students. Moreover, in marked contrast to 318PY, neither the tutor nor the students raised a discussion of module content in this environment. The 211PY tutor's role was quickly established as a technical problem solver (most of the questions asked by and of the tutor to the conference were related to technical issues) and 'module manager'. Extract 5 is a typical example of such an exchange, and was in fact the first student posting on the site after the tutor's welcome message.

Extract 5 (from 211PY forum)

Subject: re: Welcome

[Module tutor],   I can't access the link to Cerebal Lobes in the contents folder in WebCT. Any ideas??

S [Student]

Subject: re: Welcome

Off the top of my head. Are you trying to access from home and if so, do you have PowerPoint installed? If you don't then you may need the PowerPoint viewer. There's a link to it from the Advice on Printing link in contents.

Also do you get any particular error messages or does it just not do anything?

Anyone else having the same problem?

Let me know if adding the PowerPoint viewer cures the problem.

[Module tutor].

The module tutor did not present himself as a source of academic knowledge in this setting – merely the person concerned with the smooth running of the day-to-day aspects of assessment and tutoring. It seems that there is little student discussion because of the way that the early exchanges cast the tutor as 'technician' and the tutor failed to re-establish himself as 'subject expert'. Messages 2 through to 14 in this forum were all concerned with identifying and solving technical glitches within WebCT, rather than discussing the module material that they were clearly accessing. This was then replaced by a series of exchanges to do with attendance issues, and then questions about the forthcoming assessment. The tutor failed to re-establish the purpose of the forum as a site for academic discussion after these exchanges. Instead it quickly fell into a question and answer website. There was no culture of discussion or of mutual exploration of the material that they appeared to be accessing. Student activity was still perceived by the students to be individualized rather than potentially shared and collaborative.

In the Level 3 forum, the tutors were proactive in the identification of resources, but were reactive with respect to student questions and the way they engaged in discussion with the students. Initially, one of the tutors posed a question for discussion and responded to the first two students' contributions. Thereafter, the students quickly dominated the forum, asking questions of each other and the tutors, and engaging in extended discussion about aspects of the module lectures that they had found interesting. Extract 6 is an example of such an opening question initiated by a student

Extract 6 (from 318PY forum)

Subject: How can we stop Criminals re-offending?

I would just like to raise this subject out of interest, as [module tutor] mentioned in a lecture that the number of people imprisoned in Britain is increasing, but Incarceration is not effective for reducing re-offence. Surely this undermines the value of confinement and leads me to wonder what other methods people think would be effective for reducing the number of re-offenders.

[Student]

In this module forum the students can be seen to 'own' the discussions. In comparison to the 211PY forum where many of the student postings were addressed directly to the module tutor, many 318PY postings were not addressed to anyone or were addressed to 'all'. In fact, the majority of postings addressed to specific individuals were made by one of the module tutors. After beginning the first major discussion thread, the 318PY tutors entered the discussions only once the students had begun them, and although they retained an identity as 'module managers' and 'subject experts' they were not intended to be the sole audience for most of the exchanges. Few technical queries were noted in this forum compared to the 211PY forum, perhaps because in the 318PY handbook the students were referred to external sources of technical assistance, and perhaps because these students were more experienced users of WebCT.

In contrast to the 211PY forum, the 'Psychology & Crime' forum was characterized by prolonged exchanges that permitted a characterisation of the dialogue in terms of Mercer's types of talk. The students showed a willingness to engage in cumulative and especially exploratory dialogue in particular. Extract 7 illustrates the type of exploratory talk that emerged in one lengthy, student-led discussion. Note in particular the way that both 'speakers' were careful to justify their position.

Extract 7 (from 318PY forum)

Subject: re: Public responses to particular crimes

As mentioned before, I don't think that enough emphasis has been placed on the role of society, an in particular the roles played by the young boy's parents and social network.

To have been allowed and able to form any fantasy of killing a fellow human being must generate from some form of socialising that may nurture such curiosity. I believe that such a child cannot form such curiosity and carry out such an act without encouragement. The parents of these boys, and in particular the parents of the instigator of the attack, must have been aware that some form of social deviance was evident. By not investigating this deviance further, I believe that not only the parents but their social network (including social workers, teachers etc) effectively nurtured this desire by not providing any answers. This desire then *leading ultimately to a curiosity so intense that the only possible answer that boys had was to carry through with their crime, but not actually being aware of the circumstances.*

James Bulger was not the only child failed in this crime.

[Student]

Subject: re: Public responses to particular crimes

G your comments assume that the parents of Venables and Thompson were aware and socially responsible, however, they were in actual fact alcoholics , had gone through family breakdown and were not exactly the type of parents to be considering the effects of their behaviour on their children. Also, these children had some behaviour difficulties, had problems forming relationships with their peers and were regular truants from school, if their parents had been the type that we all hope and wish for these behaviours would not have been allowed to thrive.

[Student]

Subject: re: Public responses to particular crimes

In reply to your message D, although I did state that the parents had a vital role in identifying any deviant behaviours in the young boys, I also highlighted the influence of other individuals in their social network!! You state that the children played truant from school consistently. If this is the case, where were the teachers and other authorities whose job it is to monitor truancy? (which is, after all, illegal!).

[Student]

In this exchange, the tutors could have intervened to pick up on a range of assumptions and issues that were implicit in the views being stated, such as G's use of the term 'deviant' and the implication from D's contribution that alcoholism will result in lack of awareness and social responsibility. However, neither tutor did this, and as a result the conference retained a sense that while contributions may not go unchallenged by your peers, the tutors would not be excessively 'academic' about the precision with which you express or justify your position. In contrast on the level 2 module the tutor made a response to most messages. The questions that were raised required factual information and often technical answers that the tutor was better placed to answer than the students were. Moreover it could be argued that there was an *expectation* that he would answer, apparent from the fact that most questions were addressed directly to him, either implicitly as the person who would have the relevant knowledge (e.g. about coursework submissions), or explicitly by name.

The fact that the 318PY students were happy to engage in exploratory talk that necessarily included elements of dispute and justification is particularly encouraging, given Tolmie and Boyle's (2000) observation that:

"...any disagreements which occur will promote growth in understanding. Indeed, CMC might be the ideal medium for maximizing the positive effects of conflict, since it can support both reflection before responding...and on-task recombination of ideas, by providing the text of messages in reviewable and manipulable form." (p121).

The students in the level 3 forum also showed signs of confidence in that they did not necessarily see the tutor's contribution as being the authoritative view or 'last word' on the discussion of a question. This is well illustrated by Extract 8.

Extract 8 (from 318PY forum)

Subject: A law breaker or a criminal?

As I was stopped for speeding the other day I wondered whether there was a distinction between "law-breaking" behaviour and "criminal" behaviour. As I had clearly broken the law by driving faster than the limit does that make me a criminal (although in this case I was not prosecuted but lets assume I was!!) or is it only certain types of crime that are regarded as "criminal"?? Any ideas anyone??

[Student]

Subject: re: A law breaker or a criminal?

D,

Well....as you weren't prosecuted you aren't a criminal, but you are now acutely aware that you broke the law so presumably you behaviour will change in order to avoid further law breaking behaviour, thus providing some deterrence without criminalisation! As we saw earlier, definitions of law (and therefore law breaking) are problematic, but I suppose the real distinctions are going to be between minor and major crimes/offences and there will be a difference of opinion on this too (e.g. speeding may be seen as minor unless you happen to have a child who was killed by a speeding driver).

[Module tutor]

Subject: re: A law breaker or a criminal?

I believe that we're all criminals, but criminals on a continuous scale. Where at one end we have the extremely good 'never do anything against the law if I can help it' people; although if we delve deep enough into their pasts have they ever borrowed a pen which they forgot to give back?? Yes, it may have been an oversight, but it is still stealing if you have another person's property without their permission. To the other end of the scale and we have the hardened criminal, those who commit crime with intent and fearlessness. However as we are each a member of this scale we are each no better than the next person, and as such we should not judge, but treat every individual with an honesty and compassion we should hope would be afforded to ourselves should the unfortunate / unthinkable happen. D, don't worry about the policemen they are only doing their job, and if it makes you feel any better, I sport three speeding points on my licence! N

[Student]

In this exchange we see N offering her own personal view of criminality that does not acknowledge the previous contribution of the tutor. Moreover, although the tutor made her contribution two days before N, N chose to reply directly to the student with the original question, rather than posting her reply to the end of the thread that was being established. The tutor's contribution was thereby 'sidelined' into a competing thread, and the discussion was re-established as between the students.

DISCUSSION

Relative Success of the Forums

The preceding discussion raises a number of questions to do with the relative success of the forums as places for the co-construction of ideas and knowledge. Why did the 211PY fail as an arena for exploratory talk where the 318PY conference succeeded in generating student-initiated, module-related discussion and exploration? There are a number of possibilities. One relates to the amount of tutor mediation, corresponding with Soong *et al.*'s (2001) first condition. In 211PY there was a slightly higher proportion of tutor contributions to the discussions: 92.6% of the threads contained a contribution from the tutor, whereas this figure was 84.2% for the 318PY forum. However, it seems unlikely that such a factor alone would inhibit discussion. It seems more likely that it was caused by the nature of the contributions made by both the students and the tutor (more closely related to Soong *et al.*'s (2001) second condition), and the fact that the tutor did not remind and reorientate the students to maintain the purpose of the site. Although this is more obvious in the lack of module content discussion in 211PY, it is also noticeable in the 318PY discussion that, after an initial flurry of module-related discussions prior to the Christmas vacation, it contained very little similar discussion in the Spring term. Here the discussion more closely resembled that of 211PY, with many informational postings and direct questions to tutors associated with coursework and revision advice. Although the Level 3 tutors restricted their intervention in student discussion, they were proactive in encouraging this discussion by raising questions related to lectures in the forum and by encouraging use of the forum in lectures. No questions were raised by the tutors during the Spring Term and the level of encouragement to use the forum in lectures reduced throughout the duration of the module. Thus, the way that tutors cast themselves and the function of the environment is critical. It is the contributions, the discourse, that effectively creates the environment. The way that contributions are allowed to unfold will determine how the environment is perceived and the unspoken 'ground rules' and explicit advice/guidance on the use of the environment that will shape future discussion. It is also important that this environment is maintained and that as Soong *et al.* (2001) suggest, tutors constantly strive to motivate students throughout the duration of the module. However, it is also possible that other external factors led to differing levels of activity in the discussion forums, for example differing levels of assessment, pressures of nearing exams etc.

Another aspect of the students' induction into online ways of discussing and collaborating is the clarity of that induction. The Level 3 tutors took great time to clearly orientate the students to the nature and purpose of the forum, whereas the Level 2 tutor left much of this implicit. This would seem to be especially important given the dynamic nature of discussion areas: they need to have a rationale and a focus in the absence of a specific task that would give the students a focus for their activities. As a result of the lack of a clear orientation to how the tutor wanted the students to use the site, and with limited modelling of those ways, the site was used less collaboratively. As Soong *et al.* (2001) also observe, both the students and the tutors have to share the same constructivist notions of teaching and learning. This requires explicit discussion and acknowledgement of those notions and how the learning environment can be used to support learning.

It is now more widely accepted that on-line networks of students can and do take on the form of 'learning communities' (e.g. Wegerif, 1998). However, one of the major stumbling blocks appears to be the anxiety, common in face-to-face seminars, of not wanting to be seen as stupid or being conscious of not fully understanding the educated discourse that is going on within the group. The anonymity afforded by chat rooms does not exist in university based CMC settings, where contributors are automatically identified by name each time they contribute. Despite this, the evidence from this case study is that the presence of their names did not act as a deterrent to those making contributions, including those of a personal nature. However, a much larger number of students (over 75% of students registered on each of the modules) preferred to read the discussions without making a contribution. It should be noted that this is not untypical of student use of other discussion sites (see Joinson & Littleton, 2002). An indicator of the anxiety felt by some students who did post messages is the apologetic tone used when asking for help, and the suggestion made by some that they had spoken to other students who were also confused. Thus, the lack of understanding is framed as a general one experienced by many in the learning group, rather than just by the individual making the posting. Perhaps the 318PY tutors managed to alleviate some of these fears by stating in the opening posting that "there are generally no 'right' or 'wrong' answers with the complex and often controversial issues covered in the module". However the fact that three quarters of the students still failed to contribute to the forum suggests that this did not alleviate the fears of the majority. Given that the students were not asked about the reasons for their contribution or lack of contribution to the forum, it is not possible to identify these with any certainty. Clearly there could be a range of reasons why students chose not to contribute to the discussion. However, the discussions by Bonk, Wisher, Nigrelli and Häkkinen, Arvaja and Mäkitalo in this volume offer more detailed discussions on the many factors that encourage or inhibit on-line collaborative learning.

The difficulty in persuading more students to engage in the discussion forums may be related to another of Soong *et al.*'s (2001) conditions, which states that courses must be designed to encourage collaborative learning. Although the module tutors described here have encouraged students to use the discussion forums, and the students have been encouraged to use WebCT for all the psychology modules they study, creating a culture of CMC within the department, the use of WebCT has largely been added on to traditional teaching methods that have remained mostly unchanged since the addition of this facility. Perhaps a more substantial revision of the teaching and learning methods for modules/courses is required for more widespread student use of collaborative learning via CMC environments.

A key factor that seems to account for the difference in forum use was the ease with which the applied topic of crime related to everyday experiences, anecdotes, popular media and daily news. This enabled the students to initiate discussions from personal interest, or offer personal views on academic issues. The apparent familiarity of the subject matter meant that the students realized that they could make relevant contributions that may eventually be re-cast as extensions to ideas raised by the module material. Interestingly, as Bonk, *et al.* (this volume) discuss, Barab *et al.* (1999) also highlighted the importance in the creation of successful learning communities of learners being able to apply course material to personal experiences and situations.

Does this mean that courses on topics that appear to be less applied and more theoretical in nature cannot afford such rich exploratory discussion? This is not necessarily the case, but it is up to the tutor to identify the familiarity and relevance of the topics being covered. In the physiological psychology module, the topics included sleep and stress – concepts that are familiar to the non-expert (and arguably especially salient topics for students!). Had the tutor stimulated the students by highlighting this familiarity and promoted interest by the presentation of questions, issues or case studies that tapped into and validated the students' lay understandings of these terms and their personal experience of them, discussion may have been more evident. This is speculation, but it does pave the way for further investigation of this as a possible method of tutor intervention.

Levels of Collaboration in CMC Settings

Discussions of collaborative learning can assume that 'collaboration' is a unified concept. However, reflection on the account of teaching and learning presented here suggests that collaboration may be more usefully thought of as occurring at different levels. In CMC settings, collaboration must first occur between the tutor and the students: to share and agree models of 'group' learning. This has to be a collaborative exercise rather than a directive one: the students need to negotiate and sign up to the principles and methods of learning in this way and in these environments. Once this is established, the students next need to collaborate with each other during the online discussions themselves. This is both an intellectual and interpersonal enterprise, with the students having to learn how to engage in appropriate discussion of each other's ideas. This level of collaboration is limited to the context of specific discussions.

This 'online collaboration' is supplemented by a third level of shared learning. This occurs when students mutually support each other via the forum as they engage in individualized, off-line activities that are related to the course, such as writing essays, revising for examinations, or otherwise engaging in personal study. It is in this respect that online learning communities can differ from those in schools or other face-to-face settings: they have the potential to foster mutual support and collaboration beyond the context of a specific task or activity. Being a member of the student group appears to be enough for some of the students in these environments to seek to support each other in off-line contexts. This highlights the social aspect of CMC that is so often overlooked in the creation and maintenance of CMC environments, but which is an important consideration in the development of on-line collaborative learning (Bonk et al., this volume; Häkkinen et al., this volume).

CONCLUSION

What this discussion has revealed is that although it is possible to use Computer Mediated Communication to provide opportunities for collaborative learning through the use of exploratory and cumulative talk, it is not sufficient to merely provide the CMC environment. As Soong et al. (2001) argue, a number of conditions need to be present for students to make the fullest use of the learning opportunities provided by CMC. It is unlikely that students will engage in extensive exploratory talk spontaneously, or that the majority of students will even voluntarily present their views in so public a forum. And yet, CMC environments appear to offer students a 'value added' component to their studies through the potential availability of the third level of collaboration, in which the collective activity of the students extends beyond specific discussions as the group attempt to support each other in their work as individuals. Tutors therefore need to provide environments that continually motivate, encourage and support students in this type of collaborative learning activity, which is often a very different experience of learning from what they experience elsewhere in their studies. Until conceptions of teaching and learning change to become more readily aligned with notions of *discourse* as a legitimate and desirable form of collaborative activity, students need to be supported in understanding, subscribing to, and participating in the shared construction of knowledge via CMC.

Authors' Note

The authors gratefully acknowledge the support of the students and tutors who agreed to allow their contributions to the module forums to be used in this study.

References

Barnett, R. (1997). *Higher education: A critical business*. Buckingham: Open University Press.

Gagné, R.M. (1985). *The conditions of learning* (4th ed.). New York: Holt, Rinehart and Winston.

Harvey, L., & Knight, P. (1996). *Transforming higher education*. Buckingham: Open University Press.

Joinson, A., & Littleton, K. (2002). Computer-mediated communication: Living, learning and working with computers. In N. Brace & H. Westcott (Eds.), *Applying Psychology*. Milton Keynes: The Open University.

Kirschner, P.A. (2001). Using integrated electronic environments for collaborative teaching/learning. *Research Dialogue in Learning and Instruction, 2*, 1-9.

Mercer, N. (1995). *The guided construction of knowledge: Talk amongst teachers and learners*. Clevedon: Multilingual Matters.

Mercer, N. (2000). *Words and minds: How we use language to think together*. London: Routledge.

Morrison, D., & Collins, A. (1996). Epistemic fluency and constructivist learning environments. In B. Wilson (Ed.), *Constructivist learning environments*. Englewood Cliffs: Educational Technology Press.

Soong, M.H.B., Chan, H.C., Chua, B.C., & Loh, K.F. (2001). Critical success factors for on-line course resources. *Computers and Education, 36*, 101-120.

Tolmie, A., & Boyle, J. (2000). Factors influencing the success of computer mediated communication (CMC) environments in university teaching: a review and a case study. *Computers and Education, 34*, 119-140.

Wegerif, R. (1998). The social dimension of asynchronous learning networks. *Journal of Asynchronous Learning Networks, 2*, 34-49.

Chapter 12

LEARNING COMMUNITIES, COMMUNITIES OF PRACTICE: PRINCIPLES, TECHNOLOGIES, AND EXAMPLES[*]

Curtis J. Bonk, Robert A. Wisher and Maria Luisa Nigrelli

Interest in developing online learning communities and in collaborating online has certainly intensified. It does not matter if you are in school or higher education, corporate training, or military settings, there seems to be support, or at least interest in, developing online communities. Some are focused on clarifying the definition of a learning community, others on the components or signs of one, and still others on how to build one. What is clear is that greater understanding of a community will be vital to the enhancement of both education and training settings.

Of course, an important question here is why has there been this intensification of interest? Besides filling in for knowledge gaps, the development of online communities may encourage knowledge sharing among work teams and foster innovation and creativity among learners or workers as distributed expertise is brought to a commonly shared space (Blunt, 2001; Schrage, 1990). In the corporate world, faster networking and enhanced idea sharing about potential products can be determining factors in a company's survival. There are similar goals and concerns in higher education where online communities are also highly sought after and valued.

Regardless of the focus, there seems to be an assumption that developing communities and opportunities to collaborate with one's peers will enhance the online experience. Unfortunately, there are no clearly defined road maps or steps in the development of a virtual community. As a result, when one develops an online community, it may be difficult to

[*] Acknowledgements: Portions of this manuscript appear in Bonk, C. J., & Wisher, R. A. (2000). *Applying collaborative and e-learning tools to military distance learning: A research framework.* (Technical Report #1107). Alexandria, VA: U.S. Army Research Institute for the Behavioral and Social Sciences. (for a free copy, see http://www.publicationshare.com/). The views expressed in this chapter are those of the authors and do not necessarily reflect the views of the U.S. Army Research Institute or the Department of the Army.

describe how it occurred or even to know that it has. In fact, the research on the effects of online communities is fairly mixed (Chao, 2001). Moreover, there is confusion about the differences between learning communities and communities of practice (CoPs). And it remains unclear the extent to which technology plays a role in the development of either one (Hara & Kling, 2002).

Educators are just beginning to ask serious questions and engage in research related to collaborative tools and the development of online learning communities (Bonk & Wisher, 2000; Chao, 2001). Among the many questions are:

1   What conditions or social structures must be in place to foster online learning communities?
2   At what point does the learner or participant become part of an online community?
3   How can computer environments substitute for the social cues of face-to-face environments that help foster a sense of community?
4   What principles, practices, and tools spur the growth of learning communities?
5   Are there particular sizes in which online communities tend to come into being?

Given the many questions, it is becoming important to understand the factors underlying successful online learning communities. In response, this chapter will detail the emerging principles of online learning communities and communities of practice as well as the methods for researching them. Unique online learning architectures from both higher education and military settings are detailed. By grasping the common components of these projects, we can begin to understand how online learning communities and CoPs are developed and fostered.

BACKGROUND INFORMATION

There is a remarkable void in the research regarding how online learning communities are formed. In a 1994 Presidential address to the American Educational Research Association, Ann Brown (1994) outlined key learning principles of the cognitive revolution during the previous thirty years. In her speech, Brown pointed to the need for active and reflective learning in a community of discourse as well as in a CoP. She argued that "Learning and teaching depend on creating, sustaining, and expanding a community of research practice. Members of the community are critically dependent on each other. No one is an island; no one knows it all; collaborative learning is not just nice, it is necessary for survival" (Brown, 1994, p. 10).

Not only does learning theory indicate a need for online communities, but there are many practical reasons as well. In residential college settings, for example, the formation of communities is a key indicator of high quality education in residential college settings (Broad, 1999). Since the most powerful learning in university settings is achieved in faculty-student and student-student interactions and mentoring situations, Broad asked how those learning community features can be replicated, extended, and transformed from a distance.

Despite such prodding by Brown and Broad, scant research exists on the technological and pedagogical variables necessary to foster virtual communities. Unfortunately, even as institutions and instructors hurriedly place courses on the Web, the tools for e-learning interaction are not fully developed (Hughes & Hewson, 1998).

Designers of online training and education need to understand the factors underlying successful online learning communities. Bielaczyc and Collins (1998) argue that learning cultures need membership with diverse expertise, mechanisms for sharing one's learning, common goals that advance their collective knowledge and skills, and a value on learning how to learn. Each member may have different knowledge or identities that the online community should advertise and utilize. There also is a common language or socially shared knowledge base for describing and promoting ideas, processes, plans, and goals. Through shared discourse, members formulate and exchange ideas. The tools developed, therefore, should help in promoting these learning processes and interactions.

Unlike most research on learning, there is a dual focus here on both individual knowledge growth and joint products or collective efforts. From such a perspective, it is important to identify the factors that foster or negate community building in e-learning environments. How are learning communities designed and supported? What technological tools support distributed interactive learning communities? To answer such questions, a common understanding of what qualifies as a community is needed.

PRINCIPLES OF COMMUNITIES

Community psychologists such as McMillan and Chavis (1986) suggest that there are four key factors for a sense of community: (1) membership, (2) influence, (3) fulfillment of individual needs, and (4) shared events and emotional connections. They argue that a sense of belonging, community boundaries, identity, and personal investment all contribute to membership. Membership also creates a sense of cognitive dissonance associated with one's responsibility to sacrifice for the community, thereby enhancing member confidence, sense of entitlement, and loyalty to the group (McMillan, 1996). The second key factor, influence, may include influencing the community as well as being influenced by it. The notion of influence also instills some pressure for uniformity and conformity that spurs even greater member closeness. Third, communities provide rewards and reinforcers that fulfill personal needs and are critical to staying within the community. Fourth, members have emotional bonds from shared histories that connect members and encourage continued investment and involvement in the community. McMillan and Chavis (1986), in fact, developed a "Sense of Community" model that summarizes how the subelements work together to create and maintain communities.

Based on the above model from McMillan and Chavis (1986), Chao (1999) designed a categorization scheme for online communities. According to this scheme, online indicators of factor one—membership—include self-disclosure statements, acknowledging other's membership, the paying of dues in terms of time and energy, references to the boundaries of the community, and completing needed forms to become a member. Online influence might occur when referring to norms, rules, or other orders, attempting to influence or persuade others, being influenced by others, and identifying and trusting some authority. Fulfillment of individual needs is found when one is seeking common ground, expressing a personal need, acknowledging someone for needed information, or voicing criticisms, suggestions, or differences of opinion. Finally, sharing events and emotional experiences as well as identifying the spiritual bond of the group might occur when referring to stories of what has happened in the past and using special symbols or language specific to members of the group.

VIRTUAL LEARNING COMMUNITIES

As learning environments become virtual, it is vital to investigate how online communities are formed and sustained. What does an online learning community do? What are the key principles that help create a sense of learning community (Barab & Duffy, 2000; Chavis, Hogge, & McMillan, 1986; McMillan, 1996; Schwier, 1999)?

Schwier (1999) argued that electronic learning environments too often fail to develop a community of learners. Communities, he claimed, are collections of people bound together by some common reason. A learning community, therefore, is a group of individuals who are interested in a common topic or area and who engage in knowledge-related transactions as well as transformations within it (Fulton & Riel, 1999). A community of learners is apparent when learners know and value each other, discuss common interests, support each other's needs, share control and responsibility, and take risks in a trusting atmosphere (McLoughlin & Oliver, 1999). They take advantage of the opportunity to exchange ideas and learn collectively. Schwier further contends that certain conditions need to exist for nurturing a learning community such as a leader setting the tone, transparent technologies to foster task completion and the development of interpersonal relationships, a safe and comfortable environment for participation, and an emphasis on narratives and story telling. He then describes how these elements play a role in the formation, maturation, and decline or metamorphosis of the learning community.

The learning community must bring people together for some initial common interest or quest. Similarly, there is a need for both a common reference point as well as multiple entrance points for online group members (Duffy, McMullen, Barab, & Keating, 1998). The cultural and historical heritage of the community will normally include shared goals, opportunities for negotiating ideas, and common practices or rituals (Barab & Duffy, 2000). When those components are in place, there is greater opportunity for individuals to function within an interdependent system and for new members to work beside and learn from more competent members. New members inherit the goals, practices, and rituals of the previous members, and, over time, such newcomers will replace the old timers. So, there are some common goals and values, feelings of commitment and trust (Brown, 2001), and something valuable that binds the participants. In addition, members must have opportunities to contribute to and develop the online community. As such, members of the community have influence on the direction of the community and new membership.

To recap, online learning communities require membership, goals, purpose, identity, shared knowledge, member participation or contributions, and trust (Rovai, 2002). They foster interaction about course materials as well as peer-to-peer communication, resource sharing, negotiation and social construction of meaning, and expressions of support and encouragement among students (Palloff & Pratt, 1999). And the electronic community must have its own meeting or gathering place and member roles as well as norms for resolving disputes.

While much more is now known about online learning communities, a challenge facing the online instructor remains how to foster them. Part of the problem is the difficulty in determining when an online learning community really exists. For example, some may confuse an online portal, database, network, listserv, or interest group for a learning community (Stuckey, Hedberg, & Lockyer, 2002). In contrast to learning communities, Stuckey et al. (2002) contend that learning portals and hubs have varied members, limited connections between members, and a mentality of users as consumers of information not generators or contributors of knowledge. Communities, on the other hand, are interactive, nurture members who are both consumers and producers of knowledge, and foster joint artifacts and sharing of knowledge among community members.

The point is that an informal network of friends and colleagues, who simply keep in touch with each other or share information in common interest areas, is not the same as a learning community wherein knowledge is created, shared, and expanded upon (Wenger, McDermott, & Synder, 2002). An occasional guest expert is not a ritual. Sharing one or two internship experiences over fifteen weeks of a course will not be sufficient in creating a shared history. One or two opening course ice breakers may not be sufficient in building the trust and shared knowledge needed by a learning community. A high level of trust is not automatically established from access to a few useful Web links either. And using a team workspace or creating team forums will not guarantee that teams will become close knit.

While such components may combine to help foster a learning community, educators are too often excited about casual references to online communities that rarely match reality (Kling & Courtright, in press). Equally important, many incorrectly view learning communities as the same as communities of practice (CoPs). In attempting to distinguish these two areas, key aspects of CoPs are reviewed in the next section.

COMMUNITY OF PRACTICE: PRINCIPLES AND FEATURES

In business settings, the focus today is more on fostering a CoP, than on developing learning communities. According to Wenger et al. (2002), a community of practice often describes a group of people who form relationships that are essentially focused on shared objectives, concerns, interests, ideas, or a common set of problems related to a practice, domain, or topic. Members of a CoP are part of a social network that share a fervent concern about a topic or idea and who deepen their knowledge of this topic by continuing to interact about it. As a social network, a CoP lives for and through the relationships and the ties that connect people to one another. Clearly, there are many important CoP components that overlap with learning communities such as the need for trust, mutual understanding, respect, and cooperation in the development of new ideas, procedures, and knowledge. When effective, CoPs can help members share best practices, organize and distribute knowledge, or design new products.

While it is difficult to design a CoP, they have their own life cycles and evolutionary phases. For example, Wenger (1998a) detailed five specific stages of community development. Initially there is a stage where people see the potential of working together and sharing ideas after finding each other's communalities and joint interests (i.e., "Potential Phase"). Next, these interests may coalesce into a more formalized CoP with a purpose, membership, and schedule (i.e., "Coalescing Phase"). In the third stage, the identity of the CoP is more firmly established, relationships are built and maintained among members, experiences are documented, trust and commitment emerge, and new members are initiated (i.e., "Active Phase I"). Near the end of this stage, relationships and connections are more explicitly pursued outside the CoP as members interact with other practices within the company or other companies (i.e., "Active Phase II"). Fourth, member engagement in that CoP is no longer as intense and some activities dissipate or are closed out and perhaps archived (i.e., "Dispersed Phase"). Finally, when the community ceases to exist, there are some people who attempt to preserve and remember it through stories and rituals (i.e., "Memorable Phase").

While such CoP stages are important to identify, so are the components. In a study of two public defender offices, Hara and Kling (2002) found that they each had a shared vision, supportive culture, autonomy, professional identity, a common practice, and opportunities to share meaning and collectively build knowledge. According to these researchers, autonomy and shared vision were particularly important to the success of both of these CoPs. In effect, if the CoP is predesigned or manufactured by managers or administrators, it runs the risk of being ineffective or even failing.

In reflecting on various CoPs developed at IBM Global Services, Gongla and Rizzuto (2001) point out that they are typically built through shared experiences, a formal history together, common vocabulary, a repertoire of stories, roles and norms, and opportunities to learn more about each other. They are promoted through the development of trust and loyalty to the community, reaching out to new members, searching for and contributing important material or information to the community, and generally sharing relevant stories. Collaboration in the CoP is promoted through engaging community members to solve real problems, helping work groups interact with other communities, and measuring results. Ultimately, CoPs result in new products, markets, or businesses from which additional communities and associated community boundaries emerge.

As indicated, to keep the community alive and flourishing, there must be a strong identity for the CoP and ties among the members (Plaskoff, 2003). Shared history, stories, and feelings of affection for that community can help bind newcomers and old timers (Wenger, 1998b). Stories shared among IBM consultants, for instance, might not only provide practical advice and insights, but might also strike emotional chords that resonate with others in the same practice (Gongla & Rizzuto, 2001; Mack, Ravin, & Byrd, 2001). According to Plaskoff (in press), effective CoPs build intersubjectivity, or a temporary shared understanding, among their members. Online communities are one way to communicate and share insights and intuitions related to the community environment and practice; a shortcut that helps in establishing the key problem to be discussed and the associated communication possibilities among members (Cook & Brown, 1999). As such, it is vital that CoP members help develop a unique language or vocabulary which is fundamental to sharing and collaboration (Gongla & Rizzuto, 2001).

As John Seely Brown and Paul Duguid (2000) note in their recent book, "*The Social Life of Information,*" there should be opportunities to share "water cooler" stories. Brown and Duguid contend that we have overlooked context in our training programs. From their perspective, it is through shared experiences that contextualized knowledge can be acquired and later tested. Instead of such rich and engaging learning environments, most e-learning vendors emphasize the capabilities of their systems or tools to provide repositories of information and track learner progress through that information store. However, often absent are tools to help learners actually learn or opportunities for instructors to establish online communities of learning. Given the overwhelming focus on tracking and managing learners, it is small wonder that student attrition from online courses is often cited as well over 50 percent (Bonk, 2002b).

At IBM, Kulp (1999) notes that group goals and milestones are highly important in their use of Learning Space to deliver asynchronous, instructor-led learning. In effect, those in the

CoP need to problem solve, invent, create, and co-learn. According to Kulp, both experienced learners and novices should support each other through interaction and negotiation of ideas. Novices might take on more of an observer role initially as they are apprenticed into the community. From this view, a novice gradually appropriates the skills necessary for him or her to become a competent and skillful member of the community. He or she becomes acclimatized to the setting by observing in the periphery of the community and gradually taking on a more critical role. Lave and Wenger (1991) referred to this process as legitimate peripheral participation (LPP). Participating within the LPP helps explain the way the community grows and spreads in different directions according to members' interests and the evolution of their practices and expertise. In essence, a learning community is a place wherein resources and specific expertise are shared and made accessible to others.

COLLABORATIVE TECHNOLOGY

Paralleling the increase in learning communities and CoPs, is the proliferation of collaborative technologies in both work and academic settings (Bonk, 2002a, 2003). While collaborative tools do not necessarily yield highly developed CoPs (Hara & Kling, 2002), it is still important to explore where they might make an impact. Recent surveys of both early adopters of the Web in higher education as well as in corporate training environments found that tools for learner collaboration and sharing are highly valued (Bonk, 2001, 2002b). However, while the vast majority of the respondents indicated that learner collaboration and sharing best practices were useful and important, most were not yet incorporating them in their training programs. This was true of an assortment of collaborative tools including real-time chat options, asynchronous discussion forums, story telling tools, interactive feedback and annotation devices, demonstrations and simulations, and learner profile features. Instead of engaging learners in rich and intensive interaction and collaboration, most e-learning environments concentrated individualized, self-paced learning using tools for uploading and downloading of content, Web searching, online quizzing and testing, grading, and tracking learner progress.

There are many types of technologies to help online participants feel belongingness to a community such as Web sites, email, buddy lists, and instant messaging (Wellman, 2001). Common meeting places mediated by technology not only allow members to create a common history but they also enable the sharing of that history. Discussion boards and chat rooms offer opportunities for mentoring and facilitated learning where stories and experiences can be shared (Kaplan, 2002). Clearly the tools for sharing information, posting ideas, and showing off one's talents are increasing (Bonk, 2002a).

Web Conferencing and Discussion Forum Technologies

Online communities might use both synchronous and asynchronous technology. Among the asynchronous tools for an online community are a number of conferencing or threaded discussion tools (e.g., *WebBoard, SiteScape Forum, FirstClass*, etc.) that offer learners a chance to discuss issues or topics at their leisure (Bonk & Dennen, 1999). With such tools, there are no geographical or time zone restrictions on contributions. In fact, team meetings may take place across continents. And for those who want to discuss issues in real-time, conferencing technologies often include low-end synchronous chat tool options. In effect, if expertise in a company is spread throughout the world, collaborative technologies can help find individuals or groups in the community with the needed skills or expertise (Gongla & Rizzuto, 2001).

Virtual or Synchronous Classroom Technologies

The value and use of synchronous technologies in both learning and CoPs has grown extensively in recent years (Hoffman, 2001). In the corporate and military worlds, travel costs are typically eliminated since training is now locally available, instructors are not held to certain geographic boundaries, and more students can view presentations simultaneously (Hall, 2000). There are also cost savings from fewer hours away from the workplace which should quickly translate into extensive productivity gains. Synchronous conferencing technologies (e.g., *WebEx*, *Live Meeting*, *HorizonLive*, and *NetMeeting*) enable communication among learners, remote presentations from experts or instructors, online meetings, and virtual classrooms. As the need for online communities grows, it is likely that live or synchronous training on the Web will become even more cost feasible and effective.

Project Collaboration and Workgroup Technologies

In terms of CoPs, electronic meeting software is emerging that can help global teams set goals, share and record ideas, and make key decisions. Along these same lines, there are now many technologies for building teams, sharing expertise, and fostering international collaboration on diverse projects and research. A tool called *Documentum Collaboration Edition*, for instance, supports teams through a project lifecycle by using real-time chats, whiteboarding, threaded discussions, and other collaborative tools to track team member schedules and manage resources and deliverables. Along these same lines, a tool called *Quantum Collaborate* offers users different levels of collaboration (i.e., shared or private), varying degrees of document viewing and editing, and threaded discussions (Hane, 2001). Similarly, annotation tools such as *iMarkup* allow team members to highlight information, make notes, and embed other annotations. The capability to annotate directly on Web documents or pages expands the forms and types of online collaboration.

Peer-to-peer Technologies

Some believe that peer-to-peer technology will be the next major force to impact the delivery of learning. In some cases, it is already common for e-learners to hold group meetings, write and edit documents, and turn in assignments electronically. Using a tool called *Groove*, for instance, users can open multiple windows on their computer screen and discuss edits, collect additional information, and view shared data. And, if users decide to continue their work offline, it is automatically updated as part of a shared workspace when they log back in. With such functionality, peer-to-peer technologies provide the means to form online learning communities within e-learning.

Clearly collaborative technologies can serve as an aid in the development of a learning community or CoP. Table 1 provides one framework for thinking about how different principles of learning communities and CoPs might be supported by an assortment of collaborative technologies.

Table 1: Technologies and activities to support principles of
online learning communities and communities of practice

Principles of Online Learning Communities and CoPs	Supportive Technology	Sample Activities
1. Shared Goals, Purpose, Mission, Rules and Norms	Calendars, feedback tools, help systems, meeting or class archives, schedules, site announcements, streaming videos from community leaders	Create team logo and motto, post member or learner goal statements
2. Trust and Respect	Email, member profiles, shared Web links	Social ice-breakers, online introductions, member expectations, testimonials
3. Shared Spaces, Generation of Idea or Work Product, Knowledge Creation, and Negotiation	Annotation and brainstorming tools, desktop videoconferencing, discussion forums, electronic whiteboards, translation tools, virtual classrooms or online presentation tools	Learners create site glossary, learners post work in online galleries
4. Member Collaboration and Team Products	Annotation tools, application sharing, collaborative writing tools, decision making tools, drop boxes, team tools, translation tools, group announcements, virtual workspaces	Creating team product review and feedback system or procedure, post team products and new creations
5. Sense of Identity, Sustaining Diverse Membership, Expertise, and Growth	Knowledge management portals and tools, mentoring exchange systems, site pop-ups, synchronous team or group meetings, synchronous learning and instruction	Global chats, share site logo, hold special events, post both individual as well as team accomplishments, share site with friends
6. Influence and Member Participation	Discussion forums, file exchange, polling and voting, Web link tools	Change Web site based on member survey results
7. Sense of Autonomy	Cafés, chat rooms, idea forums	Allow choice in online course, allow work teams to form around interests
8. Shared History, Events, and Stories, Sense of Belonging, and Emotional Connections	Buddy lists, bulletin boards, chat rooms, discussion forums, email, FAQs, instant messaging, MUDS, newsgroups, story portals, listservs, site information	Hold historical or memorable events (famous guest expert online, online conference, etc), coordinate controversial topic discussions
9. Fulfilling Personal Needs, Rewards, Acknowledgements	Breakout rooms, intelligent agents for resource filtering, member profiles, online surveys of members, online mentoring exchanges	Use of online mentoring, post accomplishments of members
10. Embedded in Practice, and Integration with Real World	Application sharing, online cases and simulations, synchronous conferencing tools, translation tools	Reflect online on internship or job experiences, synchronous guest chats, utilize problem-based learning

MEASURING THE DEVELOPMENT OF
ONLINE LEARNING COMMUNITIES

As tools to foster learning communities and online collaboration proliferate, there is a growing need to evaluate how online communities develop. How do college students, corporate personnel, and military personnel react to online learning communities? How are electronic communities formed in different courses? What factors help with student retention in those courses? And what are some early indicators of successful online learning communities?

There are not yet many options for measuring and evaluating online communities. Some researchers look for specific characteristics or components such as "common goals" or "shared history" (Schwier, 1999) and try to determine the extent to which such features are present (Misanchuk, 2002). For instance, Rourke, Anderson, Garrison and Archer (2000) explored social presence or the ability for participants to project themselves socially and emotionally into the online community. Factors coded for social presence in that study included reinforcing behaviors (e.g., complimenting), interactive behaviors (e.g., continuing a thread), and affective behaviors (e.g., self-disclosures).

Chao (2001) found six key conditions to be important to student online experiences: 1. participation and identity; 2. learning as a priority; 3. having a sense of control; 4. tapping into a shared concern; 5. being open to learning opportunities of the respective community; and 6. openly articulating one's needs. While she found that online learning community involvement can expand and deepen meaningful learning of college students, meaningful learning can occur without learning community involvement. In effect, while they tend to be related, they are not necessary conditions for each other. Additionally, community bonding events are not always going to be reliable indicators of learning. Her findings highlight the question of whether instructors should be preoccupied with how to form online learning communities or if they should primarily concentrate on how to create meaningful activities and authentic online learning situations. Stated another way, do learning communities really matter?

A second method for evaluating communities – social network theory – explores the strength of ties between members of the group (Haythornthwaite, 1998). Using such techniques, the researcher can determine the types of interactions occurring between learners, their frequency, and their overall tone or intimacy.

Finally, as noted nearly two decades ago by McMillan and Chavis (1986), there are several ways to measure the sense of community among group members. Sense of community measures or indices for physical communities such as those from McMillan and Chavis often inquire about group cohesion, feelings of belongingness, shared history, and community purpose. In attempting to foster an online professional development community, Kanuka and Anderson (1998) developed a survey instrument wherein participants were asked to indicate their agreement with statements related to the construction of knowledge and the creation of online learning communities. Similarly, Bonk, Oyer and Medury (1995) created an instrument to explore the degree of social constructivism that students and instructors perceived and preferred in their classroom learning environments. Table 2 synthesizes items from these two scales to create an entirely new scale, the "*Social Constructivism and Learning Communities Online*" (SCALCO) (Bonk & Wisher, 2000) scale for measuring student online learning.

Table 2: Social constructivism and learning communities online
(SCALCO) scale (Bonk & Wisher, 2000)

Social Constructivism and Learning Communities Online Questionnaire
Learner Questions (Rate 1 = strongly agree; 5 = strongly disagree)
1. The topics discussed online had real world relevance.
2. The online dialogue dealt with original topics.
3. As the forum progressed, I developed a position on various topics that I did not have before the online forum.
4. The online forum dialogue offered multiple perspectives.
5. The online dialogue encouraged me to reflect on the issues.
6. I integrated new knowledge acquired from the online discussion into my existing knowledge, which resulted in a deeper understanding of the issues.
7. I made new connections to the course material as a result of the online environment.
8. I have more ideas that I can use about this topic than without the online forum.
9. The online forum nurtured my critical thinking and evaluation skills.
10. I had a voice within the discussion forum.
11. I had some personal control over course activities and discussion.
12. Online discussions were *not* relevant to my learning needs.
13. The online technology allowed me to design and create new ideas.
14. The online environment encouraged me to question ideas and perspectives.
15. I liked collaborating with others online.
16. Instructors provided useful advice and guidance online.
17. I could count on others to reply to my needs.
18. The online environment fosters an atmosphere where more than one answer may be correct.
19. I collaborated with other participants in the forum that resulted in new perspectives and a better understanding.
20. I felt that I was a member of the group.
21. The other group participants acknowledged my contribution to the discussion.
22. I felt committed with other online participants to work together in order to acquire a deeper understanding of the issues.
23. I felt the discussion took the issues to a deeper level.
24. The online forum provided opportunities for in-depth discussion.
25. I clarified my ideas by sharing them with others online.
26. I clarified my ideas by reading other participants' comments.
27. I gained an appreciation for other opinions and perspectives.
28. I received useful mentoring and feedback from others.
29. The online environment fostered peer interaction and dialogue about real-life problems.
30. The online discussions lowered the isolation and loneliness of similar learning situations.
31. The online forum fostered a sense of a collaborative learning community.
32. There was a sense of membership in the learning here.
33. Other participants and I made decisions about how we would proceed or learn online.
34. Instructors or moderators provided just enough resources to help me succeed online.
35. This environment had opportunities to prepare answers with peers or learning teams.
36. Peer evaluation and feedback was integrated into this learning environment.
37. The online environment allowed for the exploration of topics of personal interest.
38. I could share and discuss my ideas and answers with others in this environment.
39. It was interesting to see how differences of opinion were discussed and negotiated in this environment.
40. Summaries or compromise positions were facilitated in this environment.

The SCALCO is intended to measure the degree of social interaction and constructivism fostered by online collaborative tools as well as the factors leading to successful online communities. Since the SCALCO has not undergone significant validity and reliability testing, it is offered here as a notional example, not as a proven instrument. Nevertheless, such tools can provide useful information to instructors and course designers about their ability to create a learning community within an online module, course, or program.

Online Communities for the Professional Development of Teachers

So, how does one use these principles and tools to create and assess an online learning community? Barab and Duffy (2000) indicate an initial need for a mission statement, purpose, or common reference point. Second, there must be meaningful membership wherein one's questions and needs are addressed and members can learn about each other. At the same time, there usually is a learning facilitator who focuses and refocuses the group. In addition, online communities benefit from separate spaces or rooms for sharing information and for socializing and creating interesting spaces. One might also change the Web site to connote seasonal changes during the year or provide other means for conveying the feeling of time passing. New or prospective members also might be guided within the site with chats, tours, and visitor guidelines that welcome them to the online community. Members might even hold positions or responsibilities within the different areas of the community.

The Inquiry Learning Forum (ILF)

Researchers at the Indiana University Center for Research on Learning and Technology (CRLT) have used such mechanisms to create several virtual learning communities intended to support the professional development of preservice and inservice teachers (see http://crlt.indiana.edu). The Inquiry Learning Forum (ILF), for instance, was developed to support a virtual community of inservice and preservice math and science teachers (Duffy et al., 1998). Forums such as ILF take advantage of the expertise that many adult learners bring to the learning situation while providing a means to contextualize knowledge in an authentic learning environment. By using videostreaming technology with detailed classroom visits, they situate participants in a CoP focused on ownership, dynamic adjustments to user needs, participation, and inquiry. Online videos included in the site have descriptions of teaching activities, reflective teacher and expert commentary, lesson plans, and conceptual linkages. The goal is not only to create an online community rich in resource sharing, but to facilitate dialogue about teaching practices and provide timely advice. Forums such as ILF take advantage of the expertise that many adult learners bring to the learning situation as well as a means to contextualize knowledge in an authentic learning environment. Perhaps most importantly, ILF also provides a model or framework for shifting from teacher-centered instruction to an approach wherein expertise is openly shared, discussed, and critiqued among participants.

Baek (2002) researched the degree to which ILF supported teacher professional growth and found that these teachers went through four distinct phases: 1. early aspiring; 2. refocusing; 3. restructuring; and 4. concluding. Baek also revealed a number of tensions within these phases that each added to the complexity of nurturing and supporting a Web-based CoP. She found it to be more used by preservice teachers to observe samples of expert teaching than by inservice teachers as an opportunity to reflect on and discuss their current teaching practice. From a developer standpoint, the ILF evolved from a focus on assembling clever tools that help build a community to finding ways to support a community. In other research, Kling and Courtright (in press) found that ILF had ambitious goals that were often not met. For instance, it assumed that a critical mass of teachers would want to freely engage in inquiry and discussion about sample teaching episodes and that a general group identity would arise that would result in lively CoPs. What did occur, however, were break-out or bounded groups which discussed particular areas of interest within mathematics and science.

The TICKIT Program. Another attempt at developing an online community of inservice teachers within the CRLT is the Teacher Institute for Curriculum Knowledge about the Integration of Technology (TICKIT) program. TICKIT is a yearlong, school-based professional development program for rural school teachers in southern Indiana to learn about technology integration and share their ideas with their peers (Ehman & Bonk, 2002). Instead of technology driving the curriculum, here it is meant to be a factor in helping teachers reflect on their teaching approaches and philosophies about learning, while enhancing, extending, and transforming learning opportunities available to students (Bonk, Ehman, Hixon, & Yamagata-Lynch, 2002). The professional development of TICKIT teachers takes place online, at their respective schools, and at Indiana University.

Teachers receive six graduate credits from their participation in TICKIT during the academic year. As a learning community, there are many events and activities where TICKIT teachers share knowledge, reflect on their technology integration ideas, develop respect and trust between members, and identify themselves as members of the program. A recent study indicates that TICKIT has made a significant impact on degree of technology integration by the teachers who have completed the program (Keller, Ehman, & Bonk, 2003).

Despite these positive findings, it is easy to question whether TICKIT truly is a learning community. First, all teacher participants receive grades for their participation in the program. Their online interactions, therefore, are typically part of a course assignment, not self-motivated inquiry. Second, teacher participation is bounded by one academic school year. In fact, each year there is a new group of approximately 25 teachers participating within it. So while the TICKIT program has existed for over five years, it is difficult to label it a CoP.

TAPPED IN

In terms of longer-term opportunities for professional development, TAPPED IN is an environment for teacher professional development and informal collaborative activities (Schlager & Schank, 1997). This resource combines opportunities for informal and formal learning that emphasizes collaboration and social interaction within a supportive CoP. In the late 1990s, there were over 6,000 school teachers, staff, and researchers within the TAPPED IN environment. Here, teachers with diverse skills and interests can meet at any time, learn about many educational reform ideas and approaches, and find useful materials and resources (Schlager, Fusco, & Schank, 2002). Members hold real-time discussions and classes, collectively browse Websites, explore professional development options, and interact via mailing lists and discussion boards all in a single venue. Instead of relying on video conferencing or asynchronous discussions, TAPPED IN is primarily a synchronous environment with multi-user capabilities. Filled with different floors, offices, and meeting rooms, members can name and furnish these rooms, create and share documents and hyperlinked objects, and post items in their own workrooms. In effect, TAPPED IN helps overcome teacher isolation by providing a rich sharing of experiences and resources while also recognizing and rewarding participant achievements.

While TAPPED IN is a growing and thriving online community, the designers admit to problems in what to label it (Schlager & Fusco, in press). They are not sure if the environment truly constitutes a CoP or if it is more accurately called a "constellation of practices" or "a crossroads of multiple educational communities." Such questions were raised, in part, since it is unclear whether participation in TAPPED IN actually changes participant teaching practices in schools and local practices outside of TAPPED IN. Consequently, as was found in research on the ILF and emulated in the TICKIT Program, they suggest that professional development programs might move from the present focus on how technology can support global networks and CoPs, to how technology can support and enhance more local CoPs.

ONLINE CLASSES AS LEARNING COMMUNITIES

Barab, Thomas, and Merrill (1999) found that online courses can support the development of a learning community when they (1) can flexibly accommodate diverse learner needs and interests, (2) foster the co-construction of meaning through information sharing, (3) allow for student stories which are personal or filled with self-disclosures, and (4) create a positive, warm, and psychologically safe environment for learning. They also point out that, according to the adult education literature, it is important for learners to apply course content to their lived experiences and personal situations. This was crucial to the emergence of a learning community here since student identity and personal development could co-evolve with course participation and increasing competence with course material. Qualitative analyses of student posts and later member checking indicated that the design of an open, flexible, and inviting climate for learning was central to the evolution of this community.

A MILITARY LEARNING COMMUNITY

In addition to teacher professional development programs and individual classes in higher education, creating online communities is also a prominent practice in military and business settings. For instance, Phelps, Ashworth and Hahn (1991) discovered that asynchronous computer conferencing in military settings can increase student camaraderie, cohesion, connectedness, and sense of accomplishment. In addition, a recent focus group study of blended learning (combining synchronous, asynchronous, and live instruction) in the military revealed that a sense of community was important to learner retention and skill gains (Bonk, Olson, Wisher, & Orvis, 2002). Such consistency of these training studies with the previous ones in higher education is an important finding.

A leading example of a full-service learning community can be found in the military at the United States Defense Acquisition University (DAU), Fort Belvoir, Virginia. As a corporate university, the DAU coordinates education and training programs to meet the training requirements and support the career goals of more than 138,000 Department of Defense acquisition personnel. Acquisition refers to the process of procuring any item for use by the military, from paper supplies to high tech sensors to aircraft carriers. Certain items can be purchased commercially, but others are uniquely military in nature and must be engineered from ongoing research and development programs. It is the latter, of course, that requires up-to-date regulatory knowledge and sharpened technical and program management skills.

Advances in pedagogical models and communications technology assist the DAU in achieving its mission. For instance, prior to 1998, training occurred largely through programs and courses at the DAU main campus, at four regional campuses across the United States, or through special on-site offerings. Approximately 50,000 graduates per year engage in courses on contracting, technical management, program management, and business functions. Most courses are short term in nature, i.e., one to three weeks, but some can be several months in duration, such as the one on program management.

In 1998, DAU began to revamp its training programs to better prepare practitioners to apply modern business practices in the military acquisition process. At that time, the curriculum began to change to case-based instruction with a greater emphasis on critical thinking anchored in the context of realistic problems. The philosophy was to have "students learn to exercise good judgment by exercising good judgment" (Federal Times, 2001). The university began to shift towards online learning for instructional delivery rather than shuttling students to training centers.

PERFORMANCE BASED LEARNING AT THE DAU

The nucleus of the new environment is called a performance learning model (Defense Acquisition University, 2001). The model has four main components: (1) certification training, (2) continuous learning, (3) knowledge sharing/communities of practice, and (4) performance support. The environment is designed to provide an anywhere, anytime capability for learners to gain the requisite knowledge, even while on the job, through specialized offerings. It is also meant to foster learning through online interactions with others, while helping learners reach back for appropriate information and knowledge and use it at the point of application while on the job. Each of the four components is discussed briefly.

Certification Training

After its opening in 1998, online learning related to certification training accounted for only 2 percent of graduates, totaling 15,570 hours of instruction. Since then, the changes have been dramatic. During the 2002-2003 school year, online instruction is expected to increase 96-fold, to 1.5 million hours. Prior to the availability of online learning, an introductory course on the acquisition process required nine class days in residence, as well as two days for travel to and from the campus or a training center. The increased accessibility and efficiency of online instruction increased the output dramatically, resulting in the savings of millions of dollars.

Continuous Learning

The DAU provides a single portal for easy access to a multitude of continuous learning opportunities, performance support, and information. Called the Continuous Learning Center, the portal offers members of the acquisition community an unfettered way in which to fulfill the new requirement of 80 continuous learning points every two years. The continuous learning center is proving to be quite popular, with more than 3,400 users registered in its first nine months of use. More than 36 modules offering hundreds of continuous learning points are now available. Equally impressive, registrations have already grown to more than 24,000 users.

As would be expected from a CoP, another enabling component of the DAU strategy is the capacity to share knowledge and lessons learned across the workforce. Underlying this capability is the development of a public Web-based support center for knowledge assets (Defense Acquisition University, 2002). The Center will appear as a portal to CoPs, experts, tools, knowledge and learning objects, best practices, collaboration forums, and team share spaces. Access to online certification and continuous learning courses will also be available through the portal.

Knowledge Sharing/Communities of Practice

The development of CoPs within each of 13 career fields (e.g., logistics) is focused on capturing the experiential knowledge of seasoned veterans of the workforce, subject-matter experts, faculty, and alumni of the DAU. The goal is to make available performance support tools based on experiential knowledge and identify contacts for all career employees, particularly young apprentices or others new to the field. In fact, plans are underway to provide each career field with its own CoP.

The best example is the recently established Program Management community of Practice, with more than 3,000 members. Membership in that community offers access to important resources for continuous, on-the-spot learning. For example, a worker/learner can quickly connect to other professionals in a particular field, while exchanging information and knowledge with them, collaborating in discussion areas on specific topics, and creating impromptu or pre-planned private workspaces. Within the Program Management community, four principal areas, or subcommunities, have formed related to contract management, risk management, systems engineering, and total ownership costs. Of course, the many activities and continuous learning projects that result from such courses provide a follow-through learning experience, offering a place where a trade or craft is practiced in the context of a learner's immediate need. Success of this and other CoPs will be measured through the number of communities and subcommunities formed, the number of specialized topics established and placed online, the use of workspaces, and various measures of user activity using commercially available analytic software. The ultimate sign of success, of course, is improved job performance often measured at the organizational level.

Performance Support

The online and community support for learners has been addressed to a limited extent in the above three components. More specifically, the DAU plans a digital repository to provide direct performance support to the practitioner while on the job. The repository will contain knowledge objects and learning objects that conform to the Sharable Content Object Reference Model (SCORM). SCORM is a collection of specifications and guidelines that in combination are forming the basis for interoperability between multiple sources of learning content and learning management systems (Kenyon, 2002; Longmire, 2000).

WHAT IS NEXT?

As the higher education and military examples above indicate, interest in online communities and collaborative tools will continue to grow in the foreseeable future. The unfolding role of online learning communities in academic environments and CoPs in work and military training settings should prove interesting and important. Also of interest will be determining the degree to which learning communities and CoPs overlap and feed off one another. Do employees who have completed online courses with learning communities become more efficient participators in CoPs? And do those who have built new products and processes in a CoP adapt to and ask for learning communities within their ongoing training needs? Does an enhanced sense of community increase student retention in a learning community? And does this same sense of community positively relate to knowledge generation and sharing in a CoP? Such pivotal training and education questions should attract extensive research as well as significant political attention and associated funding. The final result may be wholly new definitions of learning and expectations of learners.

REFERENCES

Baek, E. O. (2002). *A study of dynamic design dualities in a Web-supported community of practice for teachers*. Unpublished doctoral dissertation, University of Indiana, Bloomington.

Barab, S. A., & Duffy, T. (2000). From practice fields to communities of practice. In D. Jonassen, & S. M. Land. (Eds.). *Theoretical foundations of learning environments* (pp. 25-56). Mahwah, NJ: Lawrence Erlbaum Associates.

Barab, S. A., Thomas, M. K., & Merrill, H. (1999). *Online learning: From information dissemination to building a shared sense of community*. Unpublished manuscript, Indiana University at Bloomington.

Bielaczyc, K., & Collins, A. (1998). Learning communities in classrooms: A reconceptualization of educational practice. In C. M. Reigeluth (Ed.), *Instructional design theories and models*, Vol II. Mahwah, NJ: Erlbaum.

Blunt, R. (2001). How to build an e-learning community. *E-learning, 2*(11), 18-20.

Bonk, C. J. (2001). *Online teaching in an online world*. Bloomington, IN: CourseShare.com. Retrieved May 28, 2003, from http://publicationshare.com/docs/ faculty_survey_report.pdf.

Bonk, C. J. (2002a, November/December). Collaborative tools for e-learning. *Chief Learning Officer.* pp. 22-24, & 26-27. Retrieved May 28, 2003, from http://www.clomedia.com/content/templates/clo_feature.asp?articleid=41&zoneid=30.

Bonk, C. J. (2002b). *Online training in an online world.* Bloomington, IN: CourseShare.com. Retrieved May 28, 2003, from http://publicationshare.com/docs/corp_survey.pdf.

Bonk, C. J. (2003). New collaborative tools: Constructing shared meanings. In A. Zolli (Ed.), *TechTV's catalog of tomorrow* (pp. 196-197). Indianapolis, IN: Que, an imprint of Pearson Education.

Bonk, C. J., & Dennen, V. P. (1999). Teaching on the Web: With a little help from my pedagogical friends. *Journal of Computing in Higher Education, 11*(1), 3-28.

Bonk, C. J., Ehman, L., Hixon, E., & Yamagata-Lynch, E. (2002). The Pedagogical TICKIT: Teacher Institute for Curriculum Knowledge about the Integration of Technology. *Journal of Technology and Teacher Education, 10*(2), 205-233.

Bonk, C. J., Olson, T., Wisher, R. A., & Orvis, K. L. (2002). Learning from focus groups: An examination of blended learning. *Journal of Distance Education,* 17 (3), 97-118.

Bonk, C. J., Oyer, E. J., & Medury, P. V. (1995). *Is this the S.C.A.L.E.?: Social Constructivism and Active Learning Environments.* Paper presented at the American Educational Research Association (AERA) annual convention, San Francisco, CA.

Bonk, C. J., & Wisher, R. A. (2000). *Applying collaborative and e-learning tools to military distance learning: A research framework.* (Technical Report #1107). Alexandria, VA: U.S. Army Research Institute for the Behavioral and Social Sciences. Retrieved May 28, 2003, from http://publicationshare.com/docs/Dist.Learn(Wisher).pdf.

Broad, M. C. (1999). The dynamics of quality assurance in on-line distance education. *Electronic Journal of Instructional Science and Technology, 3*(1), 12-21.

Brown, A. L. (1994). The advancement of learning. *Educational Researcher, 23*(8), 4-12.

Brown, J. S., & Duguid, P. (2000). *The social life of information.* Boston, MA: Harvard Business School Press.

Brown, R. (2001). The process of community-building in distance learning classes. *Journal of Asynchronous Learning Networks, 5*(2). Retrieved May 28, 2003, from http://www.aln.org/publications/jaln/v5n2/v5n2_brown.asp.

Chao, C. (1999). *Sense of community and meaningfulness in an on-line course for language teachers.* Unpublished manuscript, Indiana University at Bloomington.

Chao, C. (2001). *Toward an understanding of sense of community and meaningful learning experiences in an on-line language education course.* Unpublished doctoral dissertation, University of Indiana, Bloomington.

Chavis, D. M., Hogge, J. H., & McMillan, D. W. (1986). Sense of community through Brunswick's lens: A first look. *Journal of Community Psychology, 14,* 24-40.

Cook, S. D. N., & Brown, J. S. (1999). Bridging epistemologies: The generative dance between organizational knowledge and organizational knowing. *Organizational Science, 10*(4), 381-400.

Defense Acquisition University (DAU). (2001). *DAU Annual Report.* Fort Belvoir, VA: Defense Acquisition University.

Defense Acquisition University (DAU). (2002). *The DAU Road Map for e-Learning and Online Performance Support.* Fort Belvoir, VA: Defense Acquisition University.

Duffy, T., McMullen, M., Barab, S., & Keating, T. (1998). *Professional development in the 21st century: Preparing for the future. A strategic plan for applied research and development.* Unpublished manuscript, Indiana University at Bloomington.

Ehman, L., H., & Bonk, C. J. (2002). *A model of teacher professional development to support technology integration.* Manuscript submitted for publication.

Federal Times (2001). DoD school teaches changes in acquisition field. *Federal Times, 38*(16), December 24, 2001.

Fulton, K., & Riel, M. (1999). Professional development through learning communities. *Edutopia, 6*(2), 8-10.

Gongla, P., & Rizzuto, C. R. (2001). Evolving communities of practice: IBM global services experience. *IBM Systems Journal, 40*(4), 842-862.

Hall, B. (2000). *Live e-learning: How to choose a system for your organization.* Sunnyvale, CA: Brandon-Hall.com.

Hane, P. J. (2001). Entopia launches company, new productivity tools for enterprise. *Information Today, 18*(11). Retrieved May 28, 2003, from http://www.infotoday.com/newsbreaks/nb011029-1.htm.

Hara, N., & Kling, R. (2002). *Communities of practice with and without information technology.* Proceedings of the American Society of Information Science and Technology, Philadelphia, PA.

Haythornthwaite, C. (1998). A social network study of the growth of community among distance learners. *Information Research, 4*(1). Retrieved May 28, 2003, from http://informationr.net/ir/4-1/paper49.html.

Hoffman, J. (2001). 24 hours in the life of a synchronous trainer. *Learning Circuits,* American Society for Training & Development. Retrieved May 28, 2003, from http://www.learningcircuits.org/2001/mar2001/hofmann.html.

Hughes, C., & Hewson, L. (1998). Online interactions: Developing a neglected aspect of the virtual classroom. *Educational Technology, 38*(4), 48-55.

Kanuka, H., & Anderson, T. (1998). On-line social interchange, discord, and knowledge construction. *Journal of Distance Education, 13*(1), 57-74.

Kaplan, S. (2002). Building communities—strategies for collaborative learning. *Learning Circuits,* American Society for Training & Development. Retrieved May 28, 2003, from http://www.learningcircuits.org/2002/aug2002/kaplan.html.

Keller, J. B., Ehman, L. H., & Bonk, C. J. (2003). *Professional development that increases technology integration by K-12 teachers: The influence of the TICKIT Program.* Paper presented at the American Educational Research Association annual convention, Chicago, IL.

Kenyon, H.S. (2002). Advanced distributed learning reaches maturity. *Signal, 57*(4), 51-53.

Kling, R., & Courtright, C. (in press). Group behavior and learning in electronic forums: A socio-technical approach. To appear in S. Barab, R. King, & J. Gray (Eds.), *Designing for virtual communities in the service of learning.* Cambridge: Cambridge University Press.

Kulp, R. (1999). *Effective collaboration in corporate distributed learning: Ten best practices for curriculum owners, developers and instructors.* Chicago, IL: IBM Learning Services.

Lave, J., & Wenger, E. (1991). *Situated learning: Legitimate peripheral participation.* New York: Cambridge University Press.

Longmire, W. (2000). A primer on learning objects. *Learning Circuits,* American Society for Training & Development, Retrieved May 28, 2003, from http://www.learningcircuits. com/mar2000/primer.html.

Mack, R., Ravin, Y., & Byrd, R. J. (2001). Knowledge portals and the emerging digital knowledge workplace. *IBM Systems Journal, 40*(4), 925-955.

McLoughlin, C., & Oliver, R. (1999). Pedagogical roles and dynamics in telematics environments. In M. Selinger & J. Pearson (Eds.), *Telematics in education: Trends and issues.* Amsterdam, The Netherlands: Pergamon.

McMillan, D. W. (1996). Sense of community. *Journal of Community Psychology, 24*(4), 315-325.

McMillan, D. W., & Chavis, D. M. (1986). Sense of community: A definition and theory. *Journal of Community Psychology, 14*, 6-23.

Misanchuk, M. (2002). *Sense of community, satisfaction and performance in a distance education program.* Unpublished manuscript, Indiana University, Bloomington.

Palloff, R. M., & Pratt, K. (1999). *Building learning communities in cyberspace: Effective strategies for the online classroom.* San Francisco: Jossey-Bass.

Phelps, R. H., Ashworth, Jr., R. L., & Hahn, H. A. (1991). *Cost and effectiveness of home study using asynchronous conferencing for reserve component training* (U.S. Army Research Institute for the Behavioral Sciences Technical Report 1602). Alexandria, VA: U.S. Army Research Institute for the Behavioral Sciences.

Plaskoff, J. (2003). *Intersubjectivity and community-building: Learning to learn organizationally.* In M. Easterby-Smith & M. Lyles (Eds.), *The Blackwell handbook of organizational learning and knowledge management (pp. 161-184).* London: Blackwell.

Rourke, L., Anderson, T., Garrison, R., & Archer, W. (2000). *Assessing social presence in asynchronous text-based, computer conferencing: Chewing the phat(ic).* Unpublished manuscript, Edmonton, AB: University of Alberta.

Rovai, A. (2002). Building a sense of community at a distance. *International Journal of Open and Distance Learning, 3*(1). Retrieved May 28, 2003, from http://www.irrodl.org/ content/v3.1/rovai.html.

Schlager, M. S., & Fusco, J. (in press). *Teacher professional development, technology, and communities of practice: Are we putting the cart before the horse.* To appear in S. Barab, R. King, & J. Gray (Eds.), *Designing for virtual communities in the service of learning.* Cambridge: Cambridge University Press.

Schlager, M. S., & Fusco, J., & Schank, P. (2002). Evolution of an on-line education community of practice. K. A. Renniger & W. Shumar (Eds.), *Building virtual communities: Learning and change in cyberspace.* NY: Cambridge University Press.

Schlager, M. S., & Schank, P. K. (1997). *TAPPED IN: A new on-line teacher community concept for the next generation of internet technology.* Paper presented at the CSCL '97, The Second International Conference on Computer Support for Collaborative Learning, Toronto, Canada.

Schrage, M. (1990). *Shared minds: The new technologies of collaboration.* New York: Random House.

Schwier, R.A. (1999). *Turning learning environments into learning communities: Expanding the notion of interaction in multimedia.* Proceedings of the World Conference on Educational Multimedia, Hypermedia and Telecommunications, Seattle, Washington: Association for the Advancement of Computers in Education, June 23.

Stuckey, B., Hedberg, J., & Lockyer, L. (2002). *The case for community: On-line and ongoing professional support for communities of practice.* University of Wollongong. New South Wales, Australia.

Wellman, B. (2001). Computer networks as social networks. *Science, 293,* 2031-2023.

Wenger, E. (1998a). Communities of practice: Learning as a social practice. *The Systems Thinker, 9*(5), 1-5.

Wenger, E. (1998b). *Communities of practice: Learning, meaning, and identity.* NY: Cambridge University Press.

Wenger, E., McDermott, R., & Snyder, W. M. (2002). *Cultivating communities of practice: A guide to managing knowledge.* Boston, MA: Harvard Business School Press.

INDEX